IMAGES
of America

AROUND HONEOYE LAKE

RICHMOND, CANADICE, AND HONEOYE

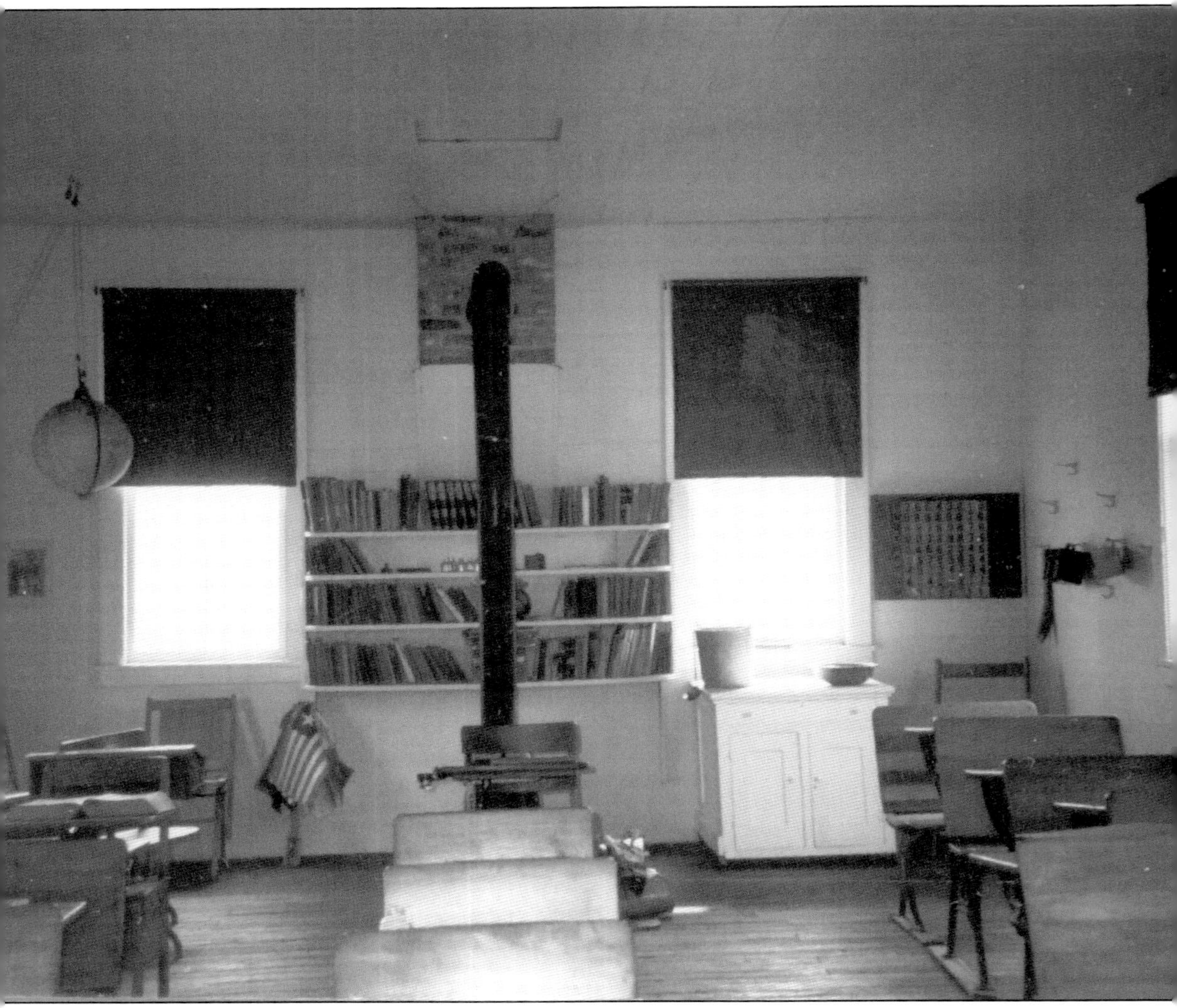

This is the interior of the one-room schoolhouse on Abbey Road in Richmond, District No. Six. It was restored by the Honeoye Historical Society and is used as a learning center for fourth graders from Honeoye Central School every spring, when they spend a day going to school as it was in the 1870s. The schoolhouse is located in its original location and was given to the Town of Richmond by Myron Green. (Richmond Historical Museum.)

On the Cover: Elizabeth Huff is seated at Burns Point on the east side of Honeoye Lake in 1929 or 1930. The hillside to the right is now Harriet Hollister Spencer Recreation Area. (Richmond Historical Museum collection.)

IMAGES
of America

AROUND HONEOYE LAKE

RICHMOND, CANADICE, AND HONEOYE

Carol J. Schoonmaker

ARCADIA PUBLISHING

ISBN 978-0-7385-7467-7

Published by Arcadia Publishing
Charleston, South Carolina

Printed in the United States of America

Library of Congress Control Number: 2010937739

For all general information, please contact Arcadia Publishing:
Telephone 843-853-2070
Fax 843-853-0044
E-mail sales@arcadiapublishing.com
For customer service and orders:
Toll-Free 1-888-313-2665

Visit us on the Internet at www.arcadiapublishing.com

To my parents, the late Marcus and Jean Lodder, who nurtured my interest in history from early childhood. Also, to my two grandsons, Forest Lang Kiger and Charles Lang Solky, who enjoy visiting Honeoye Lake as part of their childhood.

Contents

ACKNOWLEDGMENTS

Richmond and Canadice are two separate towns in Ontario County, New York. They share a common bond as they both border Honeoye Lake. Citizens of both towns contributed material to add to the information about the towns and the lake. Among the private citizens who shared material in the way of family photographs, books, and stories were: Linda Guffey, Beverly Deats, Marilyn Crast, Kitty Seablom, Laurie and Stephen Philipps, Sonja Wendt, and Dr. Preston Pierce, the Ontario County historian. Charles and Barbara Kennerson shared their vast postcard collection. The cover photograph was possible due to the kind donation of Furman and Thelma Huff to the Richmond Historical Museum. Margaret Bott, the historian of Canadice, shared the scrapbooks that are in the Canadice Museum. Appreciation also goes to my predecessor, Margaret Treble, who collected and filed hundreds of photographs and writings during her 20 years as the historian in Richmond. They proved to be very useful in preparing this book. My deepest appreciation goes to Michelle Barrett and Alan Schoonmaker for their loyal assistance in getting the book completed. My grateful thanks goes also to my editor at Arcadia Publishing, Rebekah Mower, who has been a patient listener and was always there when needed. Unless otherwise noted, materials are from the collection of the Richmond Historical Museum in Honeoye.

INTRODUCTION

Honeoye Lake may be one of the smaller Finger Lakes of western New York, but it is significant to the people who live near it, who visit it for recreation, and to those who enjoy the natural beauty of the region all four seasons of the year. Honeoye Lake is about four miles long and less than a mile in width. Its deepest point is only 30 feet. The name of Honeoye is derived from the Seneca Indian word for it—*honayaye*. A Native American legend about the shape of the lake tells the story that a young Indian brave had his finger bitten off by a rattlesnake and he left it on the shore of the lake. The shape of the lake is that of a finger in a curved position, or "finger-lying," as the story goes. The eastern shoreline lies completely in the town of Richmond and the western shoreline is about one third in Richmond. The balance is in the town of Canadice. The hamlet of Honeoye is at the north end of the lake. The outlet for the lake flows under Main Street, near the center of the hamlet. Nature trails and marshland lie between the lake and Main Street. East Lake Road and West Lake Road surround Honeoye Lake's shorelines. The marsh at the southern end of the lake prevents the roads from coming close to the inlet. They meet three miles south of the southern point of the lake.

White men claimed the land that would later become the towns of Richmond and Canadice when Maj. Gen. John Sullivan was given the order in 1789 by Gen. George Washington to "neutralize" the Native Americans residing in the area. The Sullivan campaign destroyed approximately 20 longhouses in the Richmond area, along with fruit orchards and vegetable gardens, by burning them. The Native Americans escaped, and some went toward the Niagara Frontier. A few returned to the area temporarily and the early white settlers befriended them. Some of those troops were among the early settlers of the area and are responsible for spreading the word in New England about the natural resources they had found in the Honeoye area. The early settlers often traveled to the area during the winter months when the trails were frozen and it was easier to move sleighs and oxen teams over the trails and frozen waterways.

Among the early settlers to the area were Capt. Peter Pitts and his son, William. They came from Massachusetts in 1789. Captain Pitts had won 1,000 acres of land in a lottery. It was believed to be at the north end of the lake. He erected the first log cabin in 1790. A historical marker is near the site at the corner of Main Street and Allens Hill Road. Eventually, Pitts moved his wife and 10 children to the area. In 1796, the first town meeting was held and the town was named Pittstown.

The family of Philipp Reed came in 1794, bringing a black servant with them from New Hampshire. She was referred to as Jane or Jennie Lebanon. The family did not consider her to be a slave. Philipp Reed's will dictated to his children that she was to be provided for throughout her life, and she is buried alongside the other family members in the Richmond Center Cemetery. Her tombstone has the name of Jane Lebanon on it.

In 1808, the name Pittstown was changed to the white man's version of *Honoyaye*, which was Honeoye. It was used until 1815 as the town name. It was then changed to Richmond, the maiden name of Abigail Pitts, wife of the first white settler. Richmond and Canadice were one town until 1830. Canadice derived its name from Canadice Lake.

The Native American word *can* or *con* is found in many native tongues and means water. In 1829, there was a New York state act to divide the town of Richmond, due to the increasing growth in population. The original act was amended six years later so that those who lived on the east side of Honeoye Lake were no longer included in the population of Canadice, and they returned to Richmond.

The Richmond area was known as a hotbed of abolitionists. This attracted Frederick Douglass, an escaped slave, to the area. He would visit the Pitts family and speak at the Congregational church on occasion. He also was the publisher of a newspaper named the *North Star*. The paper's name was a tribute to the star used as guidance by escaped slaves as they traveled in the night, heading north to reach Canada as part of the Underground Railroad. The home built on Main Street by Gideon Pitts in 1821, son of Capt. Peter Pitts, had a basement and cistern area used to hide escaped slaves. The escaping slaves would often travel from the village of Naples to Honeoye in a hearse with a false bottom, under the cover of darkness.

Eventually Frederick Douglass married Helen Pitts, daughter of Gideon Pitts II and Jane Wells, in 1884. It was a controversial event, as she was white and he was of mixed racial background. Douglass's mother was a former slave, but his father was white. He was also 20 years older than Helen. They lived in Washington, DC, at his home, Cedar Hill. He died in 1895, and Helen made their home a memorial to her husband. It is now known as the Frederick Douglass National Historic Site and is open to the public for tours.

In 1926, the City of Rochester, New York, announced that the property surrounding Honeoye Lake, the hamlet of Honeoye, and land north of the lake, was to be acquired and flooded to create a 16-mile-long reservoir for the city water supply. The shock of this news divided the local citizens into three distinct groups: the "Not Particulars," mostly the elderly or apathetic; the "For Rochester" group, who were approving and thought it was a chance to make easy money; and the "Against Rochester" contingent of 154 individuals who organized to fight to the finish. Their ranks soon grew. W. Scott Short had been farming land owned by his ancestors since the early 1890s, high on a hill west of the hamlet. His land was not going to be affected by the flooding, yet he led the opposition to the proposed project. A meeting was scheduled with the New York State Water Power and Control Commission in Canandaigua, New York. It lasted for a week, and some of the strong objections came from Carl Ashley, a descendent of Richmond pioneers and a civil engineer. For nearly two-and-a-half years, the Town of Richmond was in limbo over the fate of the valley. Real estate sales halted, local businesses made little profit, and home improvements were not being made. Bitter feelings developed between friends and neighbors. Finally in 1935, the City of Rochester reversed its decision. The lake area grew in popularity, and scenic locations were built upon in the surrounding hillsides.

The hamlet of Honeoye continues to be the commercial and service area of both of the towns, as it has been for more than the past two centuries. The City of Rochester has two lakes to its west—Canadice and Hemlock—as well as Lake Ontario, for its water supply.

One

Honeoye Lake

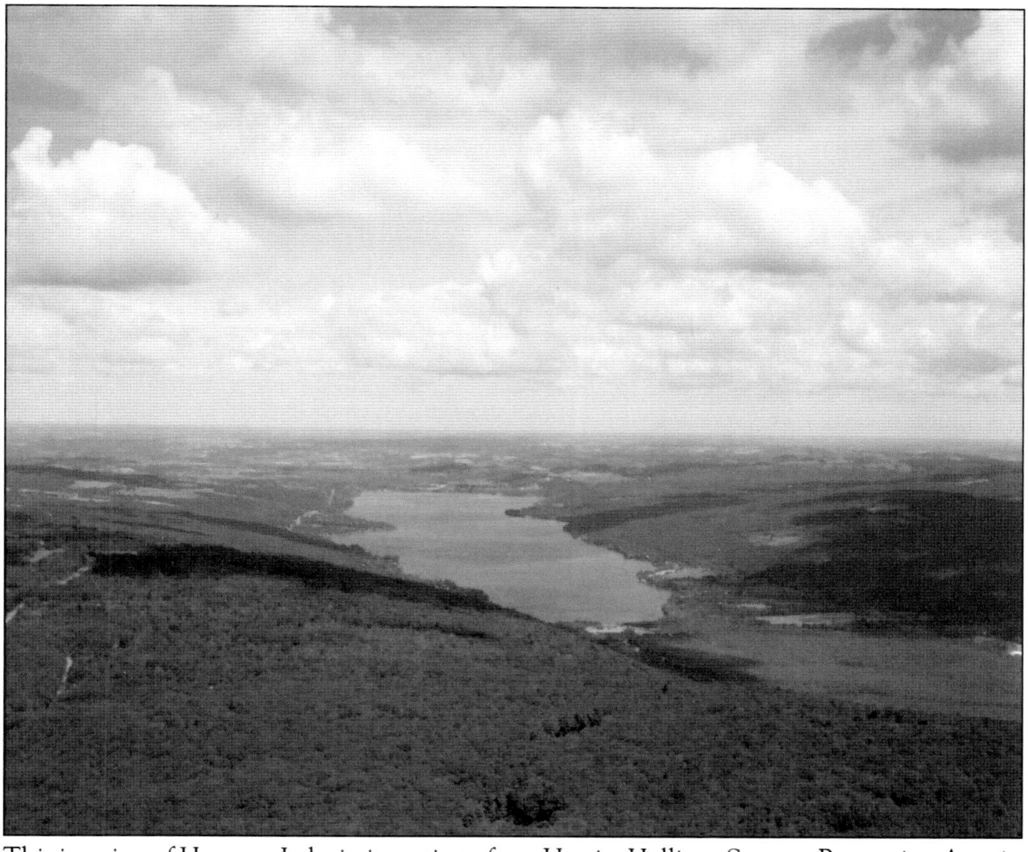

This is a view of Honeoye Lake in its entirety from Harriet Hollister Spencer Recreation Area in Canadice. Thomas G. Spencer of Rochester, New York, purchased the land in 1940. In 1964, he donated the land to the state of New York as a memorial to his wife, for whom it is named. It is 1,300 feet above the lake and consists of 679 acres. The scene is often photographed or painted by visitors through all seasons.

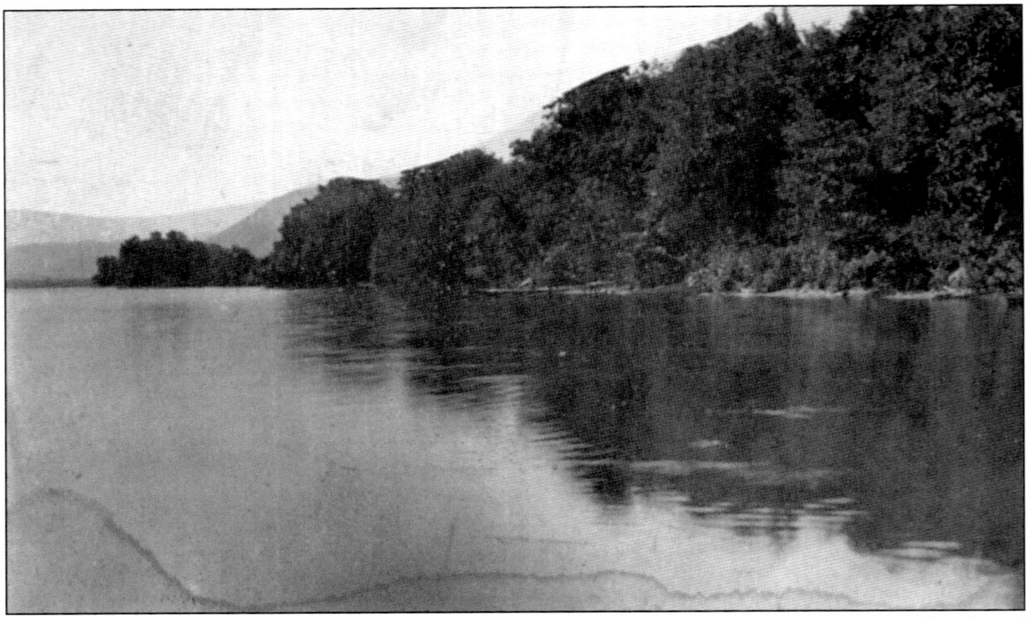

This view of the west shoreline of Honeoye Lake shows how it looked before it was developed into cottage and home sites. There were areas of agricultural land that went all the way down to the shoreline. It was not uncommon to see herds of cattle drinking from the lake. Fields of grain stretched down to the water's edge. (Courtesy of Linda Guffey.)

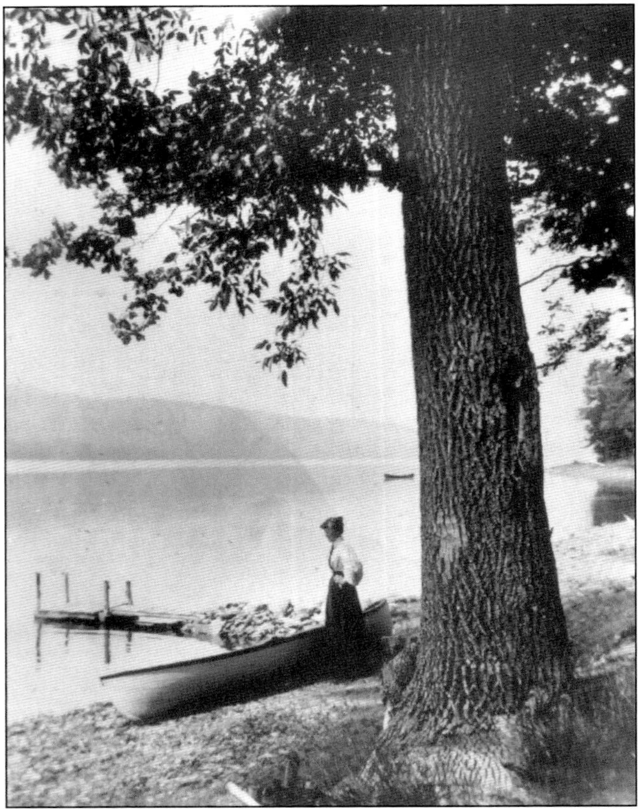

A woman visitor views Honeoye Lake from the west shoreline in the early 1900s.

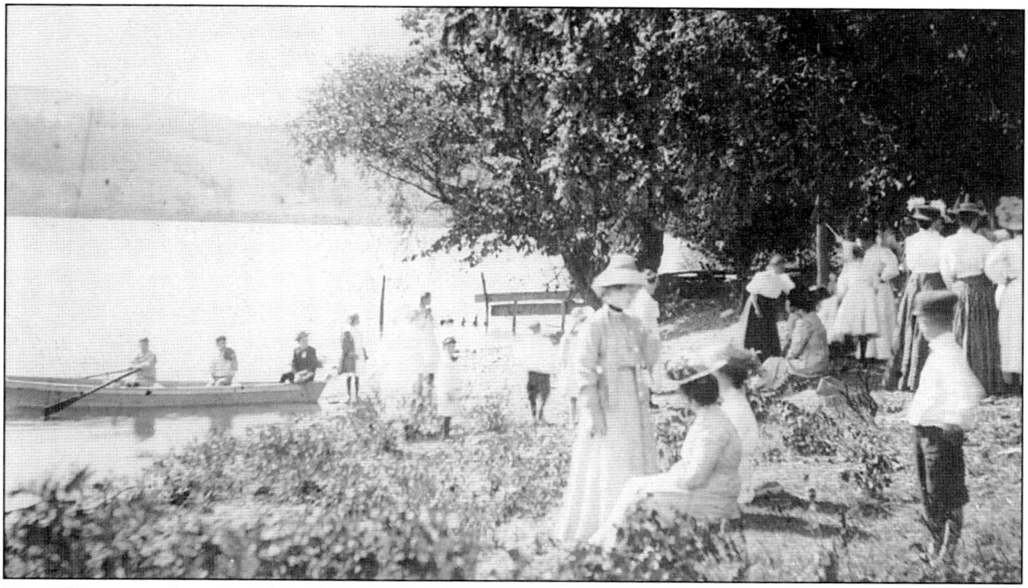

Bray's Point on the east side of Honeoye Lake was considered to be the first recreational area on the lake. In 1817, Andrew Bray and several of his 19 children came to Richmond from Cayuga County and purchased land on East Lake Road. The point became a gathering place for picnickers in the 1870s and continued as such for the next 50 or more years. It also was popular with fishermen. Before seining became illegal, Andrew Bray II claimed to have netted 7,000 fish in one night.

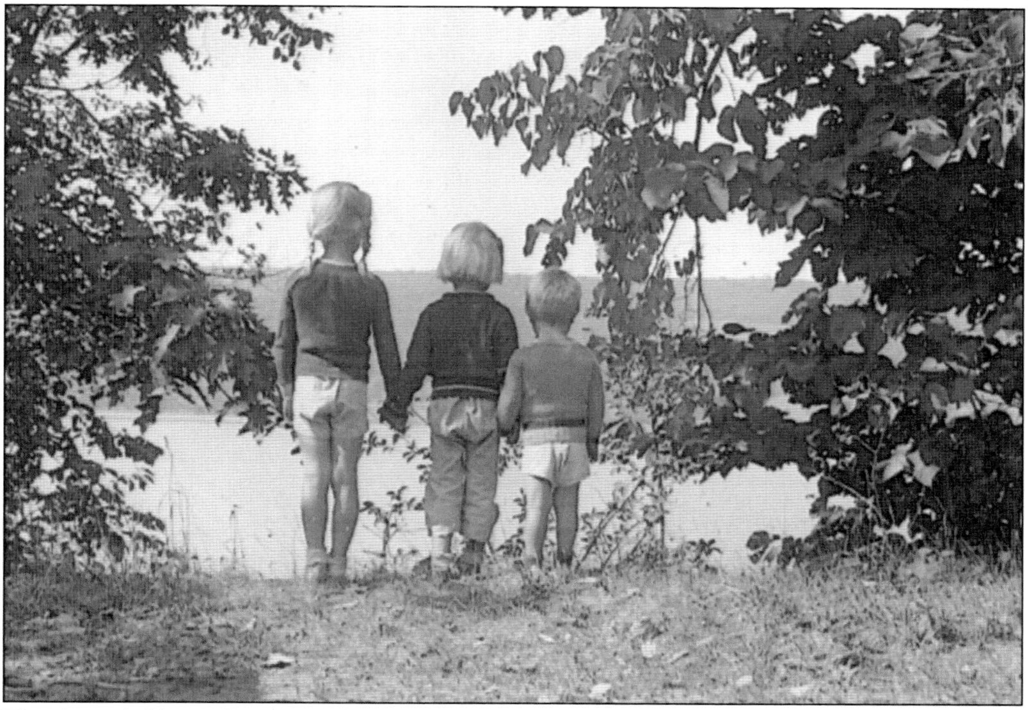

The three children of Ruth Beecher Wendt and George Richard Wendt are viewing Honeoye Lake at the family cottage on the east side, around 1937. They are Eleanor Beecher Wendt, Barbara Beecher Wendt, and Peter Beecher Wendt. Every summer they would visit their grandfather's property, where he eventually built cottages for his two oldest sons. (Courtesy of Sonja Wendt.)

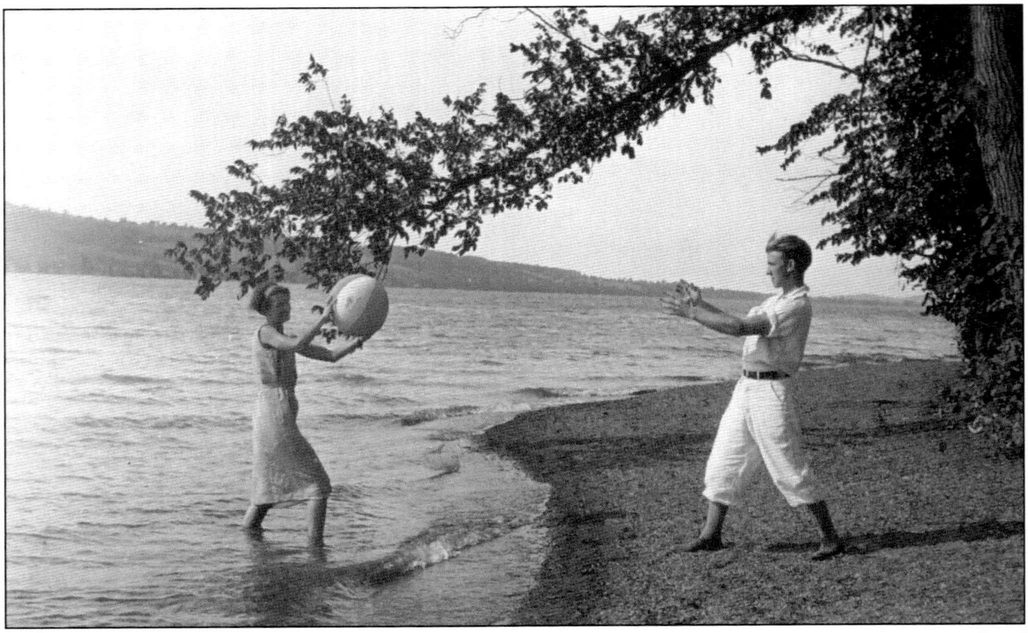

George. R. Wendt and an unidentified friend enjoy a ball game at Wendt Point on the east side of the lake in the mid-1920s. Wendt family members have been longtime residents on the east side, and there still are Wendt family members residing on East Lake Road. (Courtesy of Sonja Wendt.)

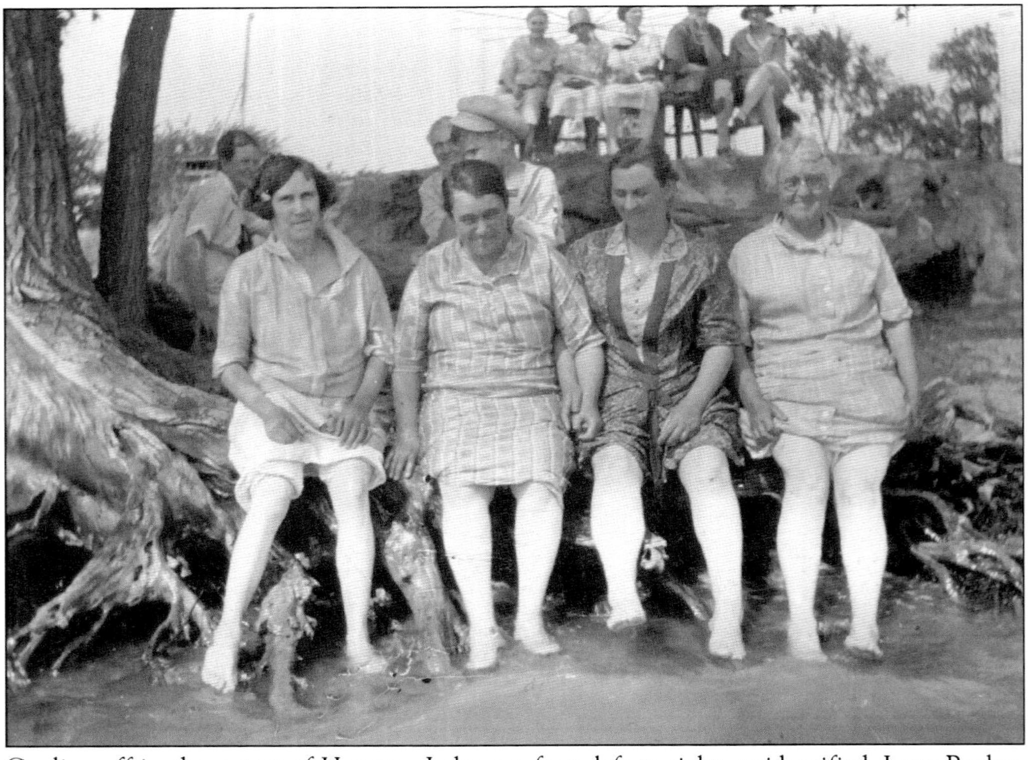

Cooling off in the waters of Honeoye Lake are, from left to right: unidentified, Lena Becker, Esther Becker, and Elizabeth Cronin. The Beckers and the Cronins were local residents in the Honeoye Lake area. (Courtesy of Linda Guffey.)

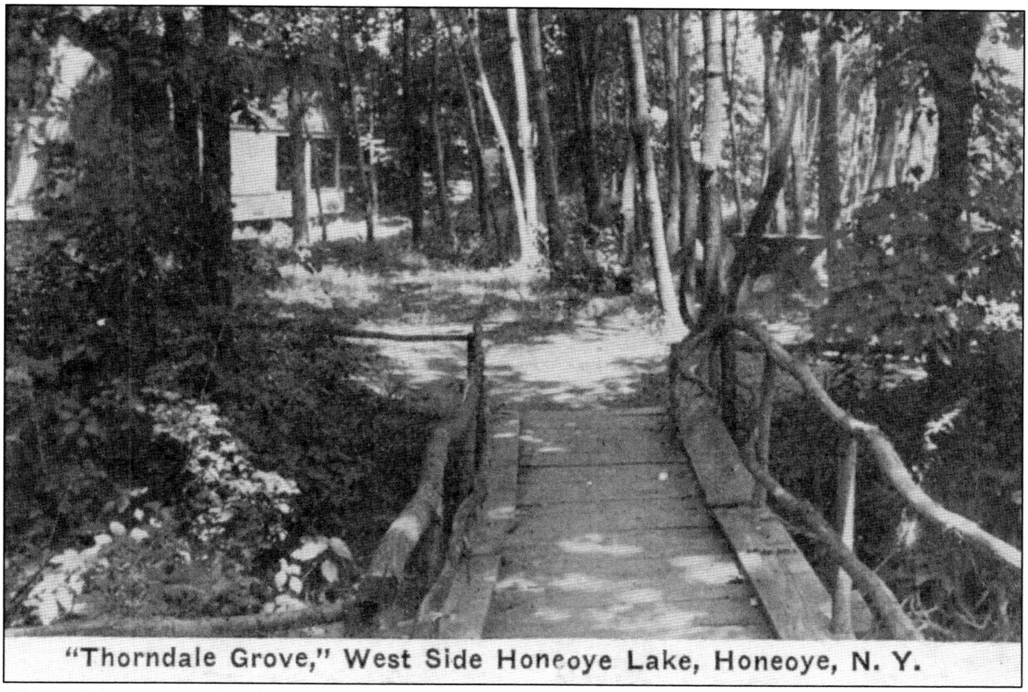

Thorndale Grove, also known as Thorndale-on-the-Lake, rented cottages by the day, week, or month and also had boats to rent for fishing. Leonard V. Colt, in Canadice on the west side, owned it.

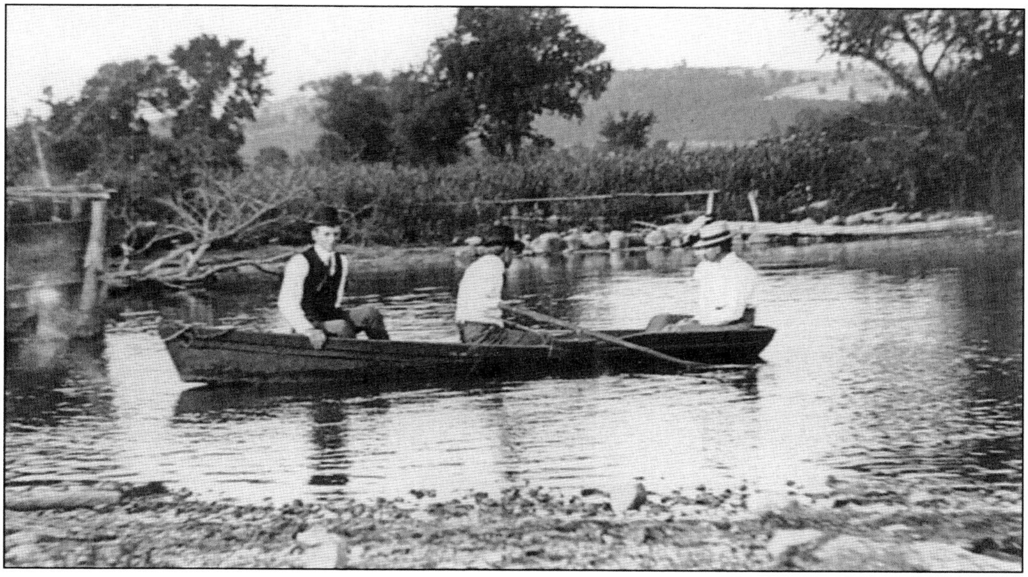

Three unidentified gentlemen are out for a boat ride at the north end of Honeoye Lake. In the years between 1900 and 1945, the Rochester Gas and Electric Company owned the property at the outlet of the lake. The company was able to control the level of the lake with a gate and by dredging the outlet. When the company sold the property to private individuals, the lake level was no longer adjusted. By 1951, some cottage owners petitioned supervisor Arthur E. Treble of Richmond and supervisor Roy G. Swan of Canadice to control the lake level. The Honeoye Lake Watershed Association was formed with 500 members to address the problems concerning the lake.

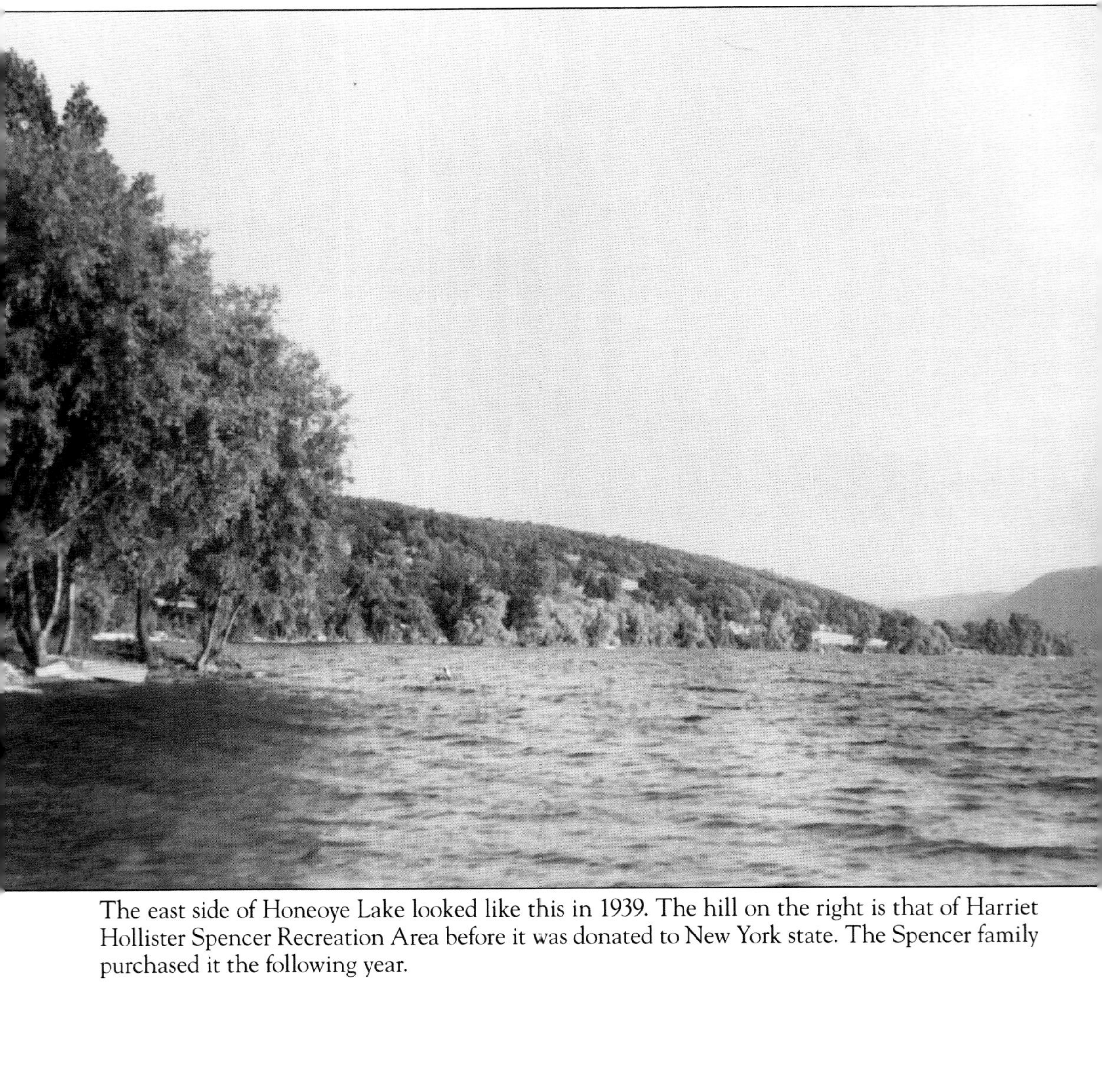

The east side of Honeoye Lake looked like this in 1939. The hill on the right is that of Harriet Hollister Spencer Recreation Area before it was donated to New York state. The Spencer family purchased it the following year.

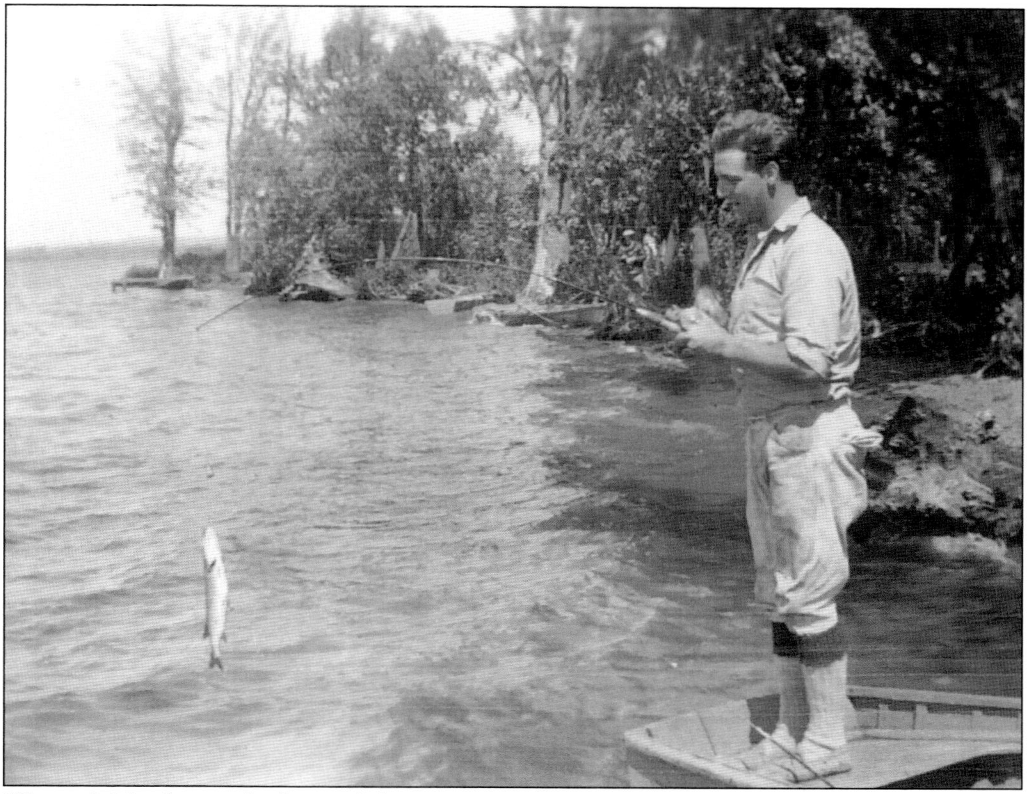

Ellsworth Morsheimer had a good day of fishing on the east side of Honeoye Lake in the 1920s. He is typical of the enthusiasts of water sports, fishing, and hunting from nearby towns who started to buy properties along the shoreline. Real estate promoters, led by Raymond T. Shafer, saw the opportunity in this area, and Honeoye Lake started its conversion from agricultural land to a resort area.

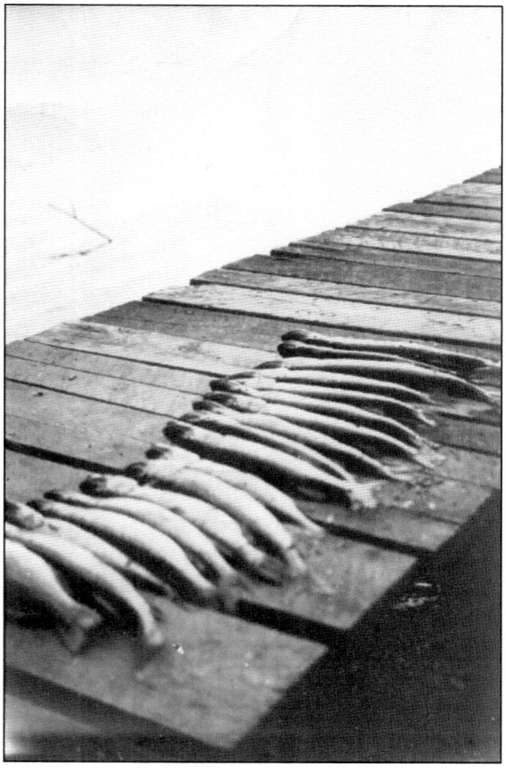

This was someone's catch laid out on a dock after a day of fishing in 1932. Local fishermen caught yellow perch, walleyes, pickerel, bass, and bullhead. This was before the lake was being stocked with fish.

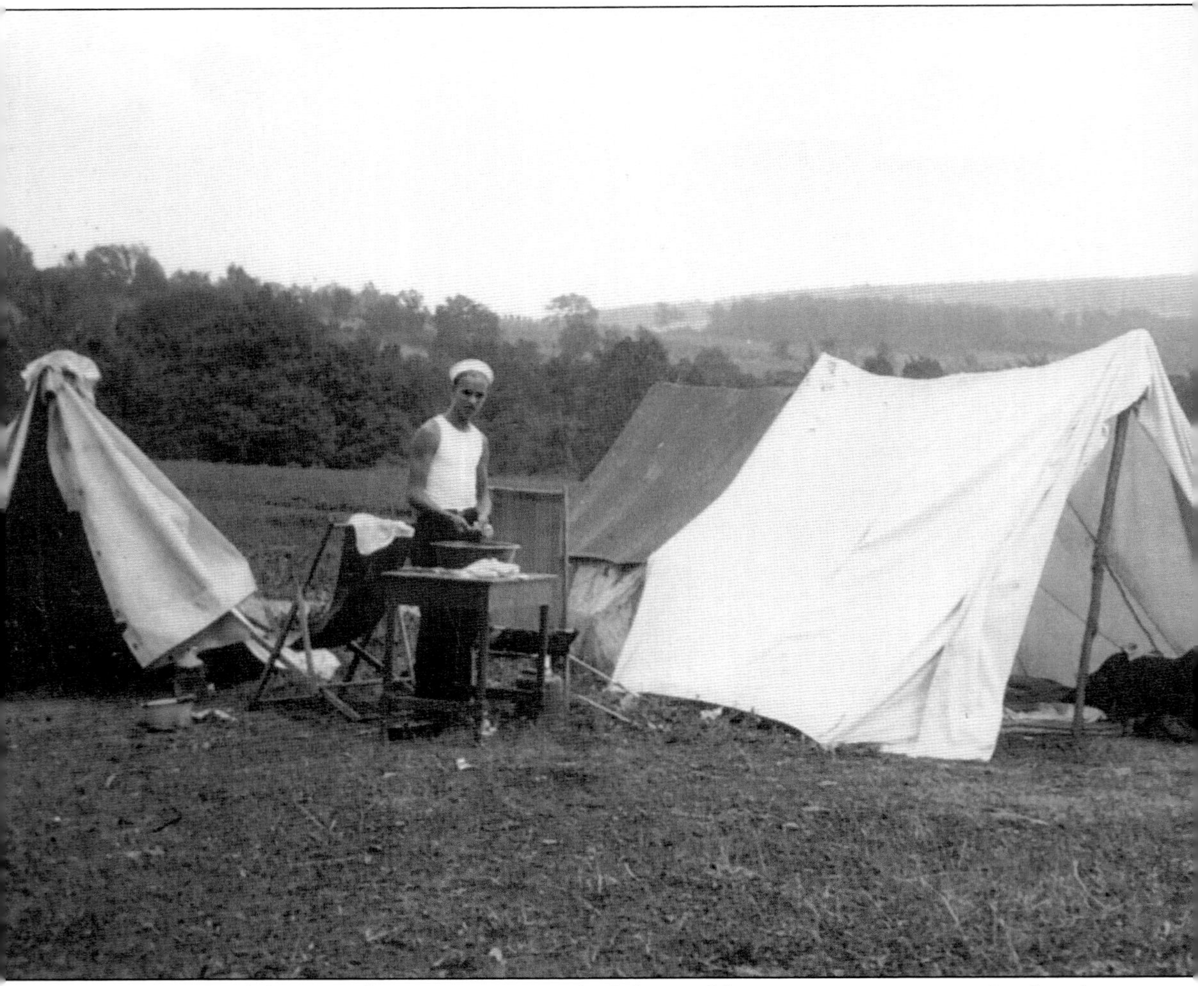

Those who did not yet have a cottage on the lake would go tent camping near the shoreline. This campsite was on the east side of the lake in 1931. The camper is unidentified. It was not uncommon to have structures along the shoreline that were part tent and part wooden building. Visitors were bringing scrap wood from wherever it could be found to use in constructing crude buildings for summer use.

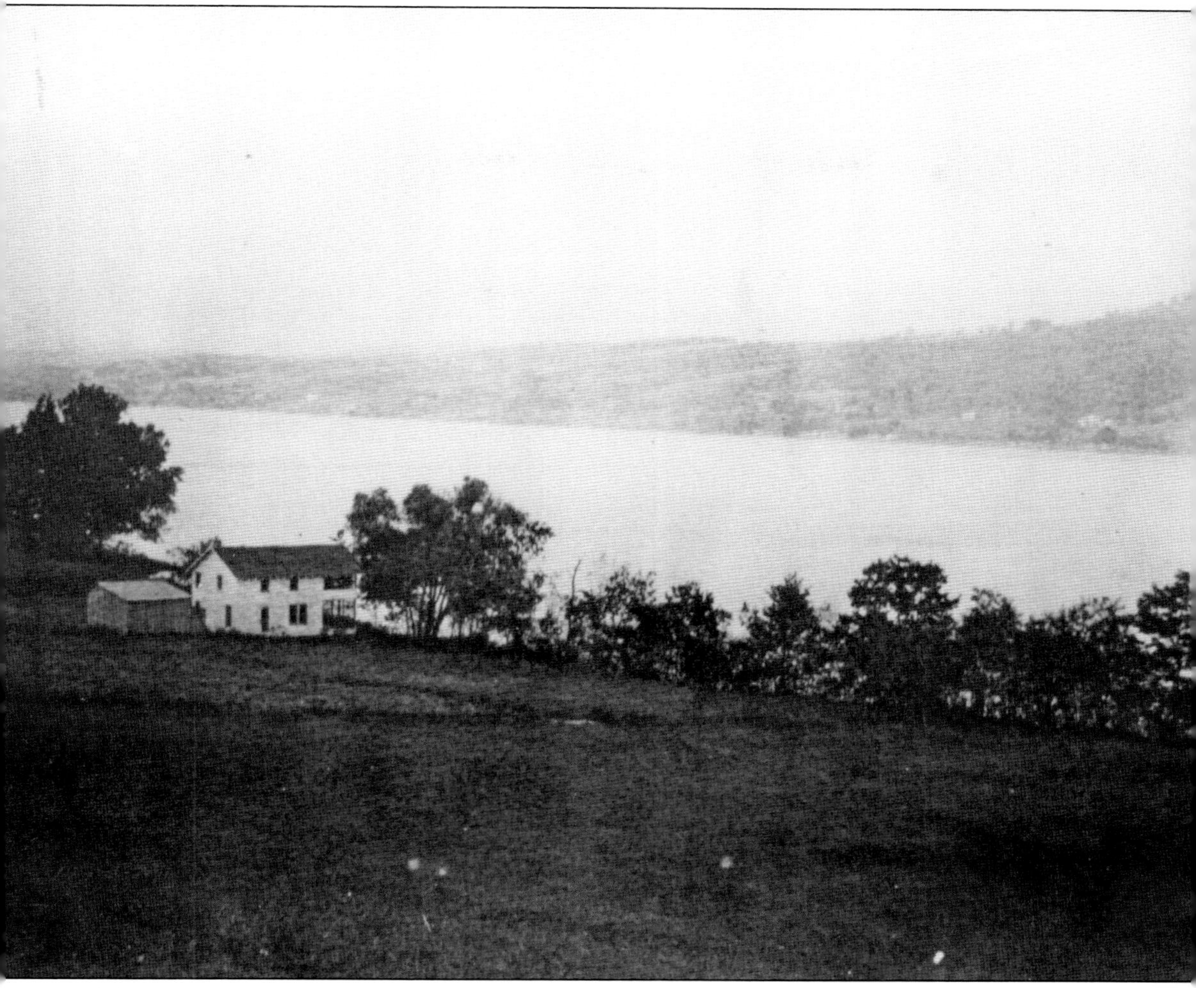

Ralph R. Young of Buffalo built the Young family cottage in 1920. It is still standing at its original location on the west side of Honeoye Lake in Canadice. The photograph was taken in 1921. Young's grandson Thomas Young and wife, Marcia, reside in their home on the lake in Canadice at the present time.

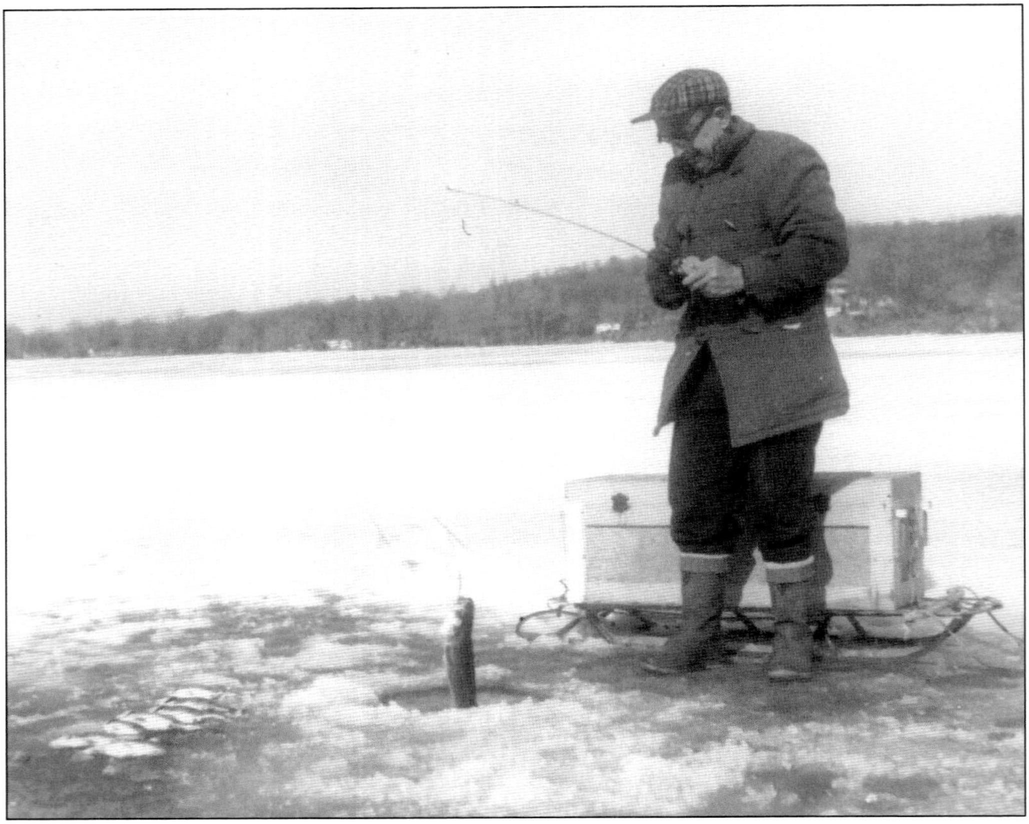

Clarence Ruppert caught a nice walleye using the jig method of fishing with a Swedish Pimple. His day's catch netted six perch and the one walleye. The date is unknown.

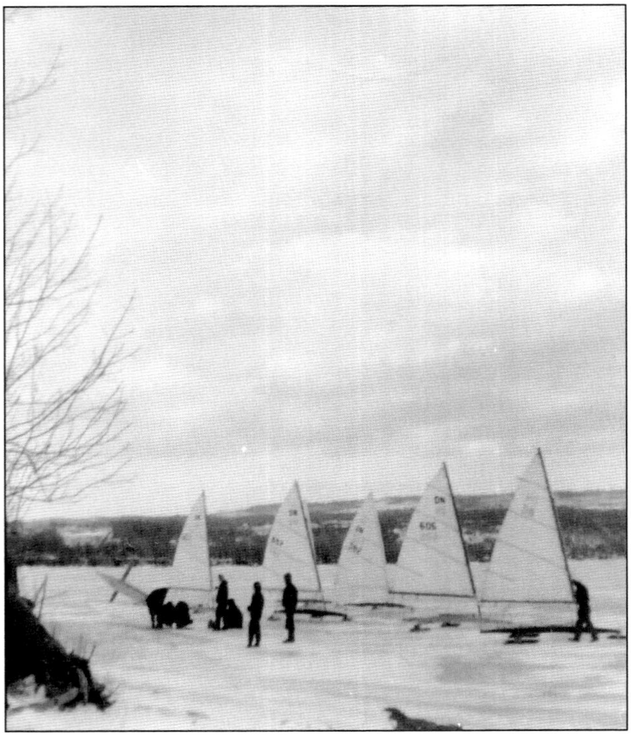

A frozen Honeoye Lake brought out the iceboats for skimming over the ice. An ice boat regatta was held for the first time to coincide with the Winter Carnival. Iceboats that previously had raced on Lamoka Lake were brought to Honeoye Lake as the ice was found to be more suitable. This shows a group of them in December 1961. (Courtesy of Betty Manuse.)

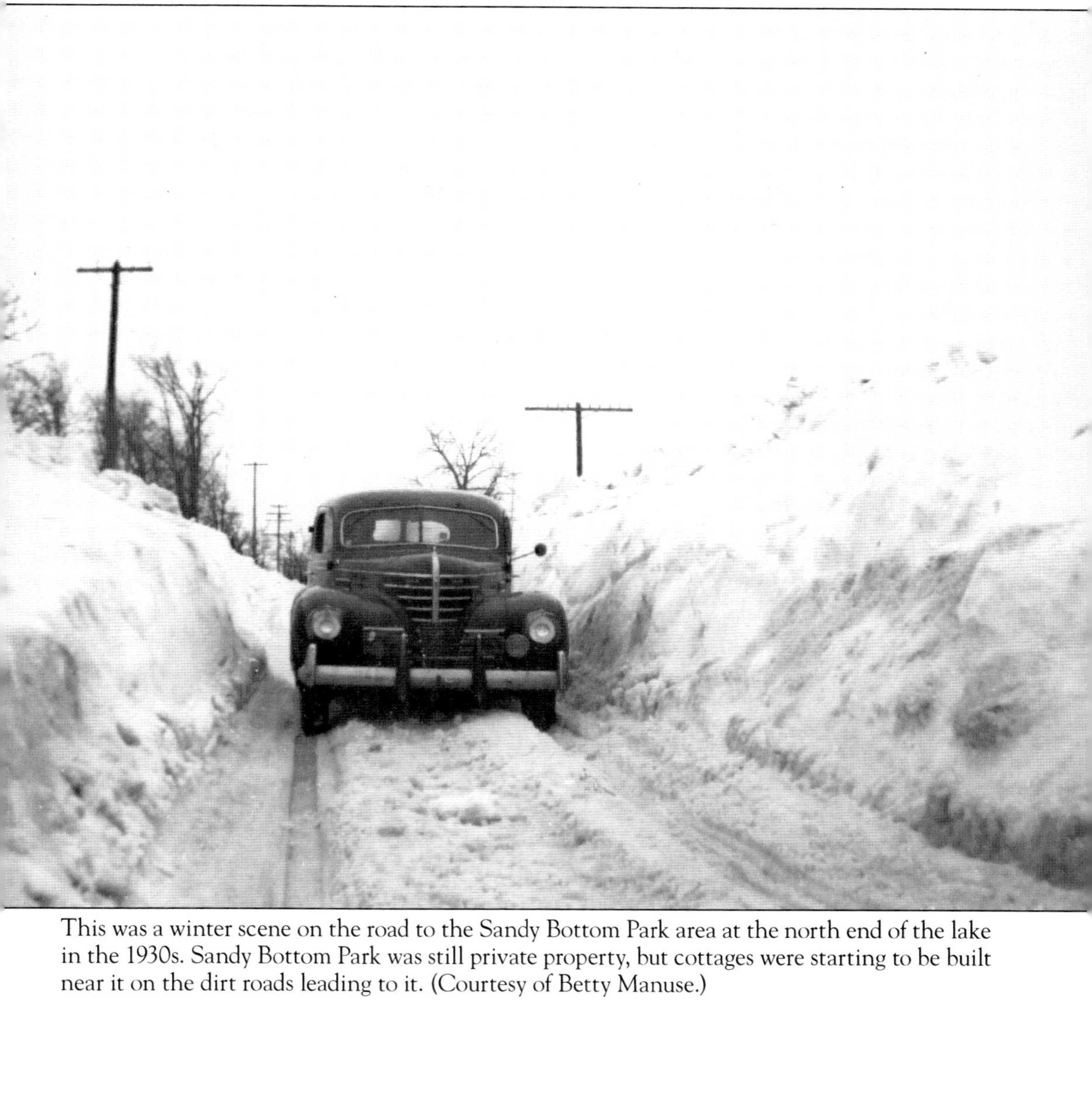

This was a winter scene on the road to the Sandy Bottom Park area at the north end of the lake in the 1930s. Sandy Bottom Park was still private property, but cottages were starting to be built near it on the dirt roads leading to it. (Courtesy of Betty Manuse.)

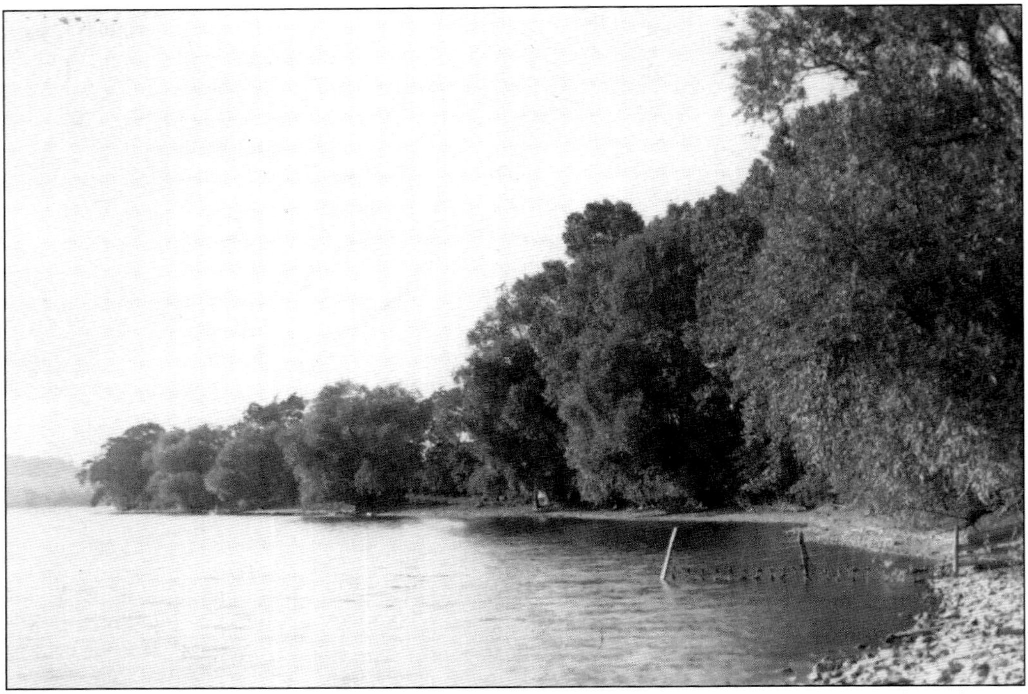

Reed Landing, on the east side of Honeoye Lake, was part of the George Reed farm. This is how it looked in 1913. It was a sheep-raising area, and hops were also grown. In the winter, farmers would cut blocks of ice from the lake and store them in icehouses nearby for use throughout the year.

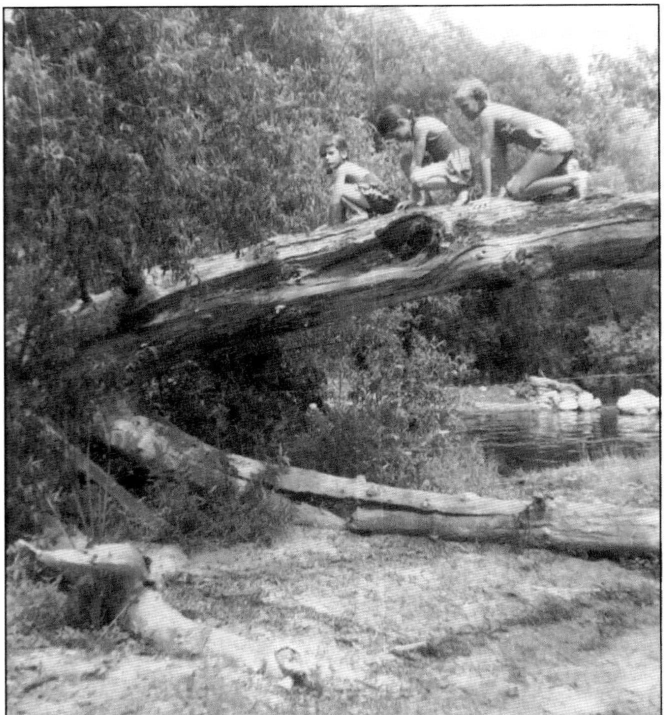

The children of Betty Manuse played at Sandy Bottom Beach at the north end of Honeoye Lake before the beach and park were developed, around 1959. The land for the park was purchased in 1973 from John and Madelyn Evans of Honeoye to be used by the Town of Richmond to develop a public park. As early as 1953, the Chamber of Commerce began to recognize the value of the lake. There was discussion in regard to the Sandy Bottom Park area being "rented" by the town and organizations to make it available to the public. (Courtesy of Betty Manuse.)

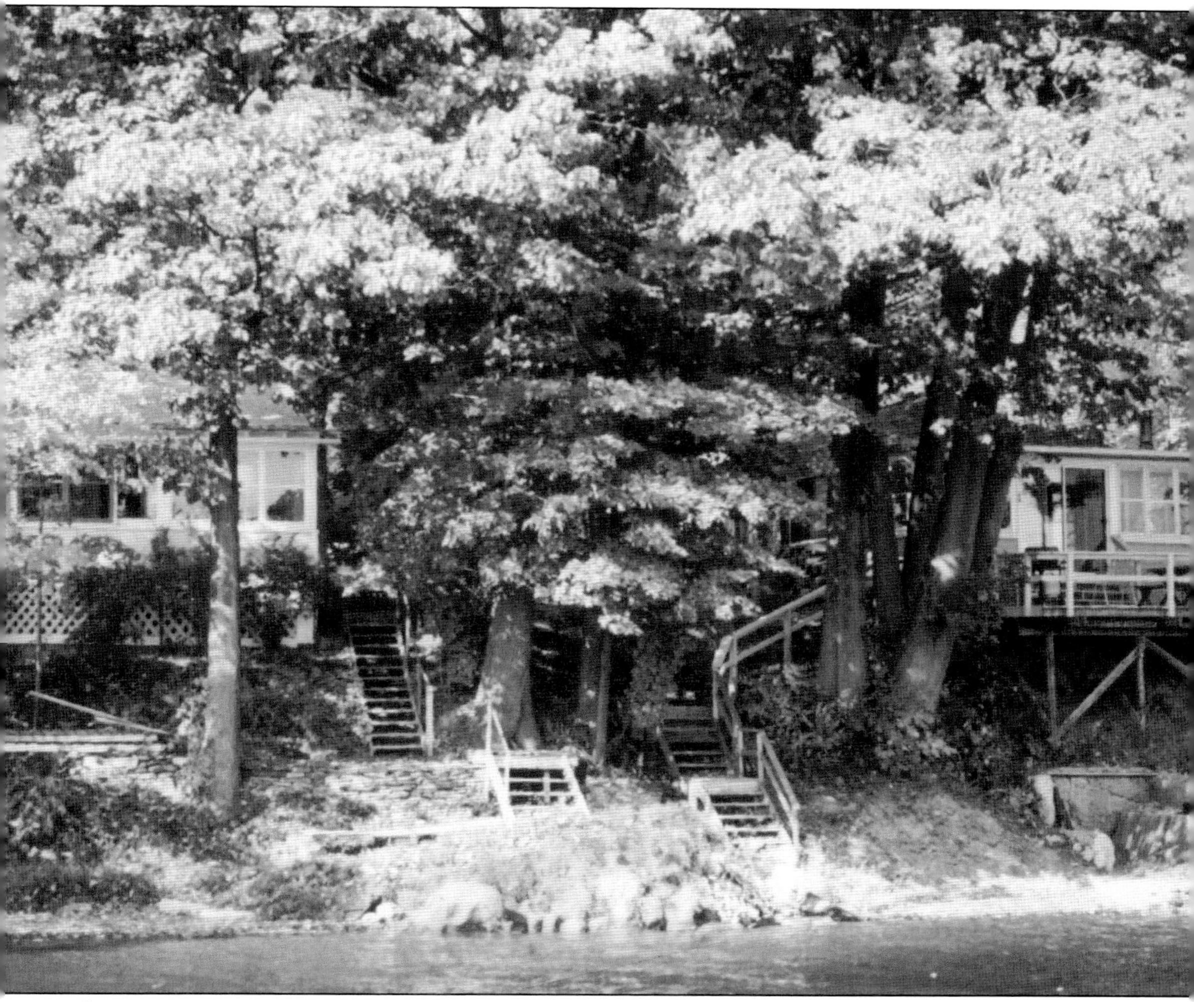

These two cottages were among several moved to the west side of Honeoye Lake when the Rochester City Water Department took over Canadice Lake for a city water supply. Many of the cottages moved over to Honeoye Lake are still being used, now remodeled and winterized for year-round living.

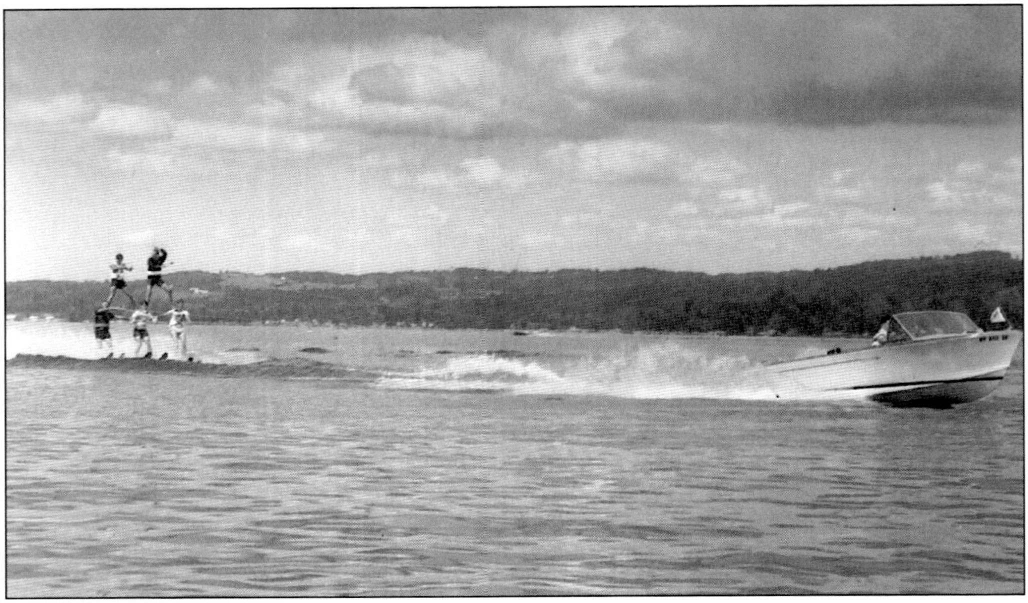

Members of a waterskiing club show some of their skills in the 1960s. Waterskiing is still a very popular summer activity on Honeoye Lake. Al Lehr, a summer resident, made what he believed was the first pair of water skis on the lake. He was a cabinetmaker for a piano company. The skis were made of wood, the bindings were a U-shaped wood block, and the top of the foot area was made from an inner tube. For a humorous touch, he painted large arrows pointing to the tips of the skis. The skis are now in the Richmond Historical Museum.

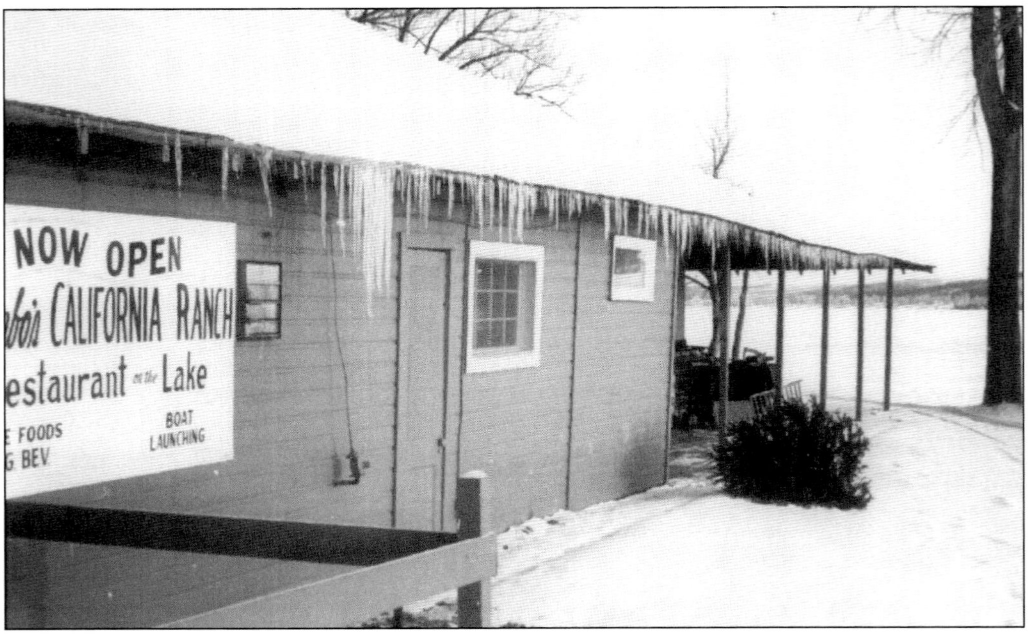

Locals and many a cold fisherman warmed up at Lambo's California Ranch on the west side of Honeoye Lake in Canadice. It has been torn down, but many happy memories remain for the lake population. The Ranch was very popular with the crowds who attended the Winter Carnival on snowmobiles. This was where they had access to the ice, and some races were held out on the ice nearby. In the summer, boat races would be held out on the water in front of the Ranch.

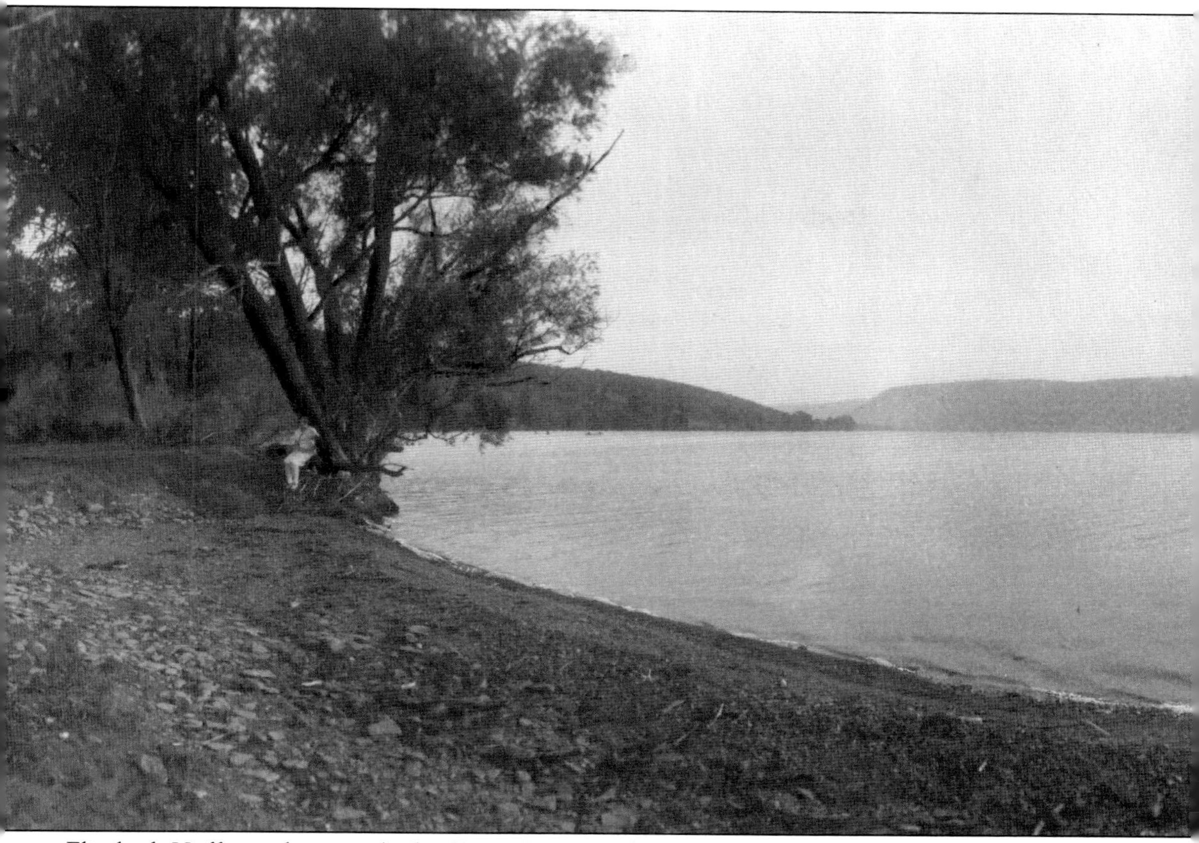

Elizabeth Huff was photographed at Burns Point on the east side in 1929–1930. This became the site of a family cottage. Furman and Thelma Huff donated this photograph to the Richmond Historical Museum.

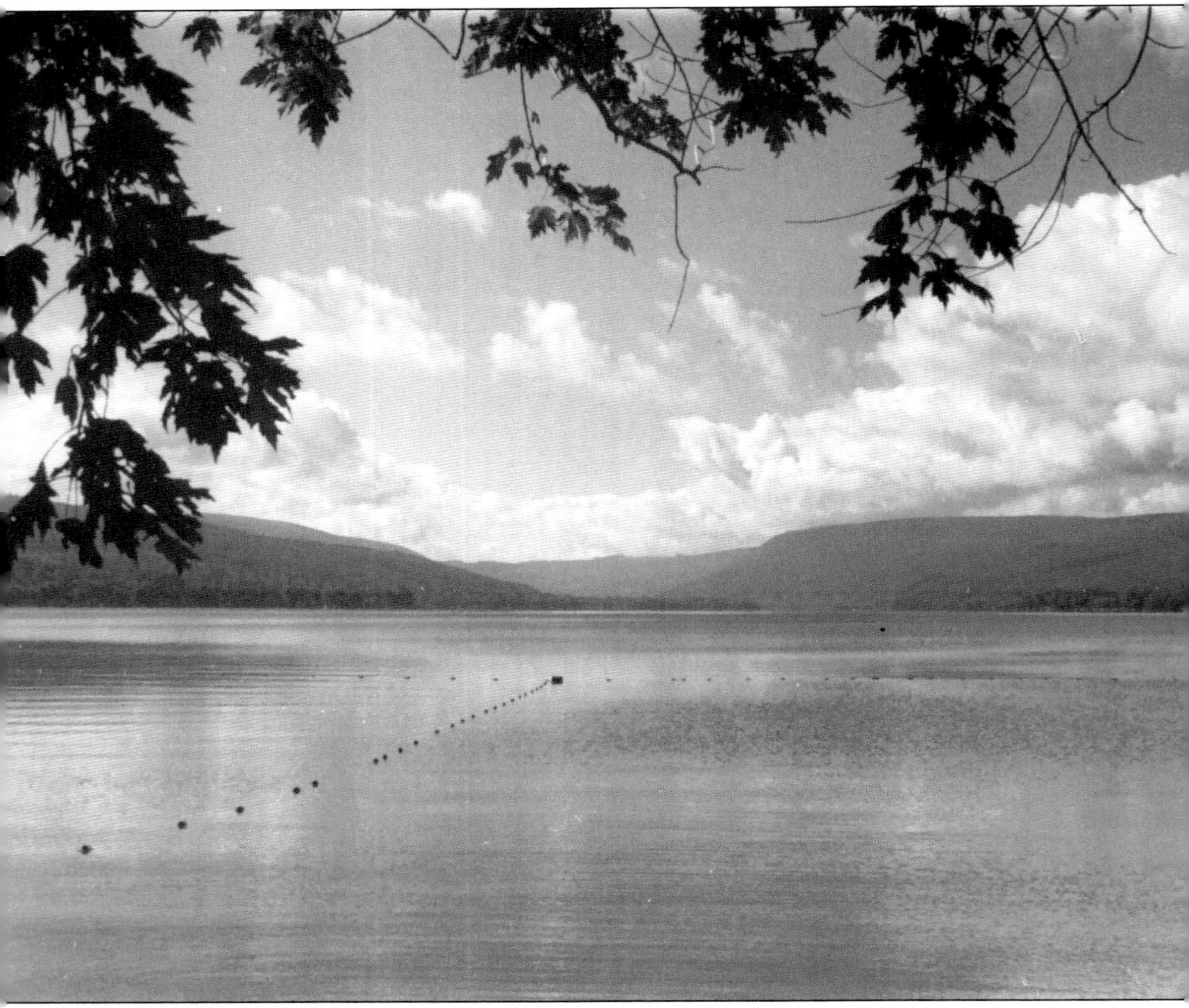

Once the Town of Richmond acquired the lakefront at Sandy Bottom Beach, a town recreation program was instituted to teach local children to swim; it also sometimes offered crafts for children and playground equipment was installed, so parents could enjoy sunning themselves on a sandy beach while the children were occupied.

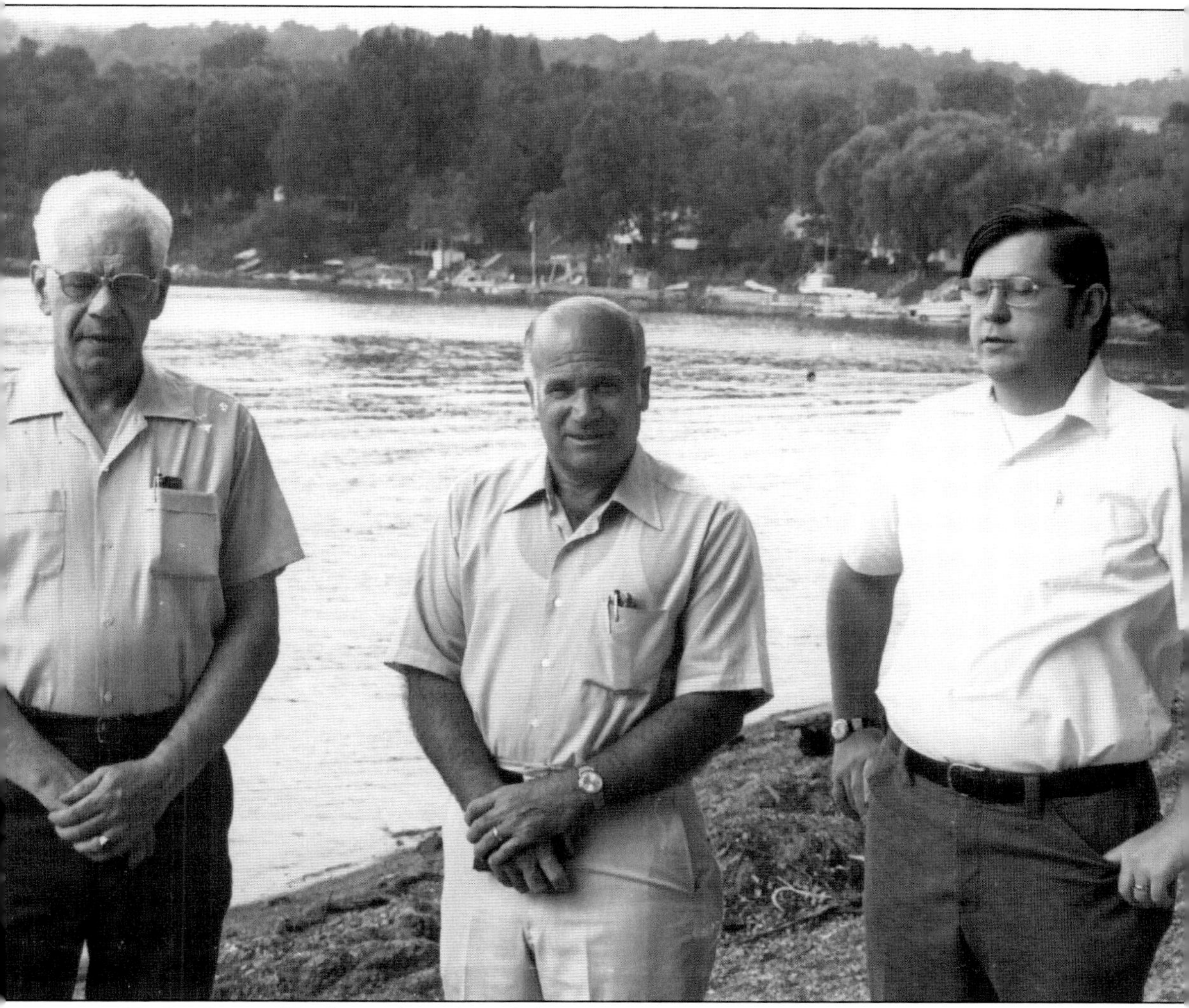

In 1973, the Town of Richmond purchased about 35 acres from John and Madelyn Evans, which was already being called Sandy Bottom Park. Town board members who were instrumental in the purchase are shown at the park, from left to right: Edmund Nighan, Supervisor Philip Rowley, and Keith Stumbo. Plans were quickly made to construct a bathhouse and sanitary facilities.

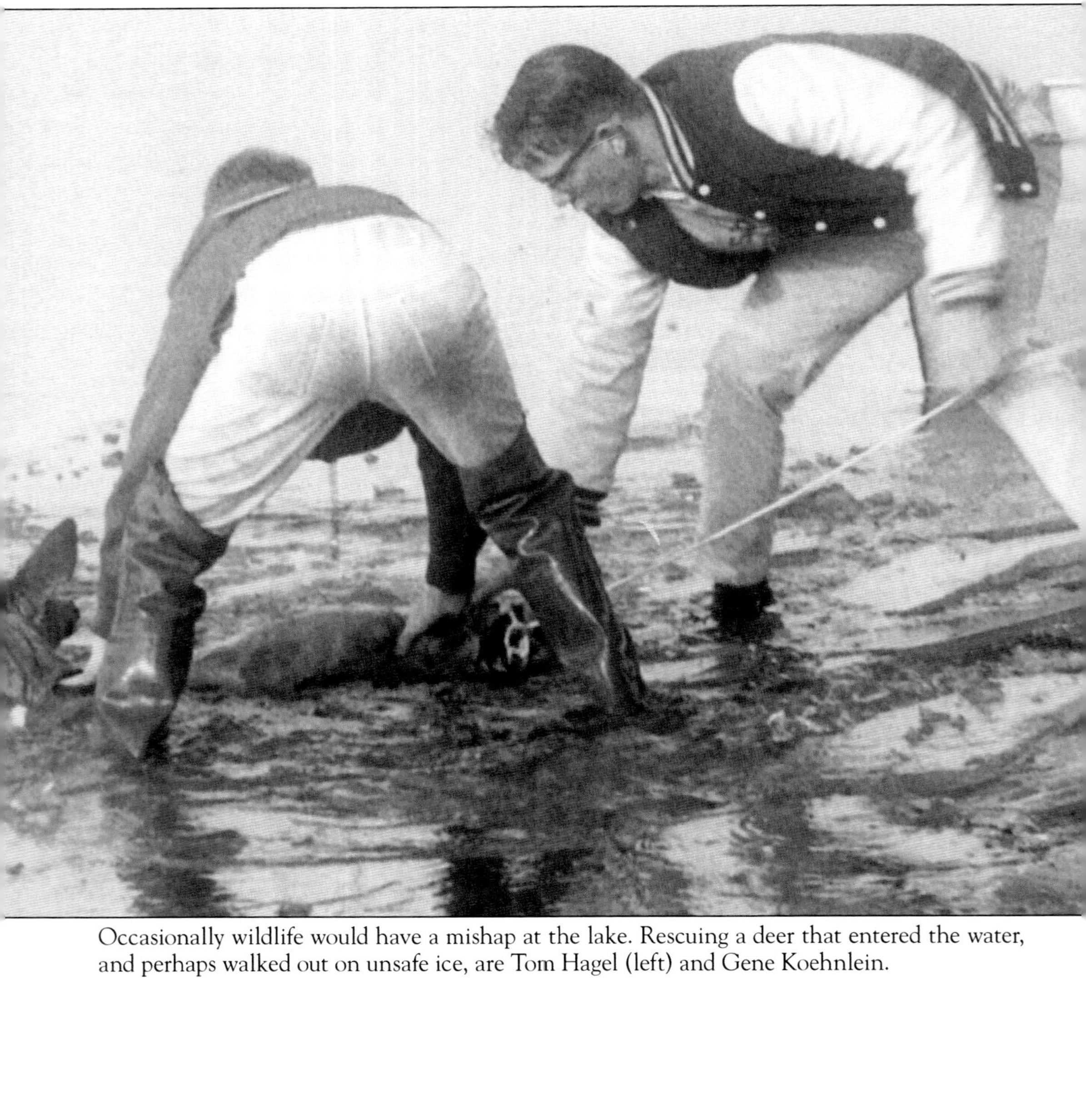

Occasionally wildlife would have a mishap at the lake. Rescuing a deer that entered the water, and perhaps walked out on unsafe ice, are Tom Hagel (left) and Gene Koehnlein.

Two

Music Groups

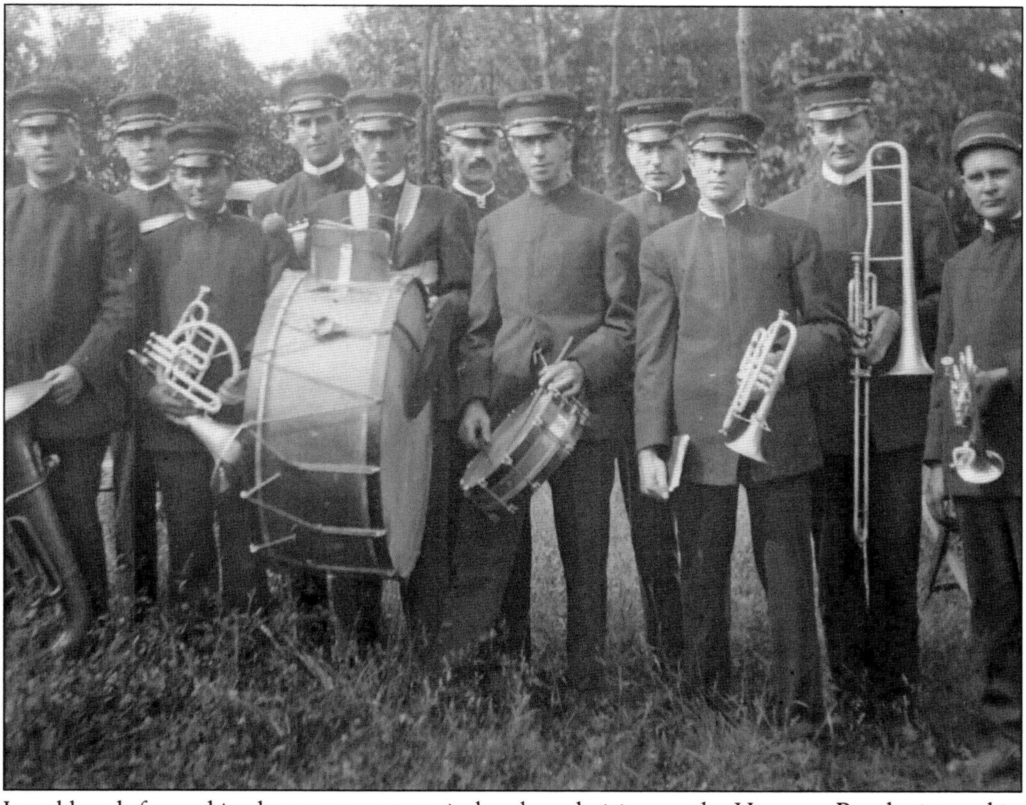

Local bands formed in the area to entertain locals and visitors—the Honeoye Band, pictured in this undated photograph, was one of the groups. Doc W. Beam of Canadice was an instructor and leader, and treasurer of the group. James Southgate and Charles Stillwell were other members. A group of young men formed the Silver Cornet Band of Honeoye in 1889. Cornet bands were popular in area towns. Enough money was raised to help with the purchase of instruments and to build a bandstand.

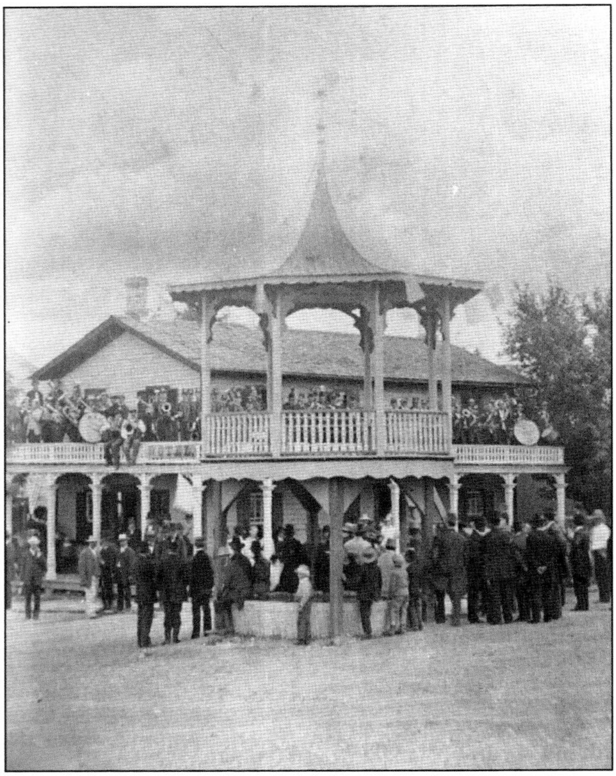

The crowds would form in the roadway around the bandstand. Notice its location in the intersection. It remained there for 49 years. It was slightly off-center of the intersection to allow for the passage of the horses and carriages in use at the time. After 49 years, it was moved to the Sandy Bottom Beach area and remodeled for use as a bathhouse. It eventually was torn down.

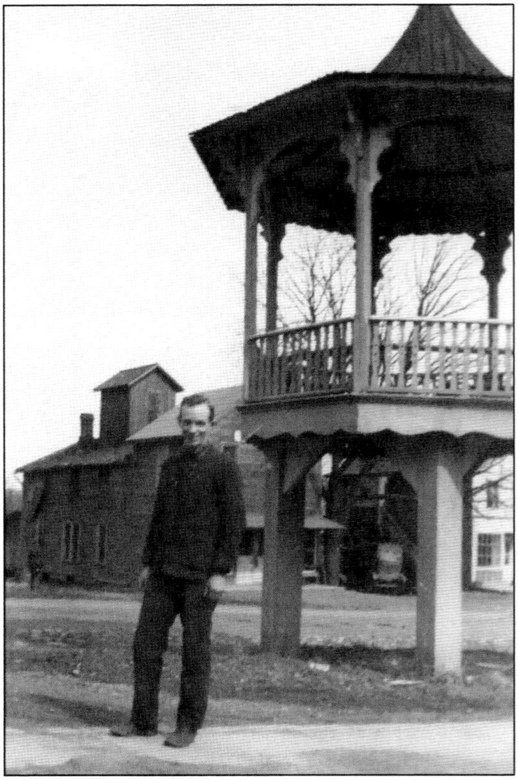

Clarence Bennett is shown in front of the bandstand in this undated photograph. Two-story bandstands were popular at the time, until there were incidents involving falls from the second level. Later bandstands in the area were built as one-story structures. The metal horn decoration on the top became an unofficial symbol in Richmond. The original one is now located in the Richmond Historical Museum.

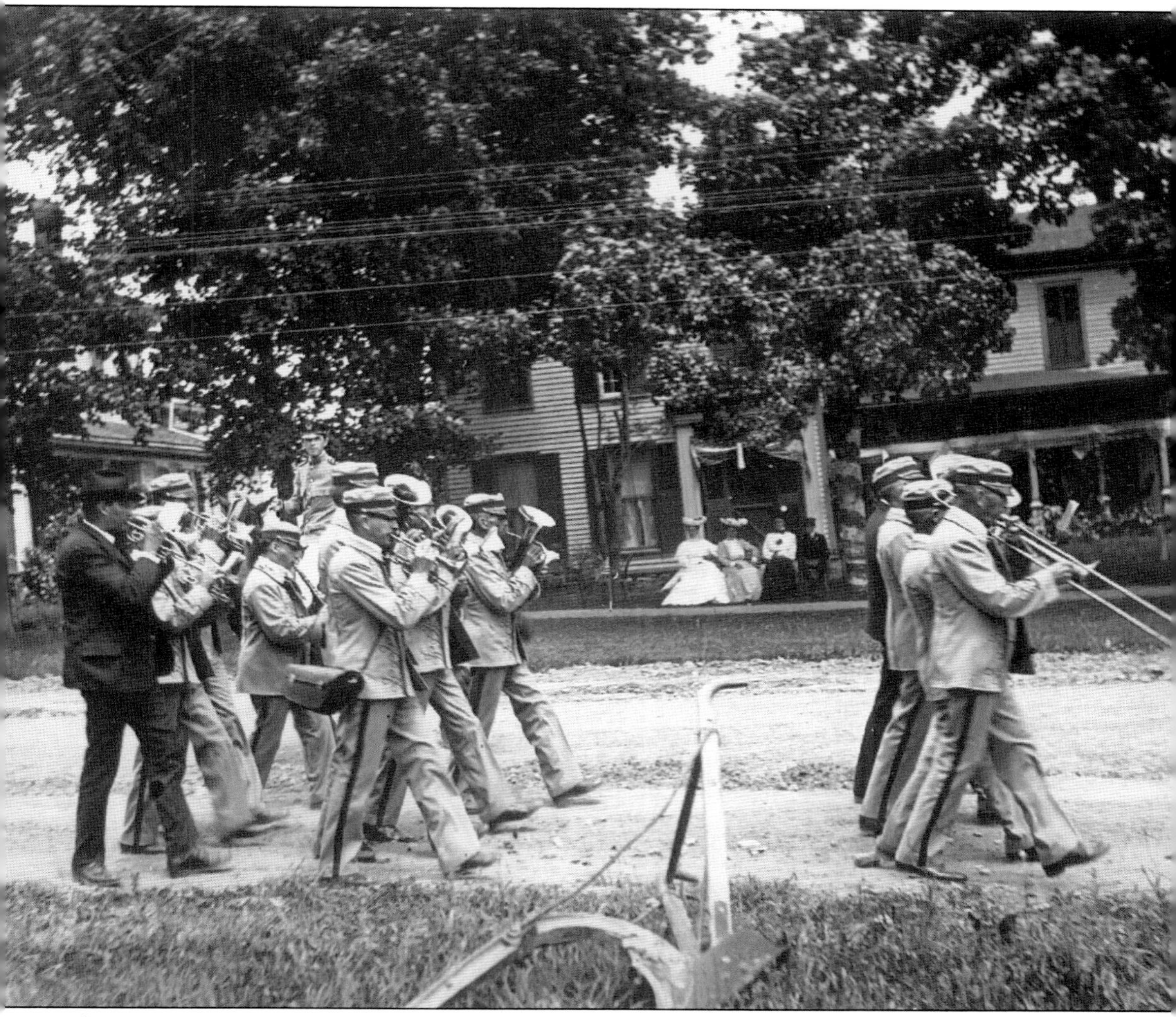

The Honeoye Band marched down Main Street in 1906. The home in the background was that of Gideon Pitts II. It is where Helen Pitts lived as a girl growing up in Honeoye. It also was the house where Frederick Douglass would visit for discussions with Gideon Pitts and other abolitionists in the area.

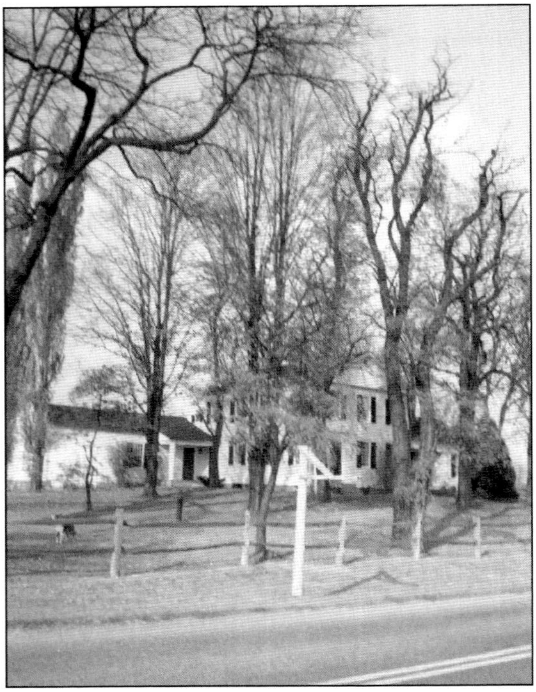

The Tally-Ho Music Camp was run at the home of Fred and Dorothy Bradley on Richmond Mills Road from 1948 to 1965. High school students from all over New York and some adjoining states attended the music camp; concerts were held for the community on Sunday evenings with attendance sometimes approaching 1,000 guests. Many of the attendees went on to become professional musicians all over the world. There were daily rehearsals, private instruction, class lessons, and recreation. The faculty was chosen principally from the Eastman School of Music in Rochester. Fred Bradley was a French horn player in the Rochester Civic and Philharmonic Orchestras for 31 years. The main house was built in 1816 of New England architecture. Additional buildings were added to the property for use as dormitories. An open-air band shell and a swimming pool for the campers were also added.

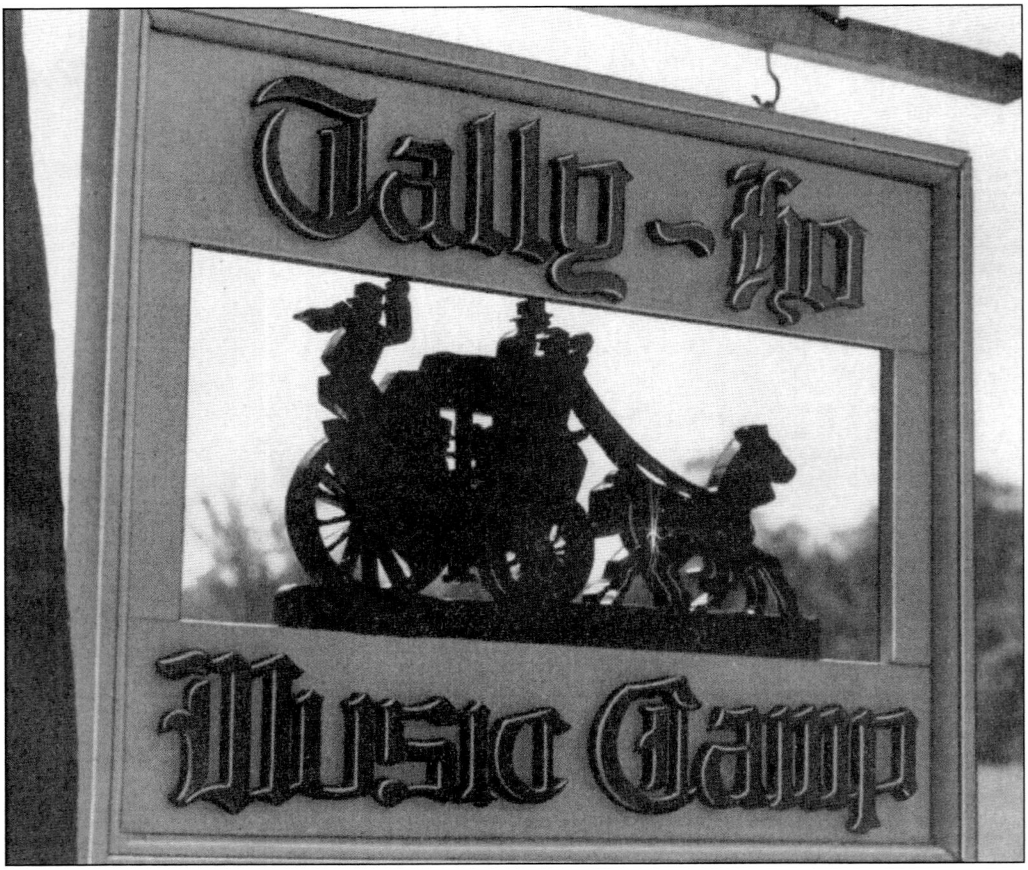

Three

SULLIVAN'S MARCH

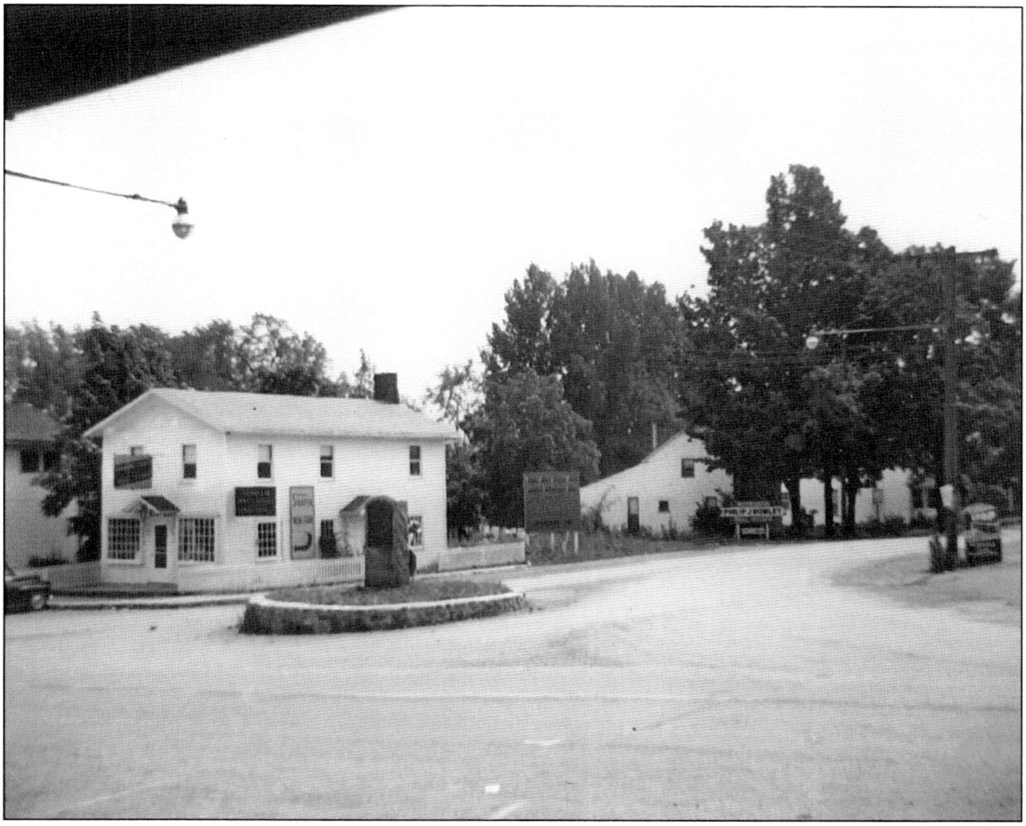

New York state erected several monuments in various towns Gen. John Sullivan and his troops had marched through during their attempt to remove the Native Americans living in the territory. Honeoye's monument was first erected just off center of the main intersection of Main Street and West Lake Road. It was there from 1929 to 1961, when it was moved to the front of the school on East Main Street.

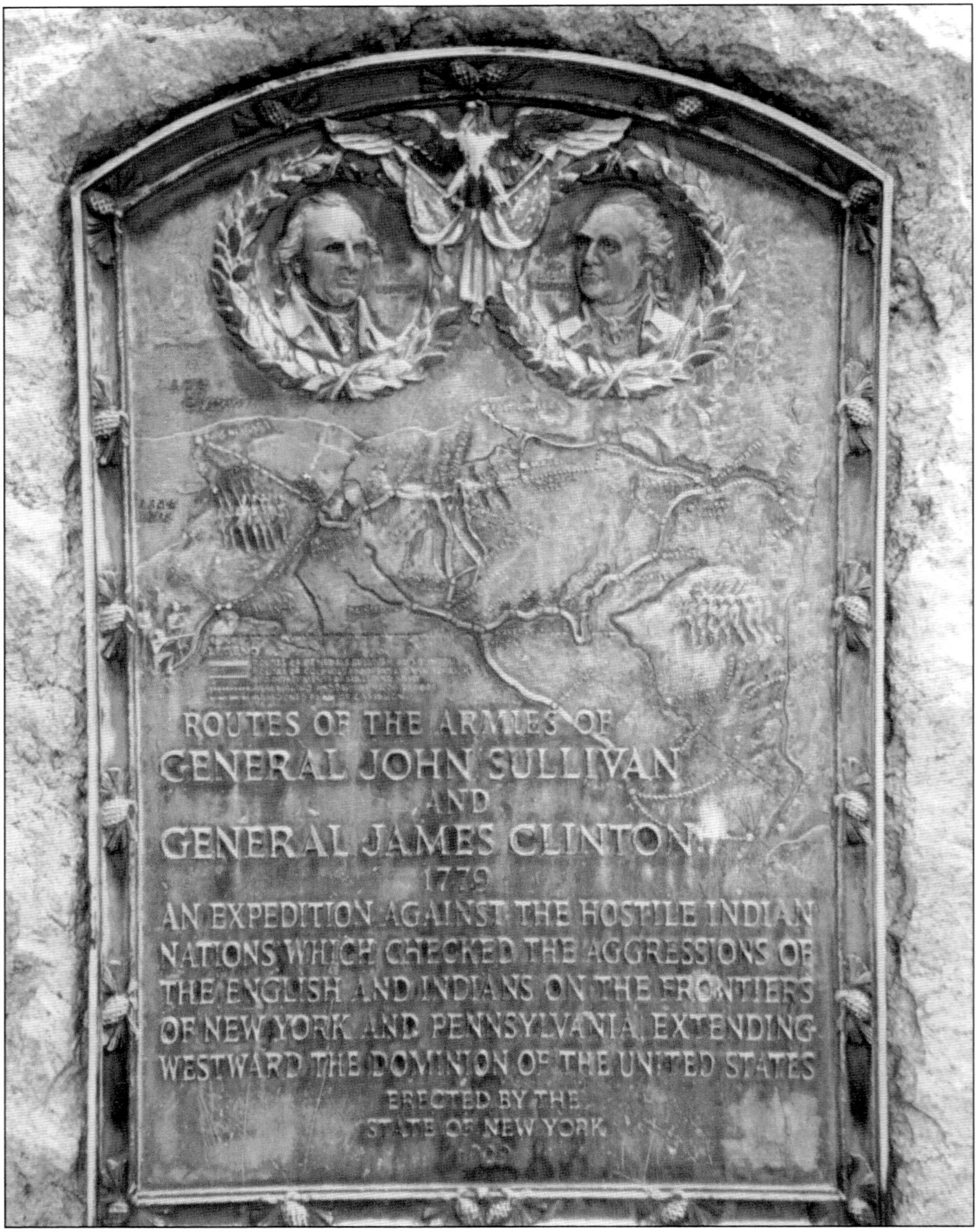

General Sullivan and his assistant, Gen. James Clinton, are shown on the front of the monument. The expedition of 1779 is described as being "against the hostile Indian nations." Some locals have questioned the need for such a monument, given its wording.

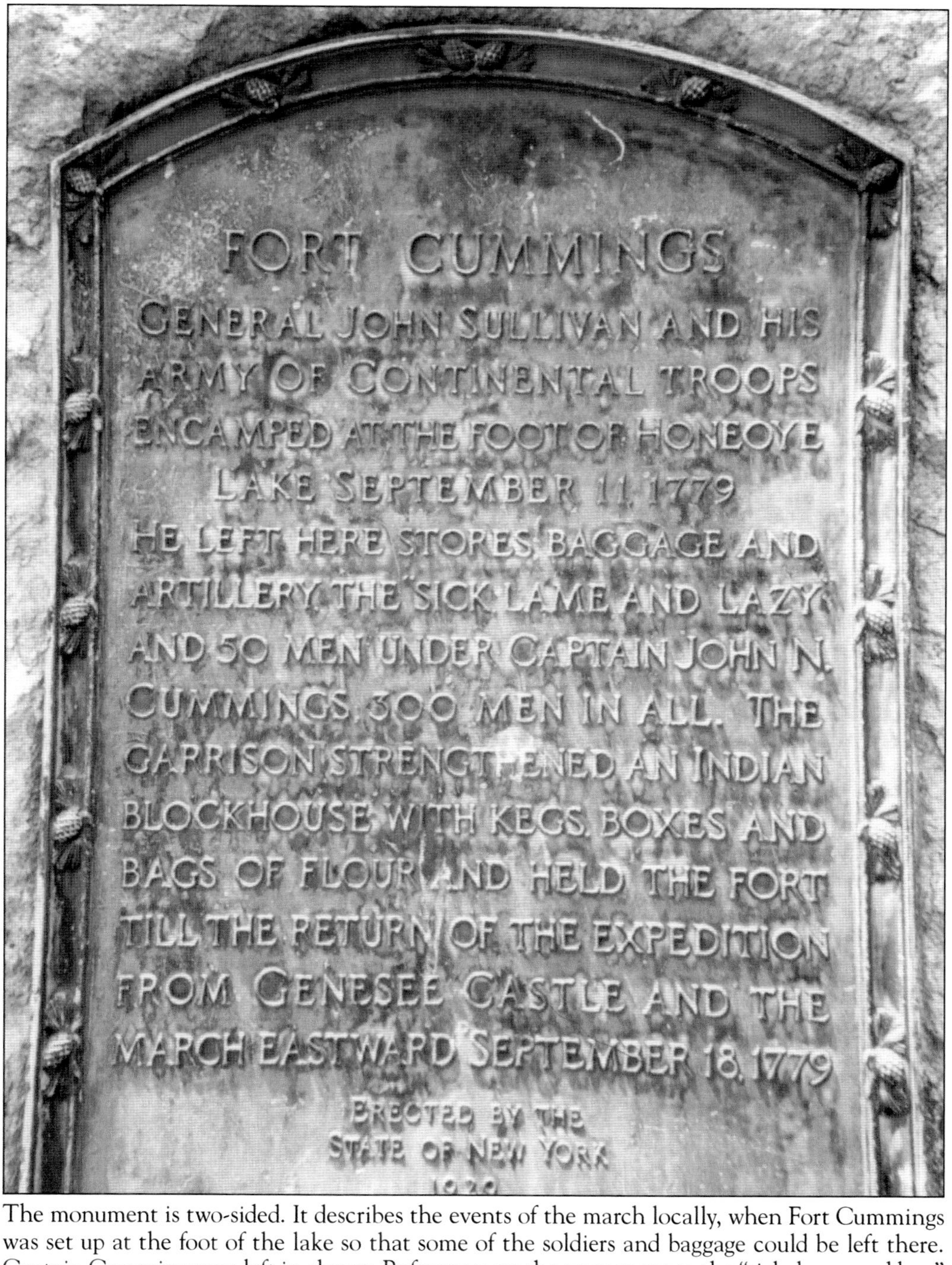

The monument is two-sided. It describes the events of the march locally, when Fort Cummings was set up at the foot of the lake so that some of the soldiers and baggage could be left there. Captain Cummings was left in charge. References on the monument to the "sick, lame, and lazy" soldiers who were left further upset some locals. It is possible that some of those who were left were among the early settlers of this area.

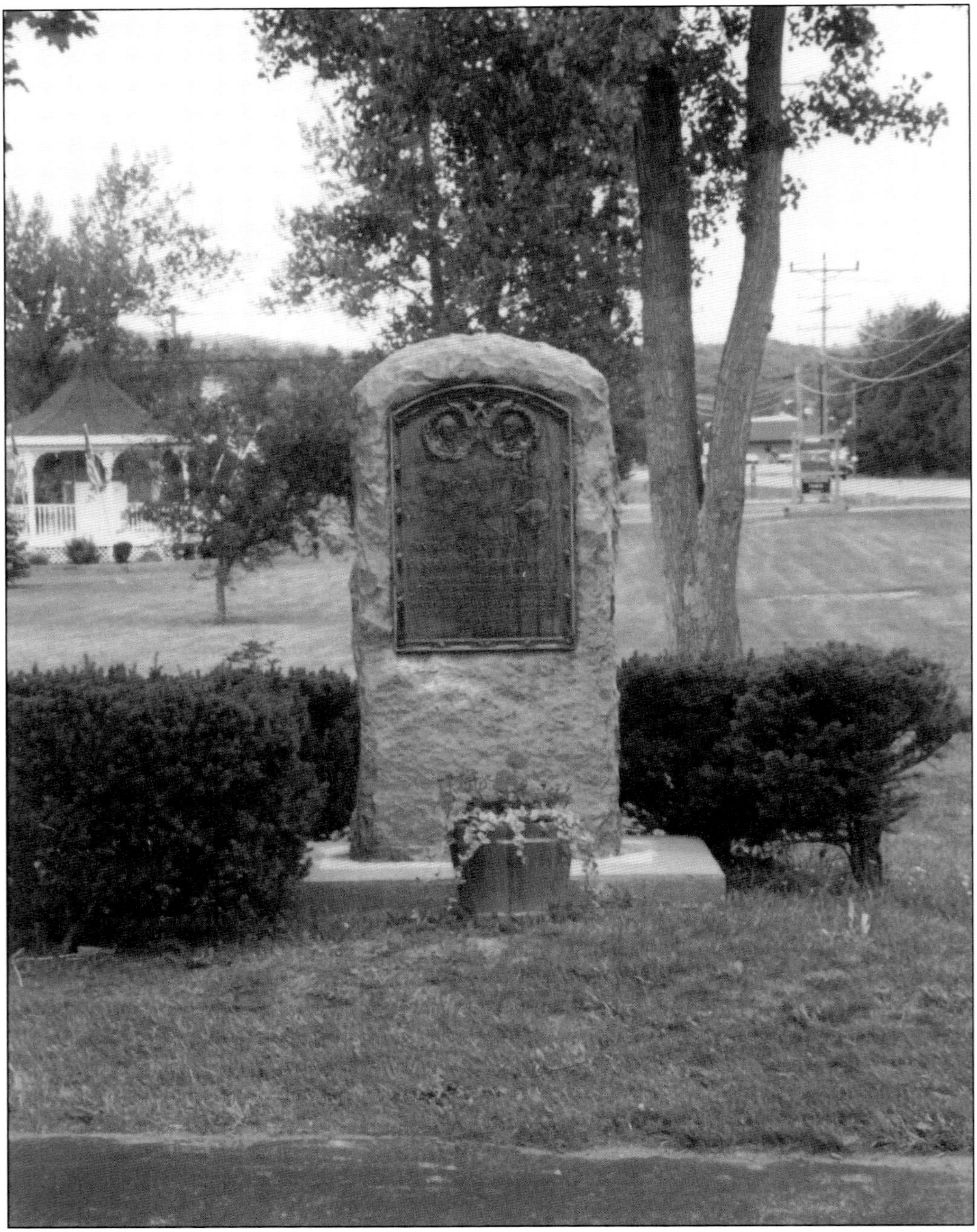

The Sullivan monument was moved once again from the school to the front of the Honeoye Public Library, where it now sits. George Washington's orders to General Sullivan were to destroy and devastate settlements and capture as many prisoners of every age and sex as possible. General Sullivan became ill on the expedition and at times slowed it down. He resigned his commission in 1780 and returned to his home in New Hampshire. In 1929, a 2¢ postage stamp was issued commemorating the 150th anniversary of the expedition, with Sullivan's picture.

Four

Businesses

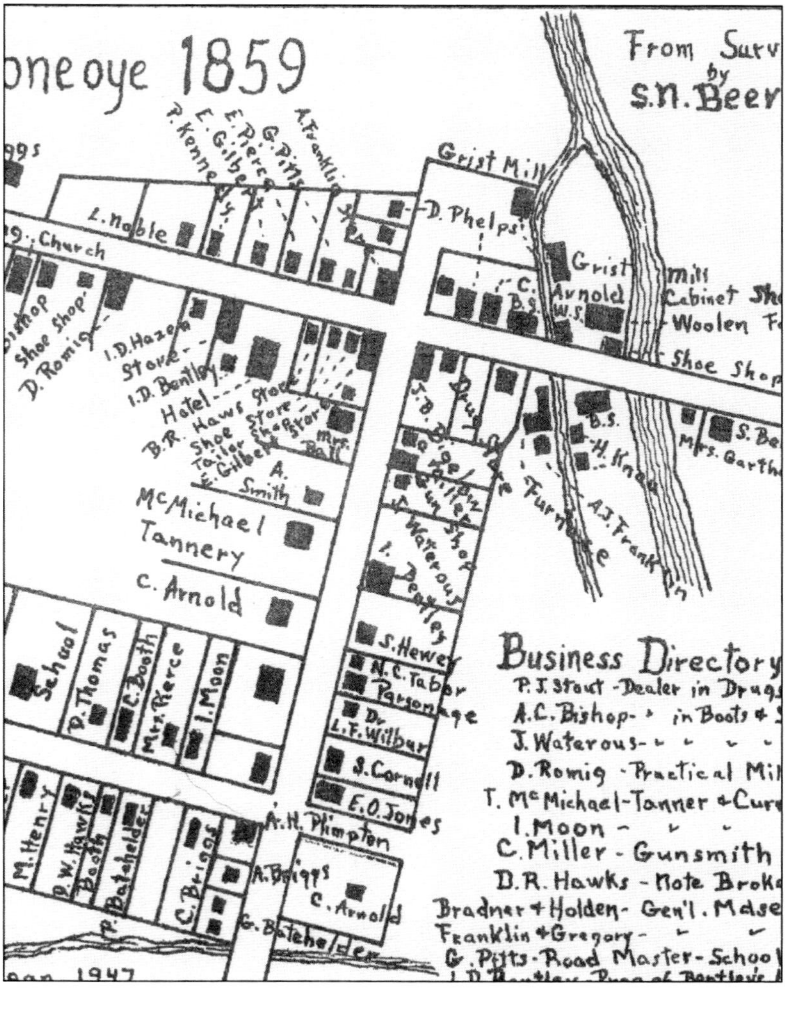

This map of the hamlet shows where the concentration of homes and businesses occurred in the early years of Honeoye. Canadice has no central business area even up to this day. The concentration of businesses continues to be in the same general vicinity as shown on this map.

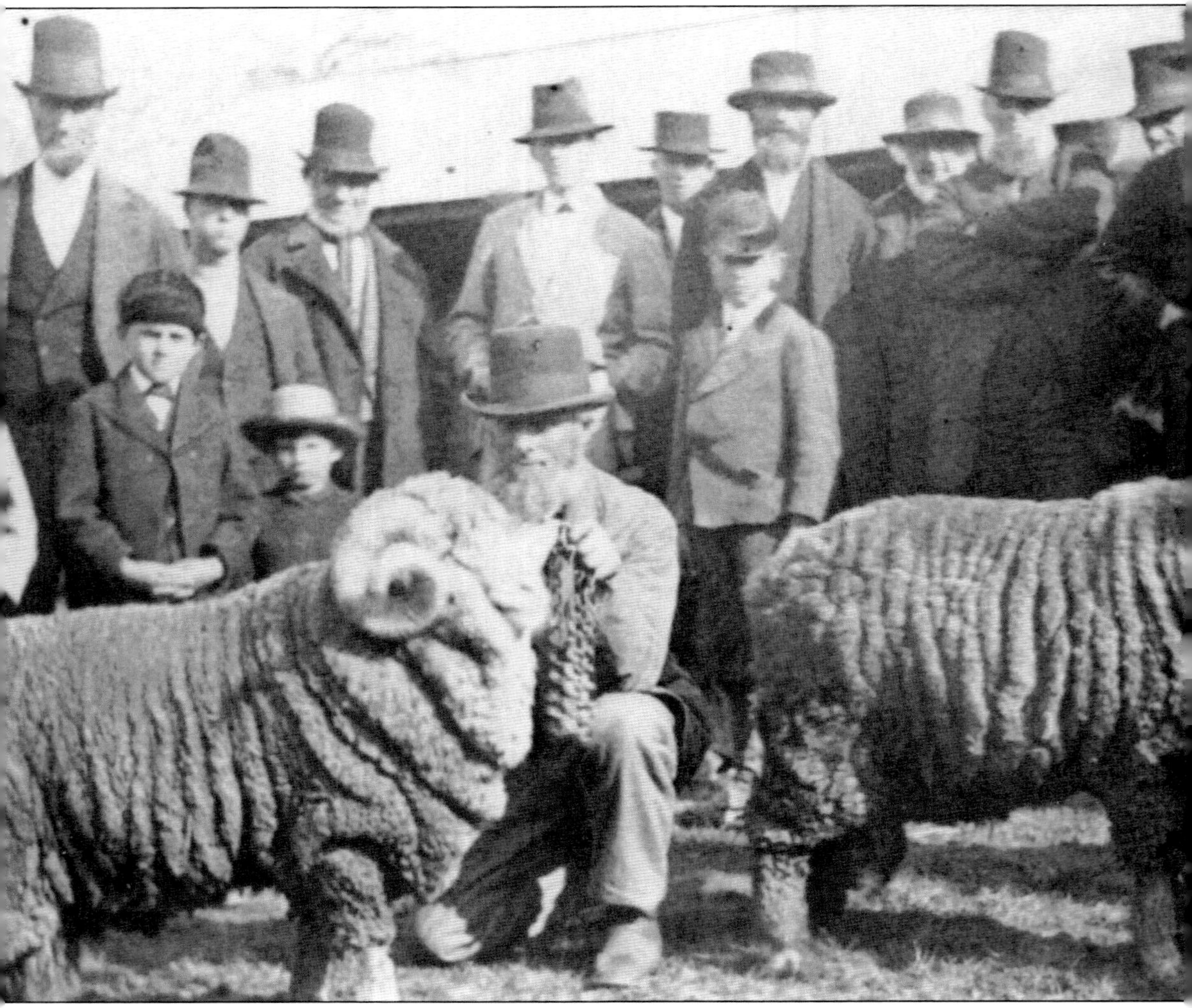

Sheep-raising was a major business in the 1800s and early 1900s. There was an active Wool Growers Association in the Richmond area. Summers provided the chance for the sheep raisers to get together at shows and let each other see their sheep and judge the quality of wool that was sheared. One Richmond farmer, John P. Ray, provided wool for President McKinley's inauguration suit in 1897. That also was the first inauguration to be recorded on film. Sheep shows were sometimes held behind the Congregational church in Honeoye, where Merino sheep were sheared. Band concerts were added in the later years. Farm machinery was on display and horse races were run on Main Street. Eventually, the Hemlock Fair, to the west of Honeoye, absorbed those activities.

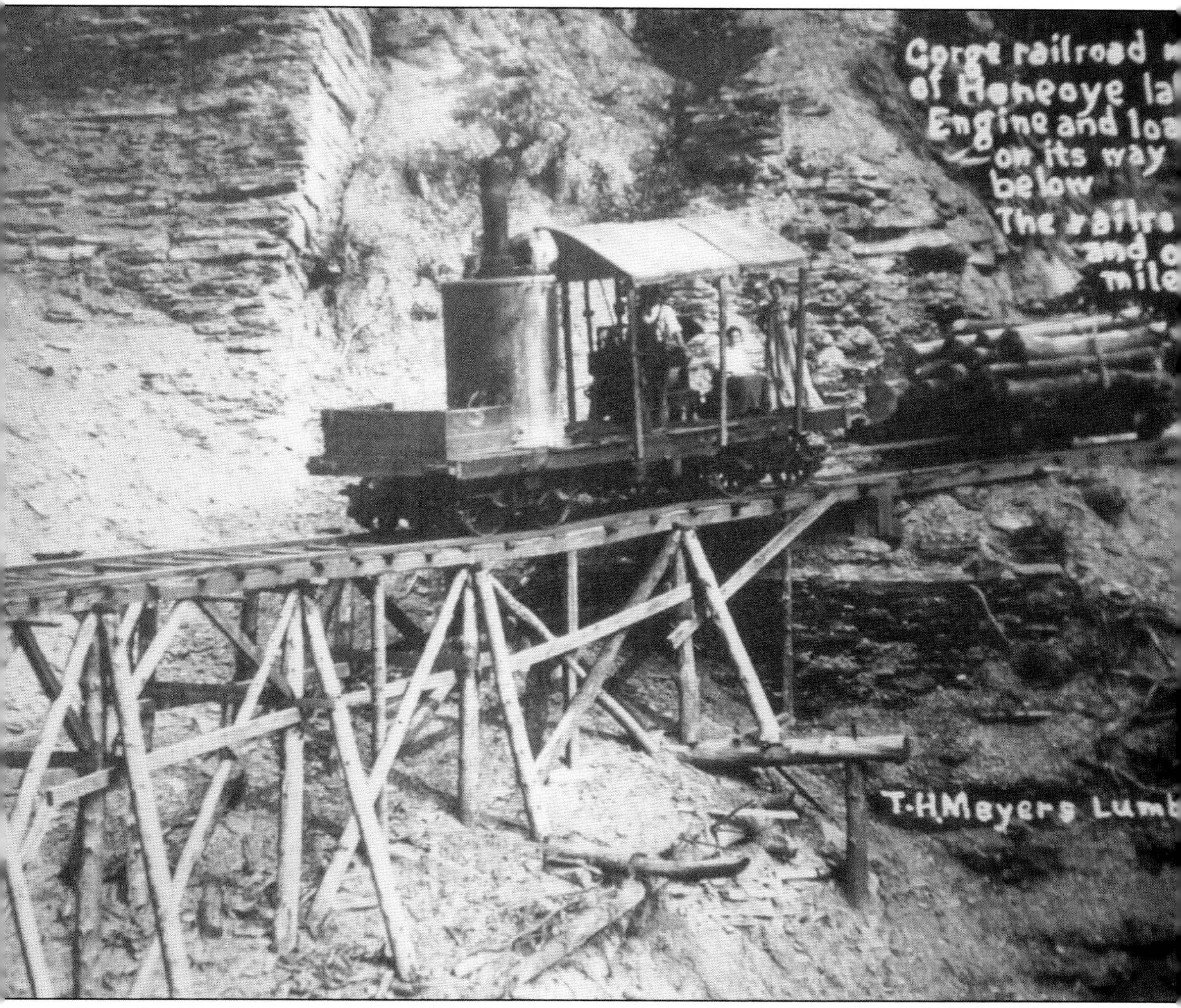

Meyer Lumber Company was in the southeast area of Richmond around Brigg's Gully. Some of their equipment, such as this engine, was considered to be quite crude. The Meyer Lumber Company was in the area for about 10 years, until the area they had been logging was finished. On the west side of Honeoye Lake, another company started logging in the area but did not stay long. It was called the Klondike Company.

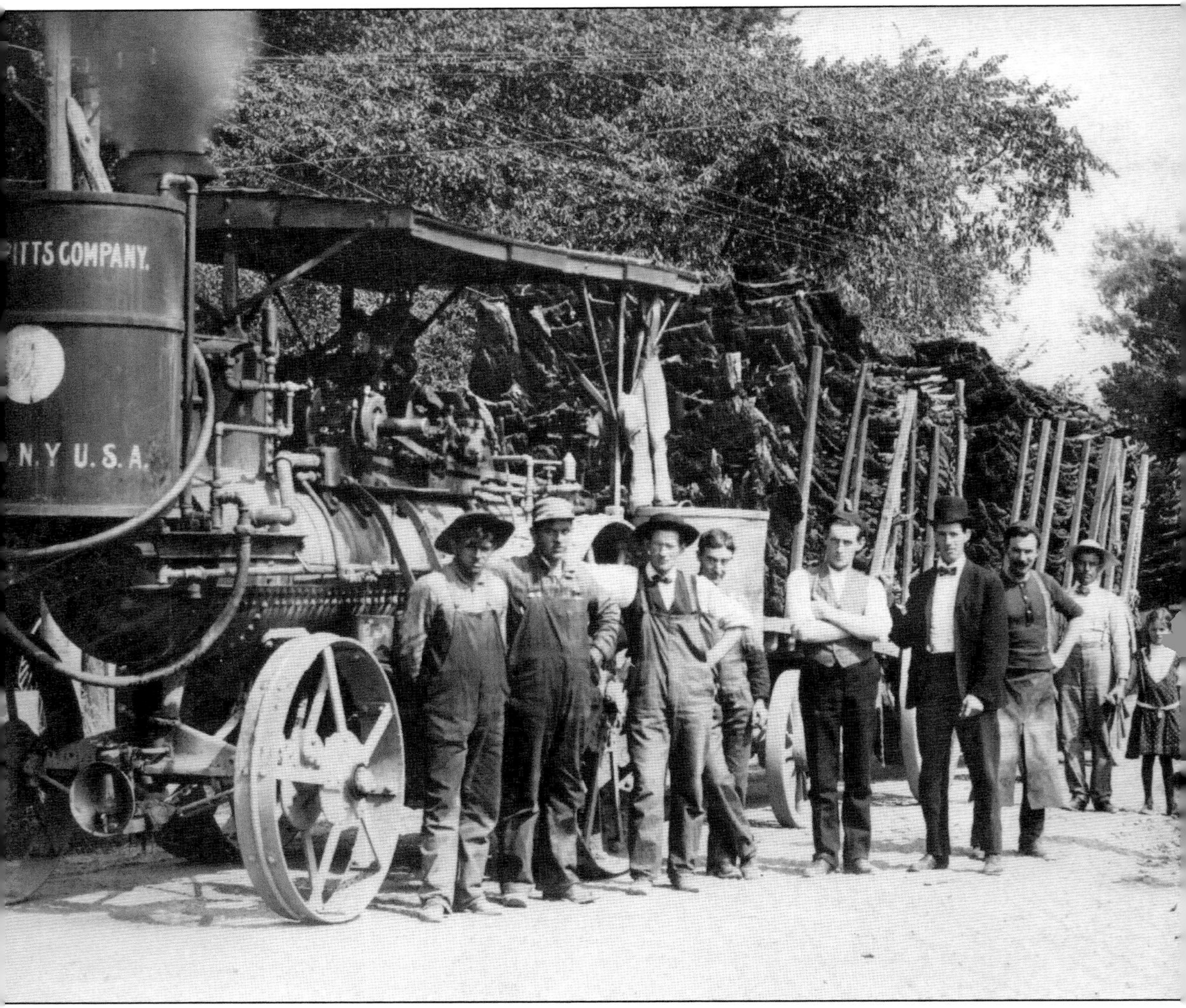

These were some of the hardworking employees getting the lumber out of the gully area to be transported down to the lumber mill. The gully is still a difficult area to get into. A hiking trail now exists along its top ridge as part of the Wesley Hill Nature Preserve, which is part of the Fingers Lake Land Trust.

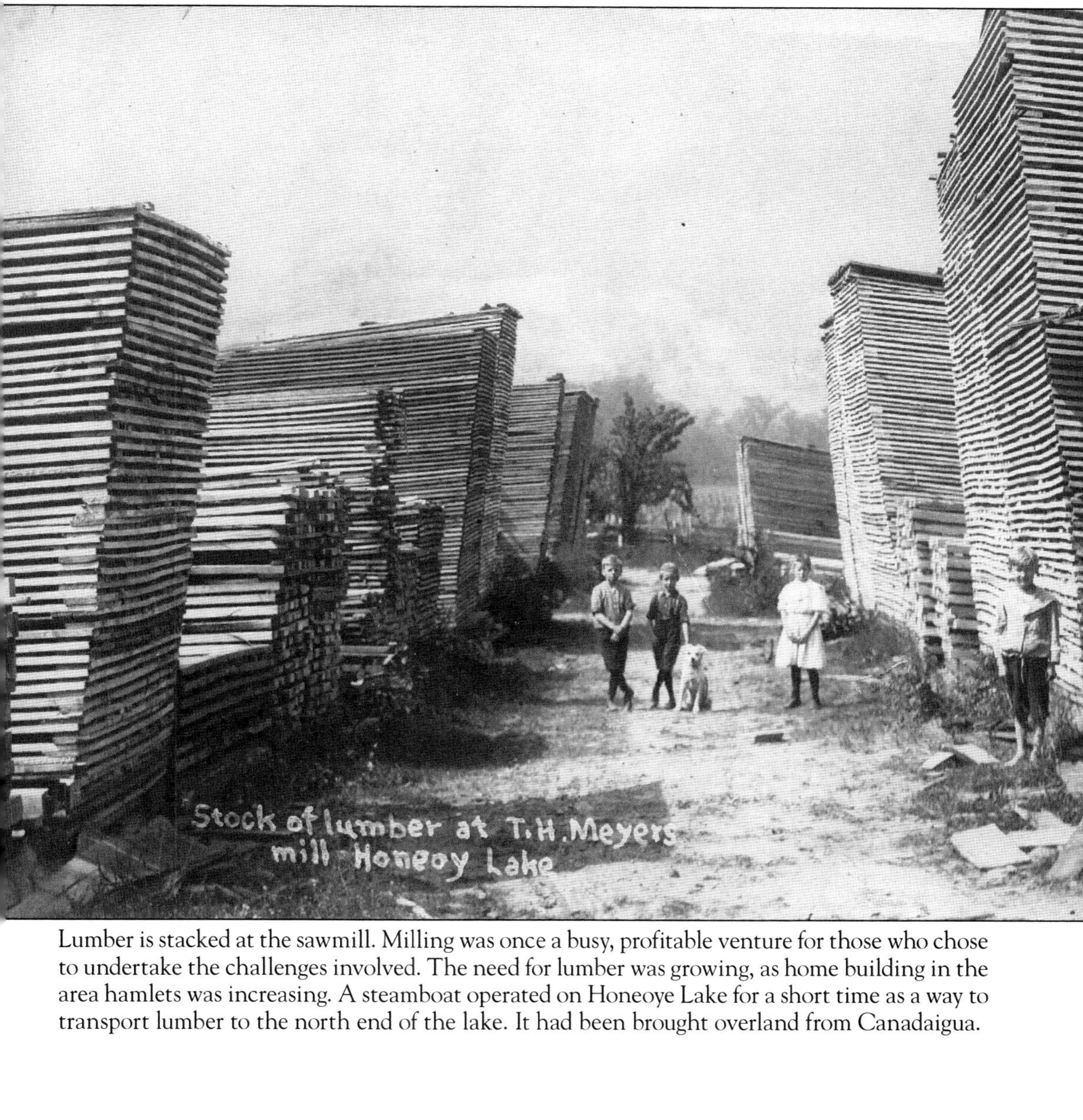

Lumber is stacked at the sawmill. Milling was once a busy, profitable venture for those who chose to undertake the challenges involved. The need for lumber was growing, as home building in the area hamlets was increasing. A steamboat operated on Honeoye Lake for a short time as a way to transport lumber to the north end of the lake. It had been brought overland from Canadaigua.

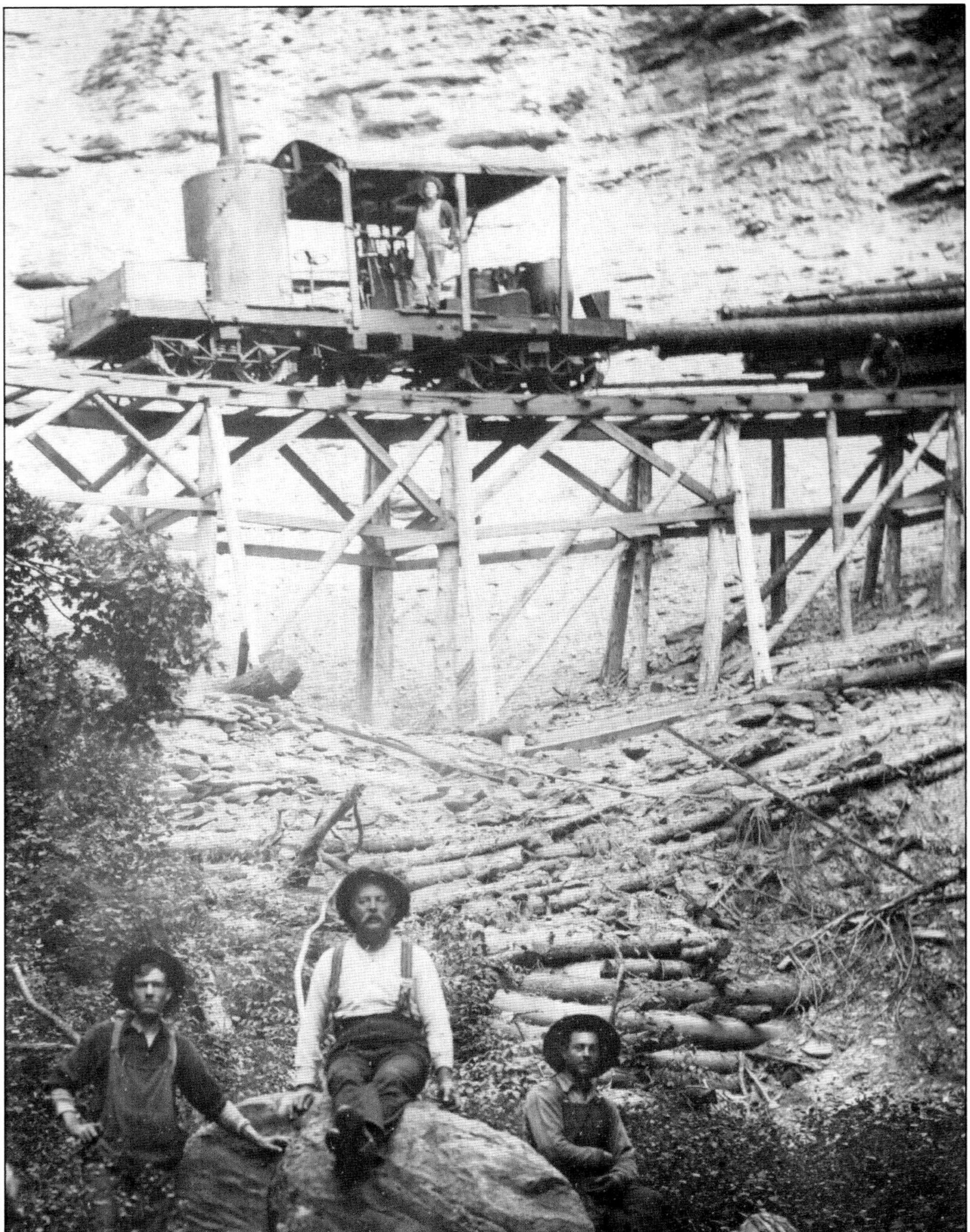

The train that was built in the gully was crude and short lived. No evidence of it exists. It ran for a mile and a half back and forth from the upper terminus of the gorge to the mill located below the gully. The engine was powered by steam, a common way to run equipment at that time. By the early 1900s, the logging venture had shut down in Brigg's Gully. There were other smaller operations in the area by individuals who sought the vast amount of timber available at the time.

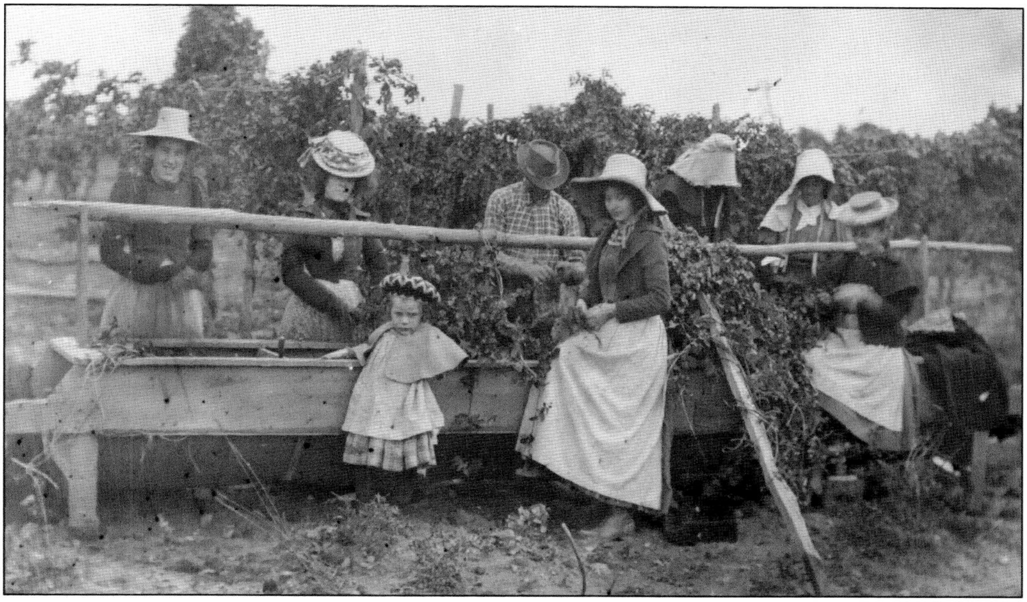

Hops were being grown on nearly every family farm in the 19th century and the farms around Richmond were no exception. Hops were a leading agricultural crop in the late 1800s and early 1900s. The hops would be sold to area breweries to use in the production of beer. Hops are actually a flower grown on perennial vines. The vines would be trained to grow up poles, wire, and string. The plants could grow as much as two feet per week and reach heights of 40 feet. Hops would be ready to pick in late August and early September. One single hops plant still grows at the northwest corner of the Agricultural Museum on Main Street in Honeoye.

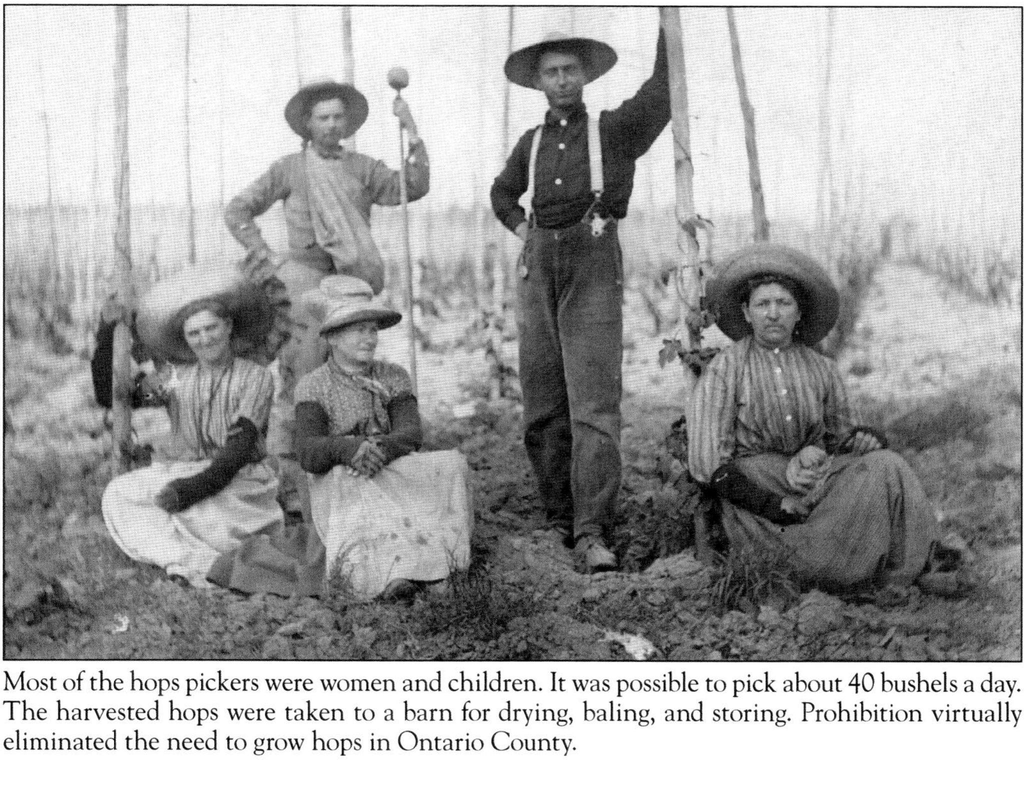

Most of the hops pickers were women and children. It was possible to pick about 40 bushels a day. The harvested hops were taken to a barn for drying, baling, and storing. Prohibition virtually eliminated the need to grow hops in Ontario County.

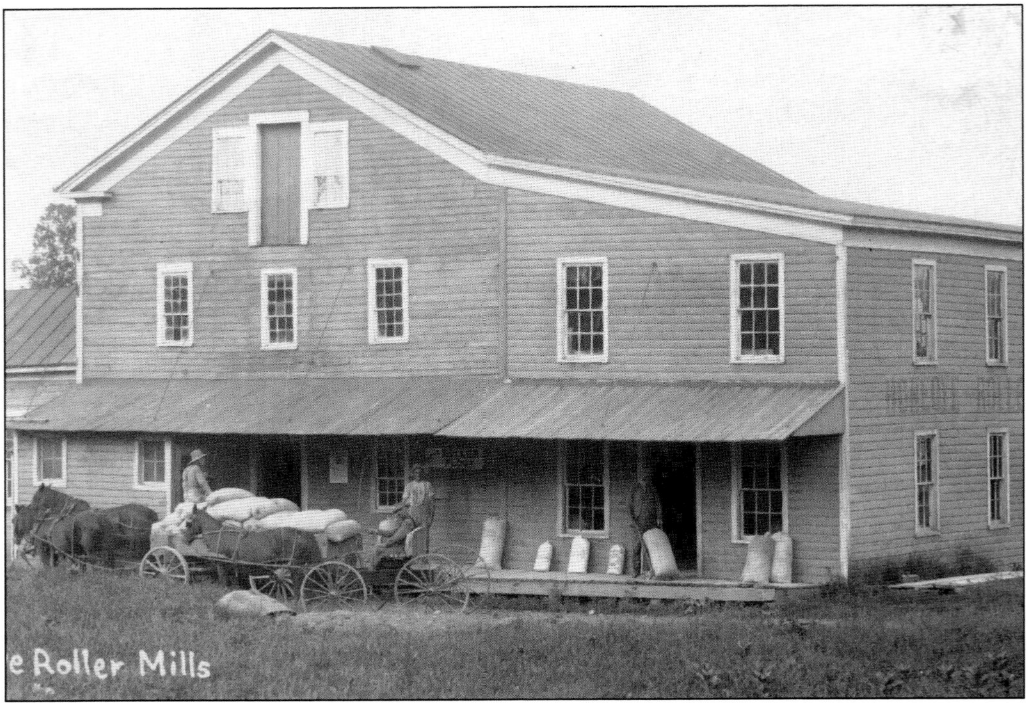

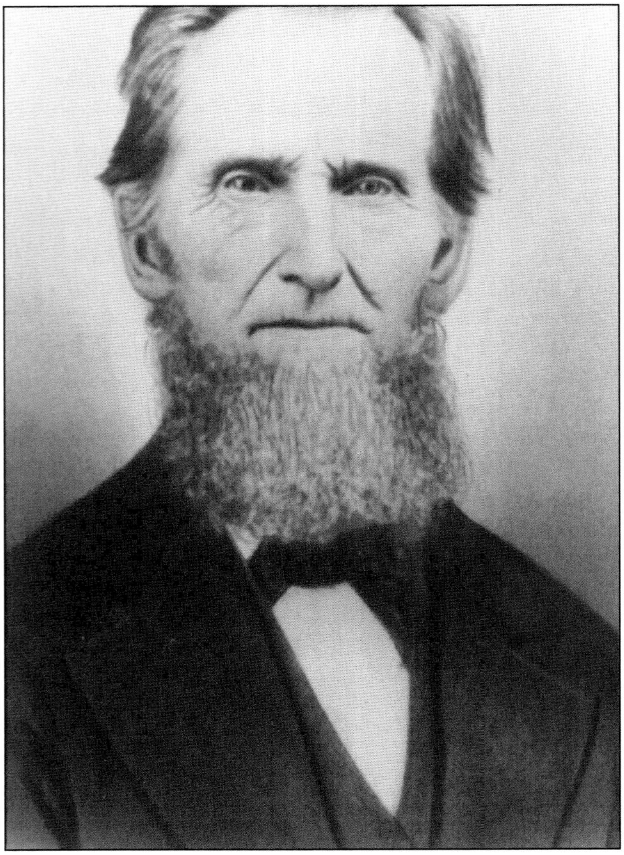

The Honeoye Roller Mill (above) stood near what is now Briarcliff Square. In 1815, Gideon Pitts, son of Peter Pitts, built the first gristmill in Honeoye. In the early 1840s, Capt. Hoshua Philips purchased the mill and owned it for several decades. John Quick (at left) purchased the mill in 1876 and made improvements by putting in a complete roller system. A few years later, he enlarged the mill. In 1899, due to failing health, Quick leased the mill to Woodruff and Backus, a partnership that continued until 1901 when John W. Backus became the sole proprietor. He supplied his customers with several grades of flour, his best being Cream of the Valley. The best winter wheat flour was White Rose. After the mill stood vacant for several years, it is said that a local citizen grew tired of looking at the building and burned it down.

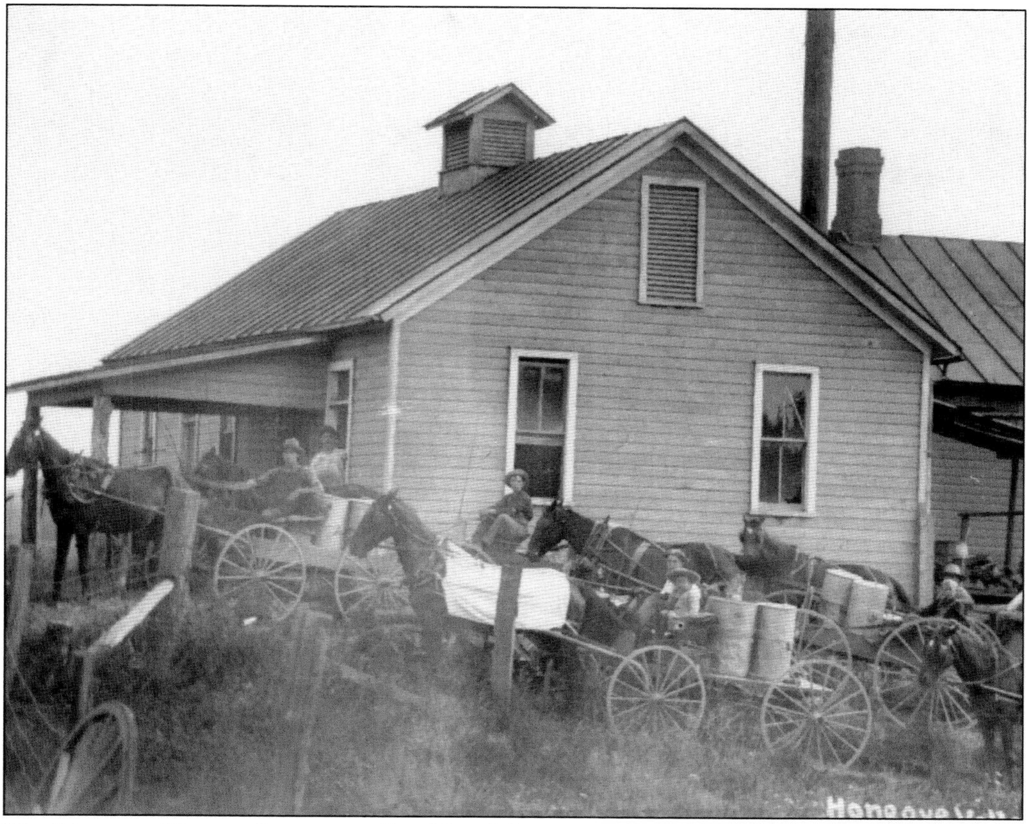

The Honeoye Cheese Company offered local farmers a place to sell excess milk. They would come with their wagons, going through what is now Briarcliff Square, and travel to the end of Church Street. It actually was a cooperative enterprise where farmers were invited to provide milk for which they were paid according to its quality. James Gardner, a 45-year-old bachelor, was chosen to be the cheese maker. In June 1897, the first wagons carrying cans of milk to the factory made a delivery. It took 1,500 pounds of milk to be transformed into four cheeses, each weighing 44 pounds. They would be cured in the curing room, and in a month, would be shrunk to about three pounds.

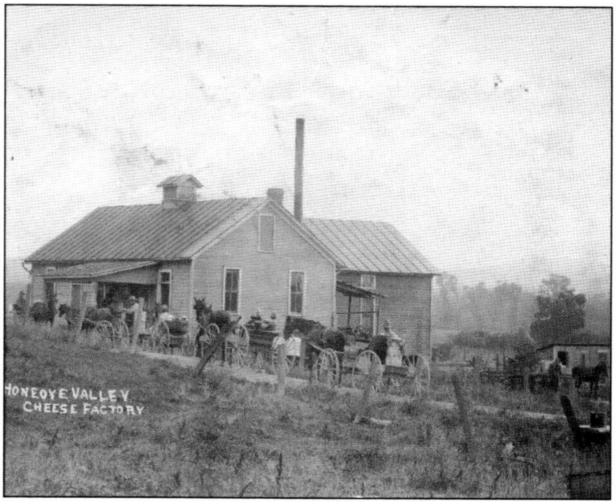

This photograph shows additional farmers delivering their milk to the cheese factory. The cheese manufactured at the Honeoye Cheese Company was considered very fine in quality. James Gardner was also complimented on the cleanliness of the factory. In April 1908, 57-year-old Gardner married Ellen Hatch of South Bristol, who was the same age and had also never married. The marriage was brief, as Gardner died in April 1909. Part of the cheese factory remains as the last house on Church Street.

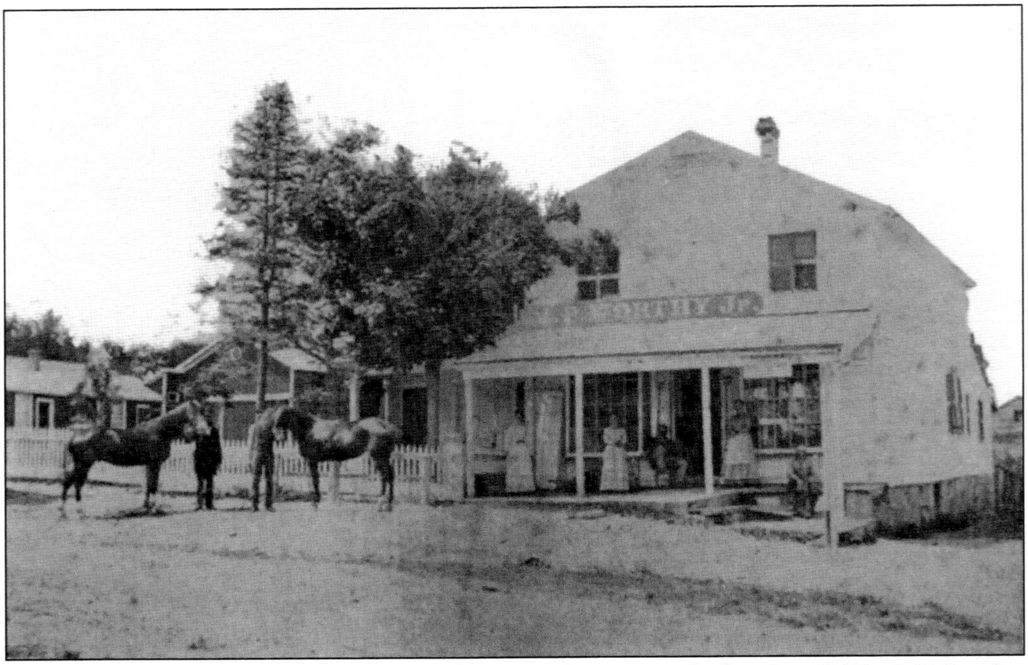

Worthy's Store was one of the businesses that were thriving in the hamlet of Allen's Hill, a few miles north of Honeoye. There also was a tavern, two churches, and a one-room schoolhouse. The tile factory was located to the south of the hamlet.

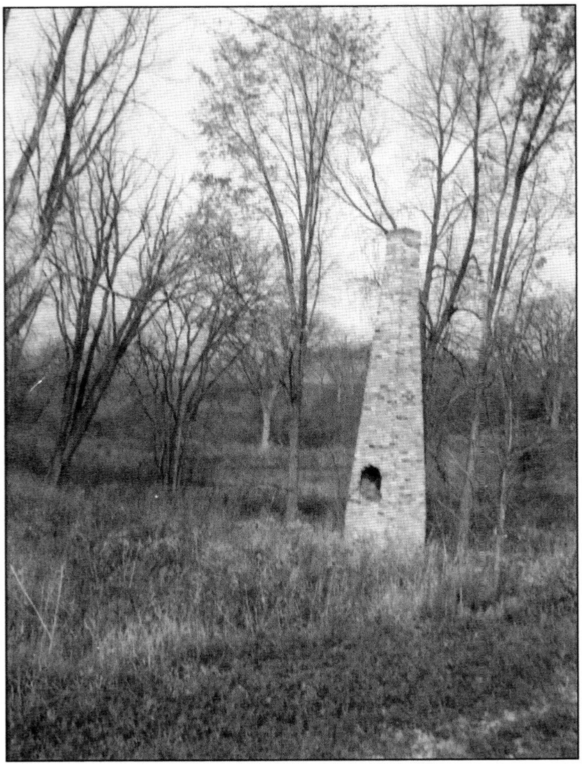

Nelson Ogden purchased a tract of land in 1855 and built a tile and brick factory near Allens Hill. A nearby creek provided the necessary water for manufacturing along with a deposit of fine quality clay, another essential ingredient. The business was an instant success. A sawmill, an evaporator, and a cider mill were added to the business over the years. By 1912, the business was no longer thriving and the current owner retired. Part of the factory was dismantled and moved and the other buildings were taken down. All that remained of the tile factory was the landmark chimney, leaning precariously to one side. By 2006, the chimney had collapsed and the owners of the property cleaned up its remains and the tile factory became history. A few of the tiles manufactured there are currently in the Agricultural Museum located in the one-room schoolhouse on Main Street in Honeoye.

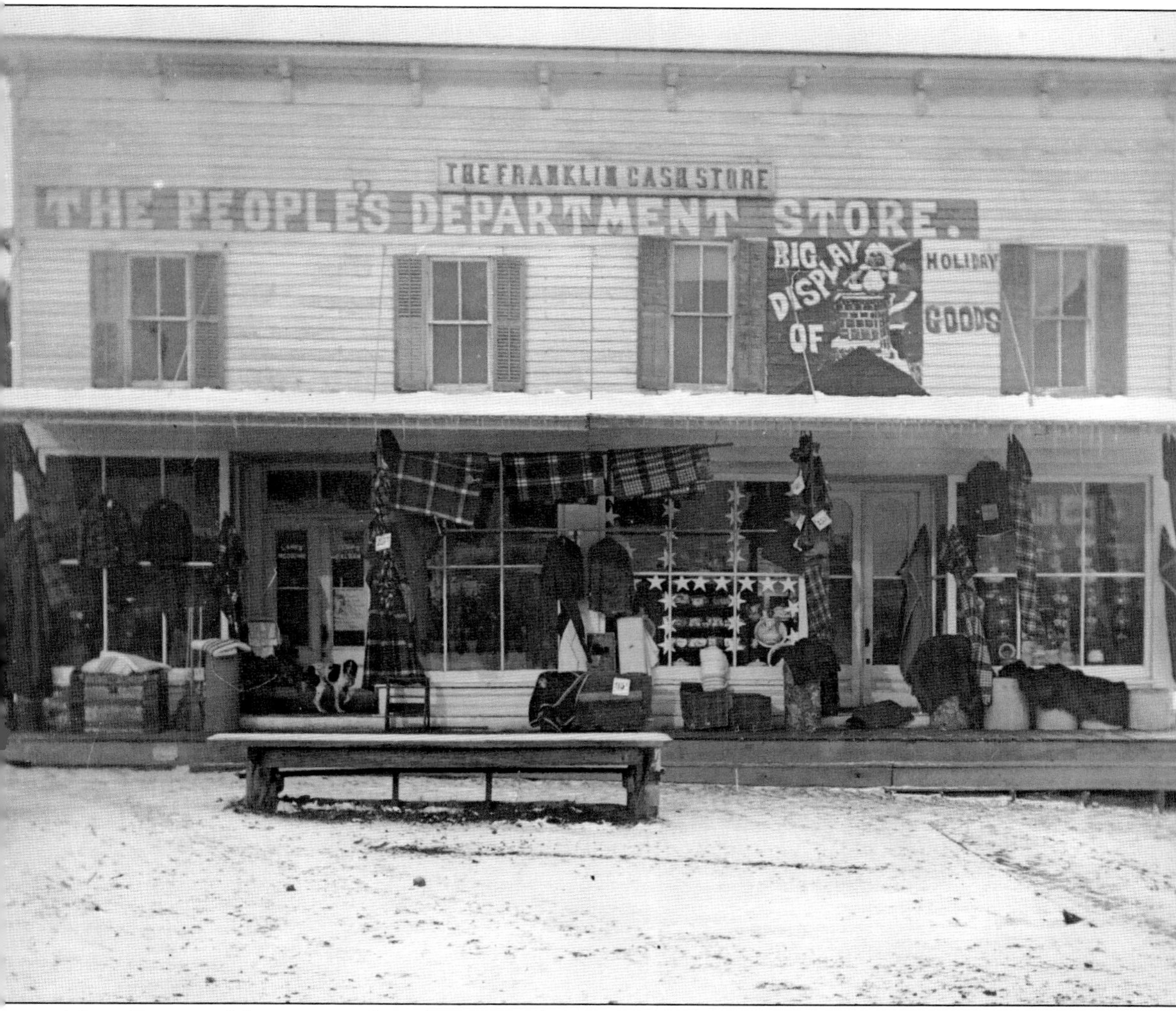

Main Street in Honeoye is where businesses began to sprout up. One of them was the Franklin Cash Store or People's Department Store. Cash was not always required for a purchase as bartering was common in the early 1900s. In 1905, the store burned to the ground after a hanging kerosene lamp dropped to the floor. A clerk in the store tried to put the fire out using a broom soaked in water. The building was soon engulfed in flames. It was rebuilt in 1906, and the Eagle Lodge purchased the building in 1909. The lodge established a meeting room on the second floor, and the lower level was a dry goods store for a short time. It then became a grocery store until 1919. The building was vacant until 1924, except for two years when the Ku Klux Klan rented the northwest area of the first floor to hold their meetings. The Klan created dissension in Honeoye. In 1924, Rexford Drain, Clarence Bennett, and Mortimer Clement rented the store, operating a grocery area on the east side and a meat market on the west side.

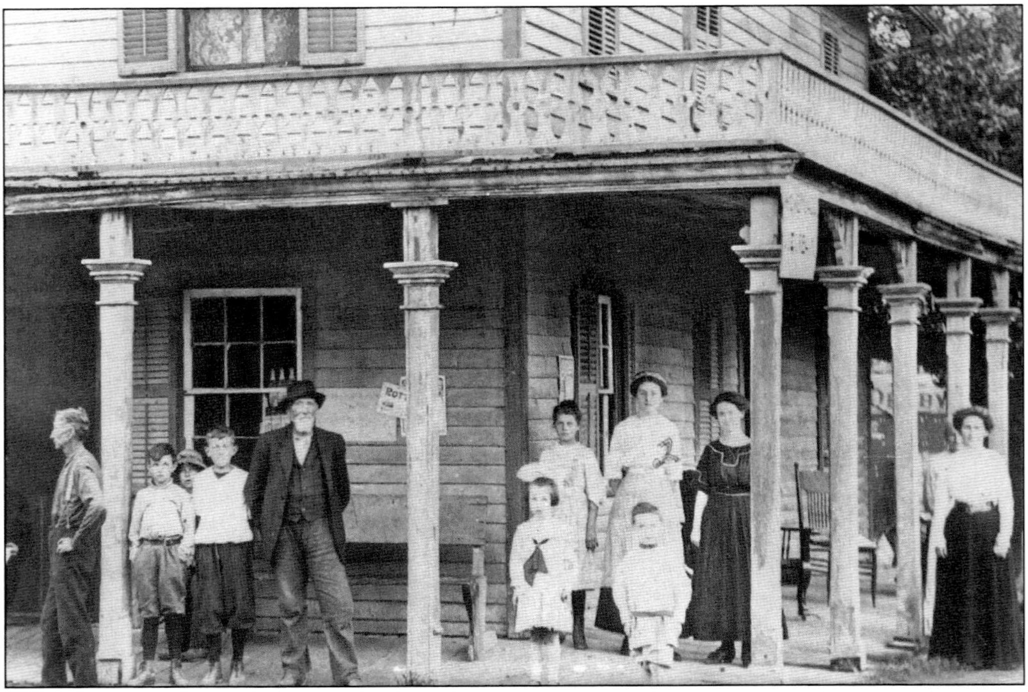

In 1876, Philip James "P.J." Stout and his son, James, who were popular druggists in Honeoye, added a first-class hotel on the southeast corner of Main and Lake Streets (West Lake Road). It became a popular stopping-off place for "traveling men." A livery stable was behind the building. The hotel became known for its food, which was prepared by Adelia Stout and her aunt. A hall above the hotel was where dinners and public dances were held. A grocery store was also operated in the building by a son of P.J. Stout. Over the years, the porches have been removed.

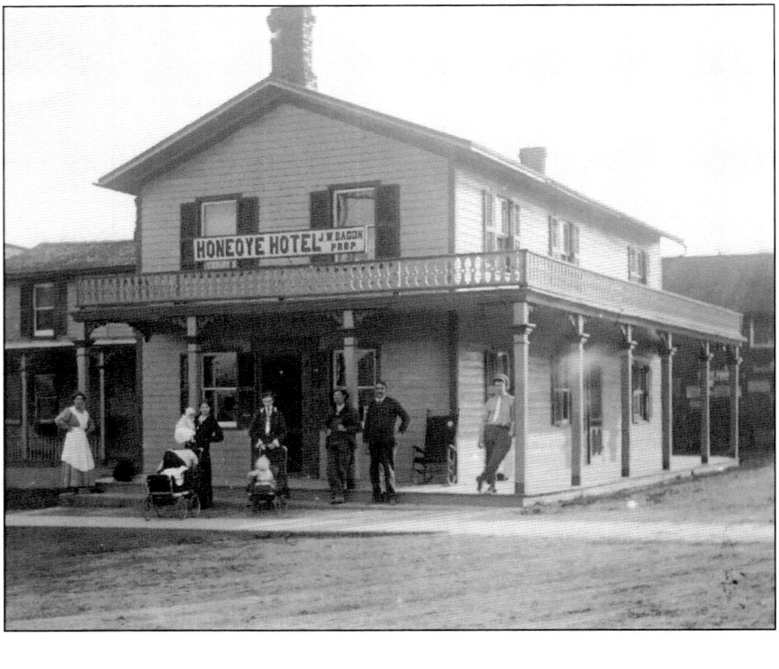

At one time, the Stout Hotel was called the Honeoye Hotel. Over the years, it has been the home of varied businesses. Occupying the historic building have been a coffee shop, a hairdresser, an antique dealer, a gift shop, and a travel agent. It is currently occupied by a real estate agency.

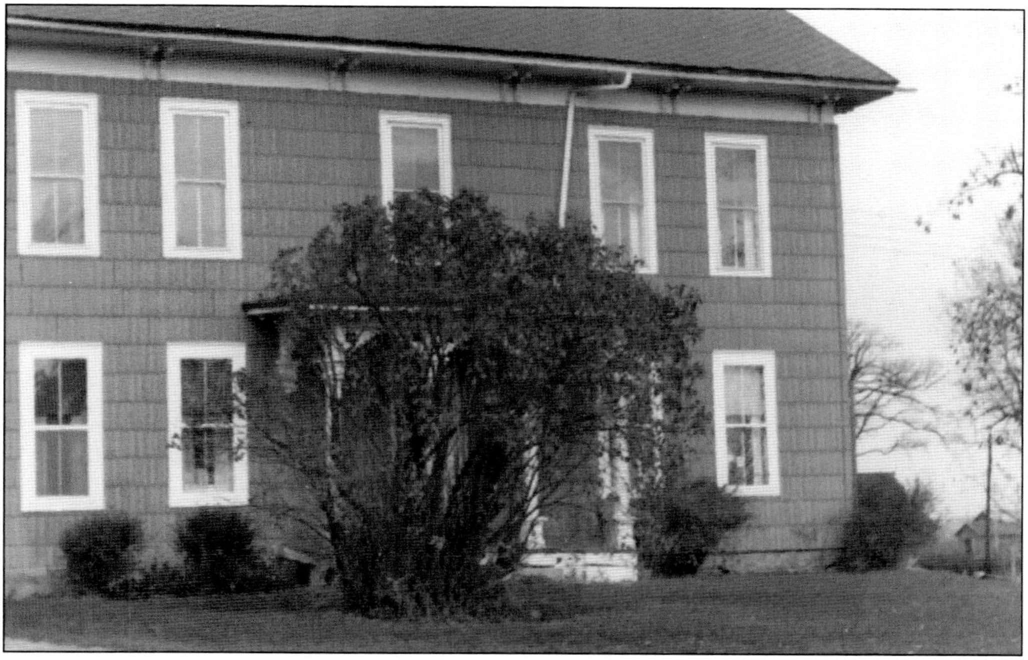

The Dennison's Corners Tavern was located in this home. It was on a major route from Canandaigua to points west. Asa Dennison was licensed in 1831 along with 10 other tavern owners to "retail strong and spirituous liquors and wines." The license cost $5 and was signed by Hiram Pitts.

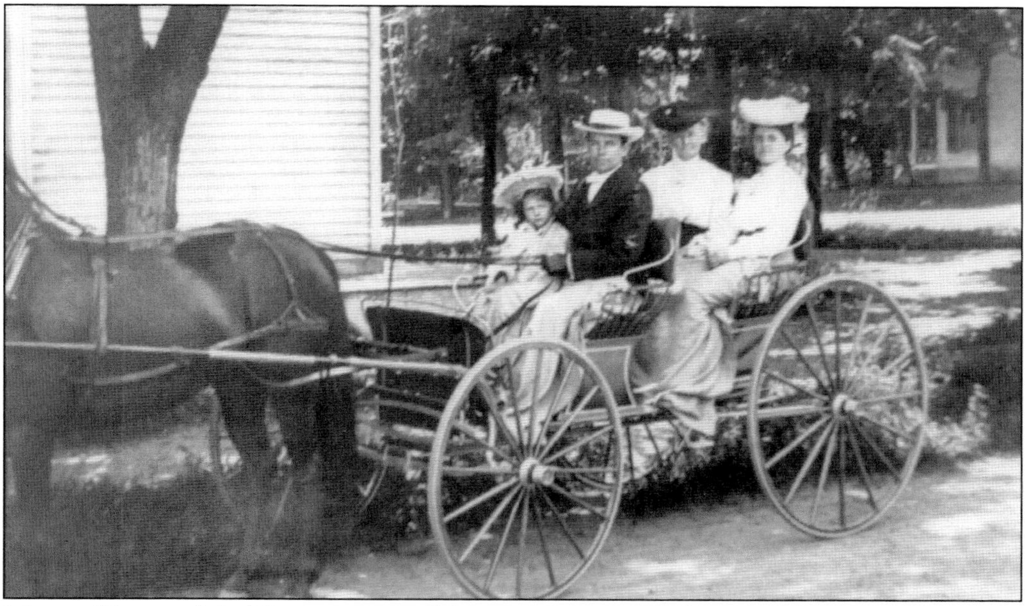

John and Lenora (May) Burton were well known in Honeoye. They are shown here with family members. John Burton had been born in Honeoye Falls in 1867 to Asahel and Catherine Fish Burton. He was in the undertaking business for 11 years in Honeoye Falls and then moved to Honeoye, where he was in the undertaking business for 39 years. In 1895, he married Lenora May of Holley. They had two daughters, Catherine Burton and Pauline Beam of Hemlock. Lenora intended to continue the business in accord with her husband's wishes after his death. It is not known if she did.

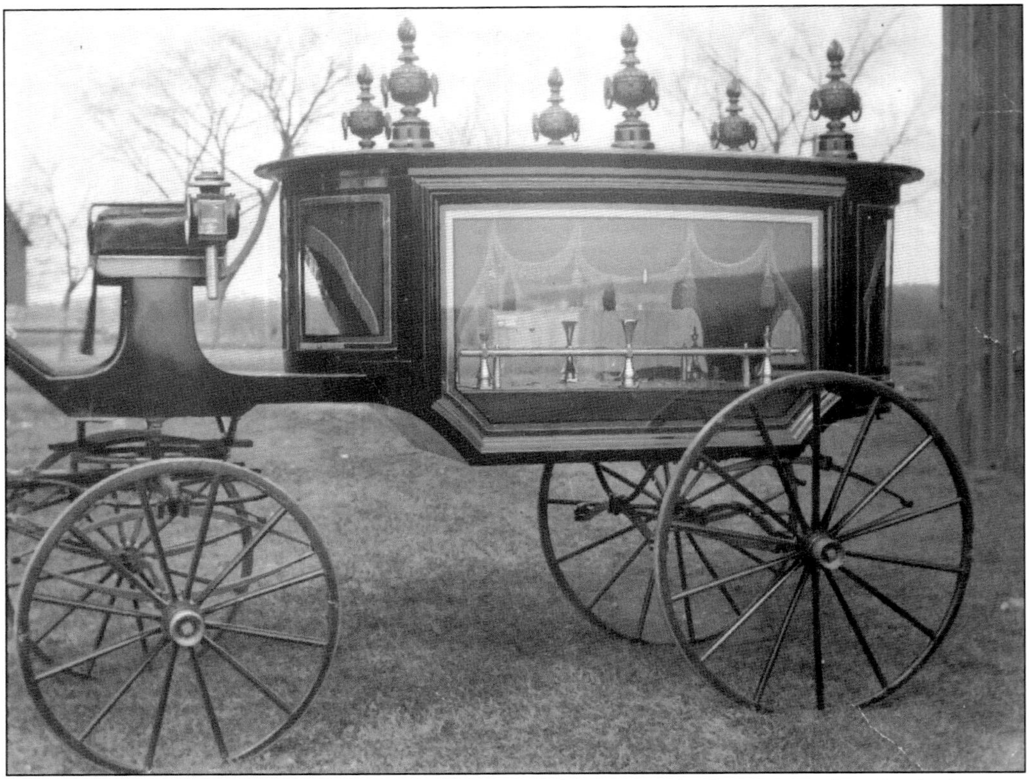
John Burton owned this hearse for his undertaking business. The hearses in that day had a trap door in the bottom—not for escapees, but to be able to wash the windows from the inside.

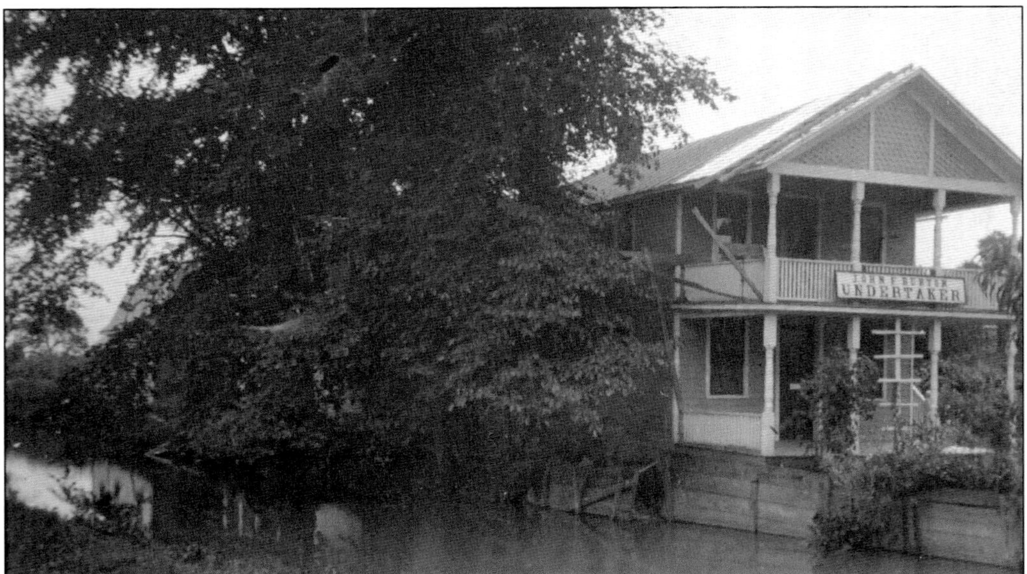

The Burtons' home and funeral parlor were both located in this building on Main Street. In those days, it was rare that a funeral was held in the funeral home. The embalming was done on one floor and the family lived on the second floor. Caskets were stored in a building to the west of the home.

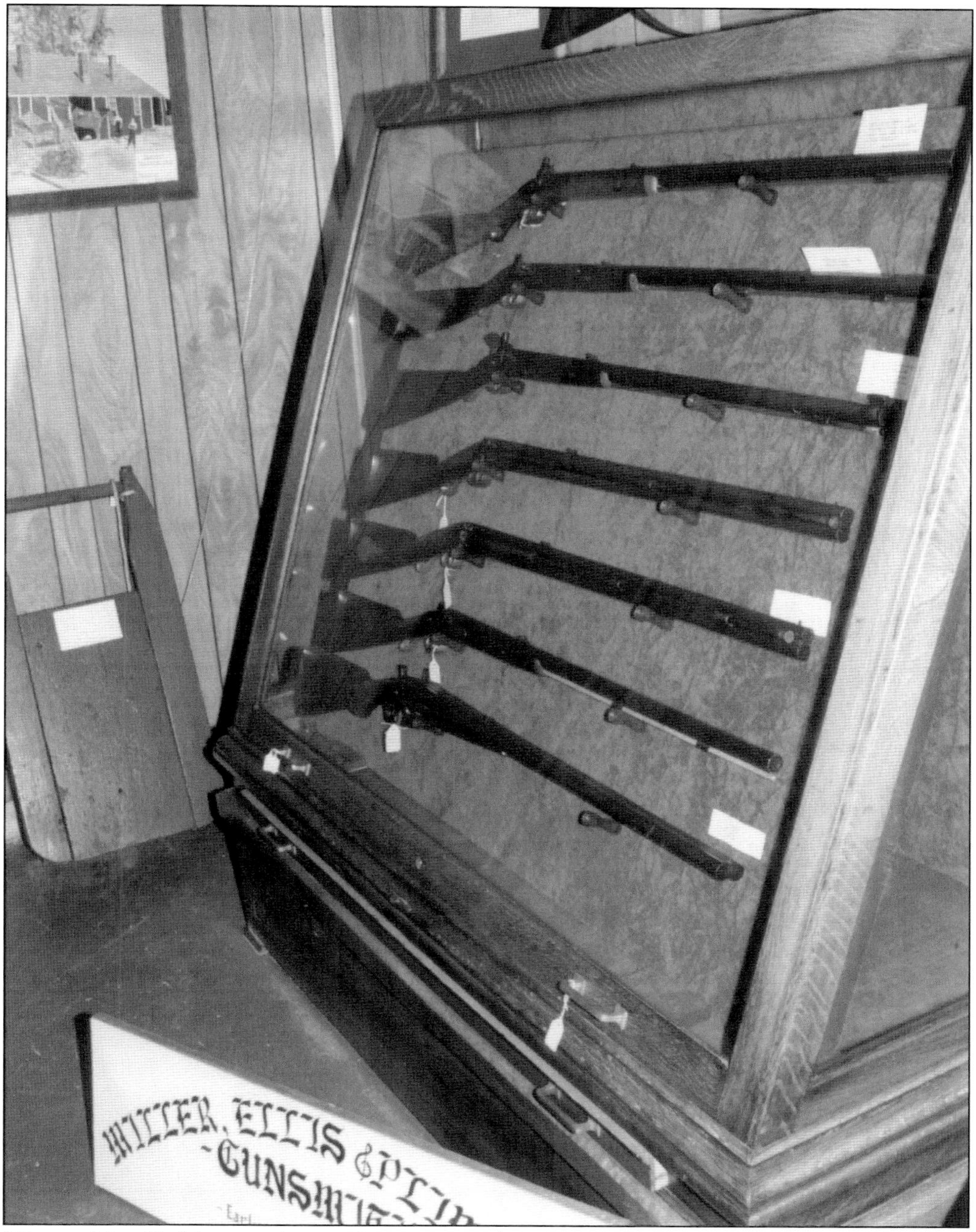

Western New York became known for its gunsmiths. Among them was Amasa H. Plimpton, who was born in Ontario County around 1837. He served briefly in the Civil War and was discharged in June 1865. He was a farmer on West Lake Road and lived down the street from Calvin Miller, a noted gunsmith. Plimpton decided to get into the gun business and purchased Miller's home and gun shop in 1871. He made combination sporting guns similar to the guns Miller had been making. He later operated a gun repair shop. Several of the guns by the early gunsmiths are in a collection at the Richmond Historical Museum and are from a collection donated by Alan Stone.

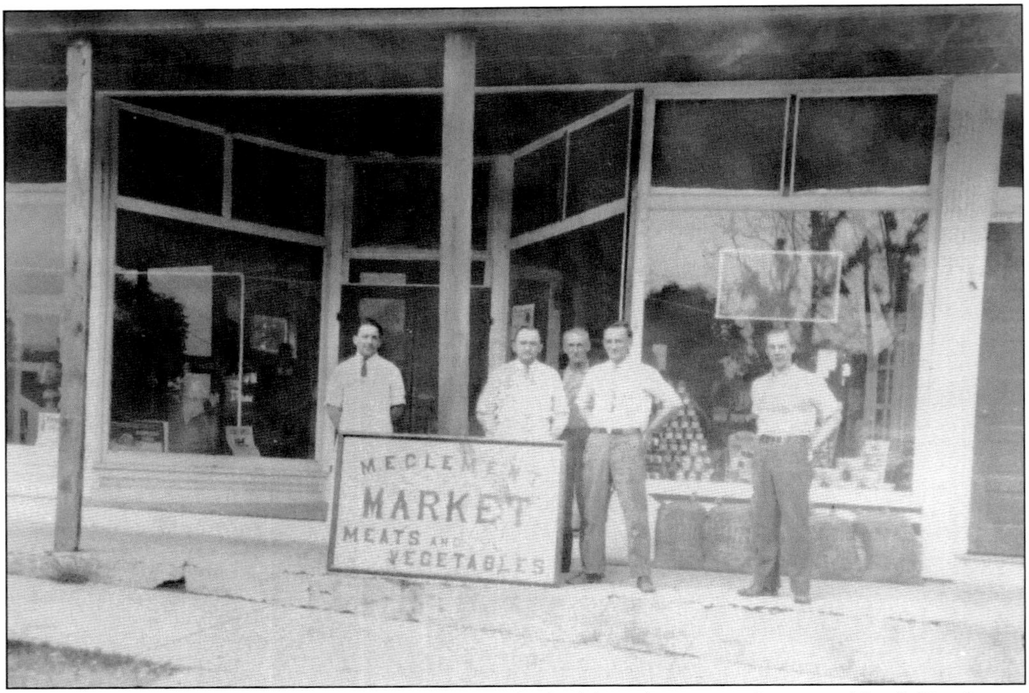

The Market on West Main Street was located in the building that was to become Alger's Hardware. This photograph shows, from left to right, Sid Ingraham, Marty Clement, Sam Drain, Rexford Drain, and Carl Pingrey in 1925.

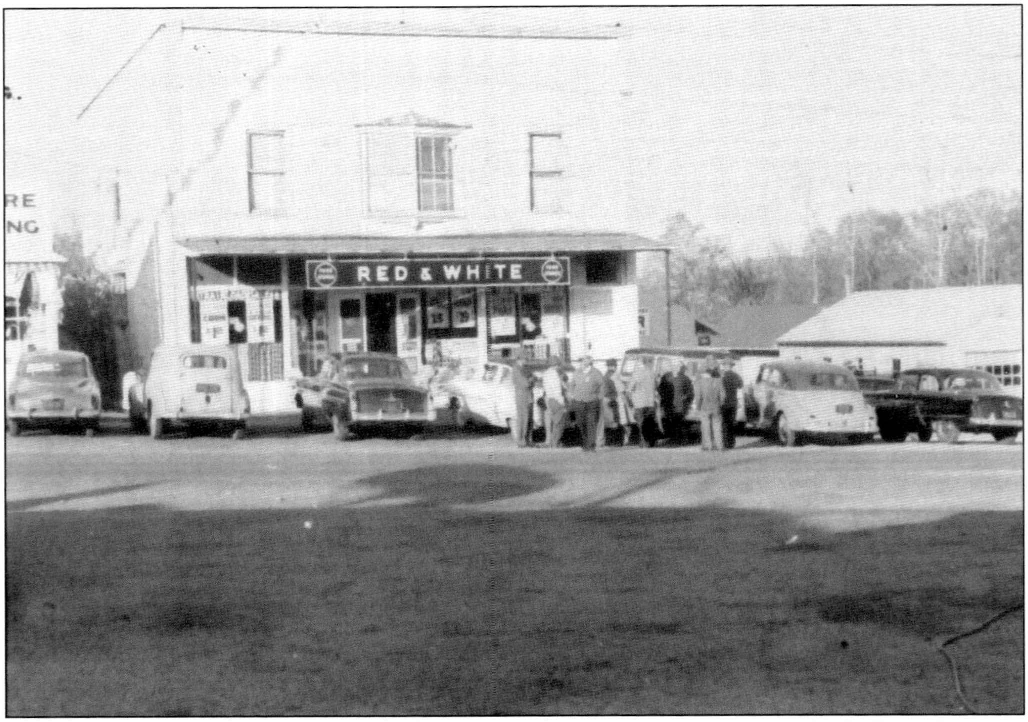

Treble's Red and White Store was located in the Alger building in the 1950s, before relocating farther up East Main Street.

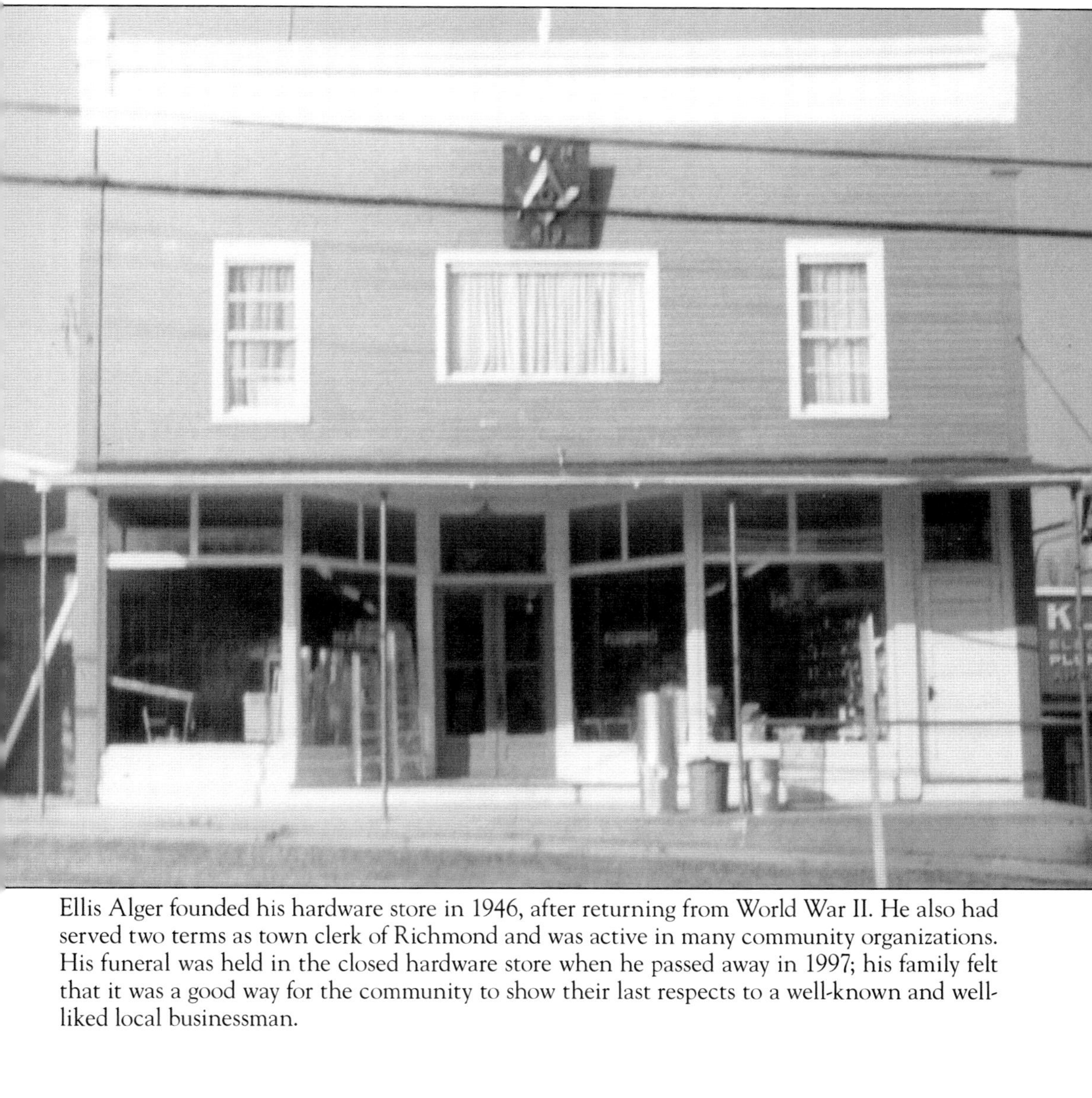

Ellis Alger founded his hardware store in 1946, after returning from World War II. He also had served two terms as town clerk of Richmond and was active in many community organizations. His funeral was held in the closed hardware store when he passed away in 1997; his family felt that it was a good way for the community to show their last respects to a well-known and well-liked local businessman.

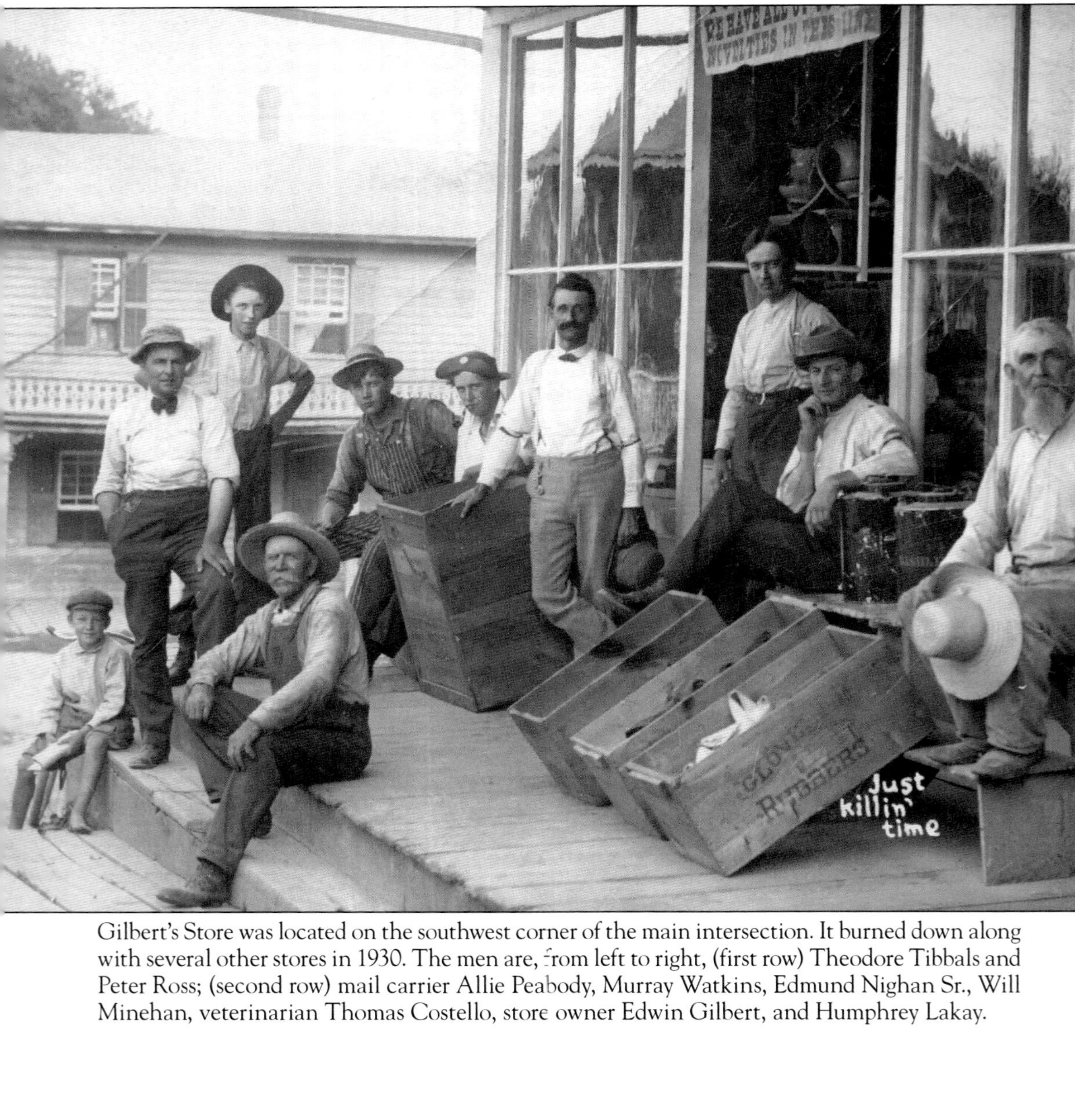

Gilbert's Store was located on the southwest corner of the main intersection. It burned down along with several other stores in 1930. The men are, from left to right, (first row) Theodore Tibbals and Peter Ross; (second row) mail carrier Allie Peabody, Murray Watkins, Edmund Nighan Sr., Will Minehan, veterinarian Thomas Costello, store owner Edwin Gilbert, and Humphrey Lakay.

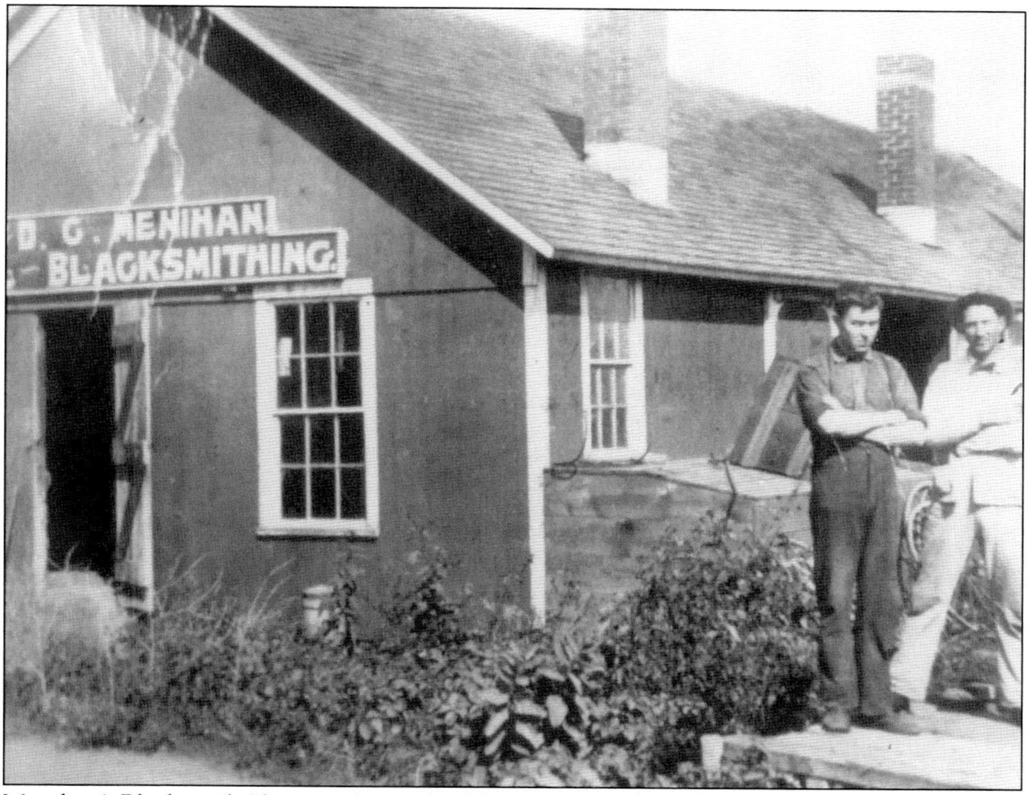

Menihan's Blacksmith Shop was located in Honeoye near where the library now stands on Main Street. Their ad in 1901 stated that they were "practical horseshoers" who did general blacksmithing, woodwork, matching, and planing.

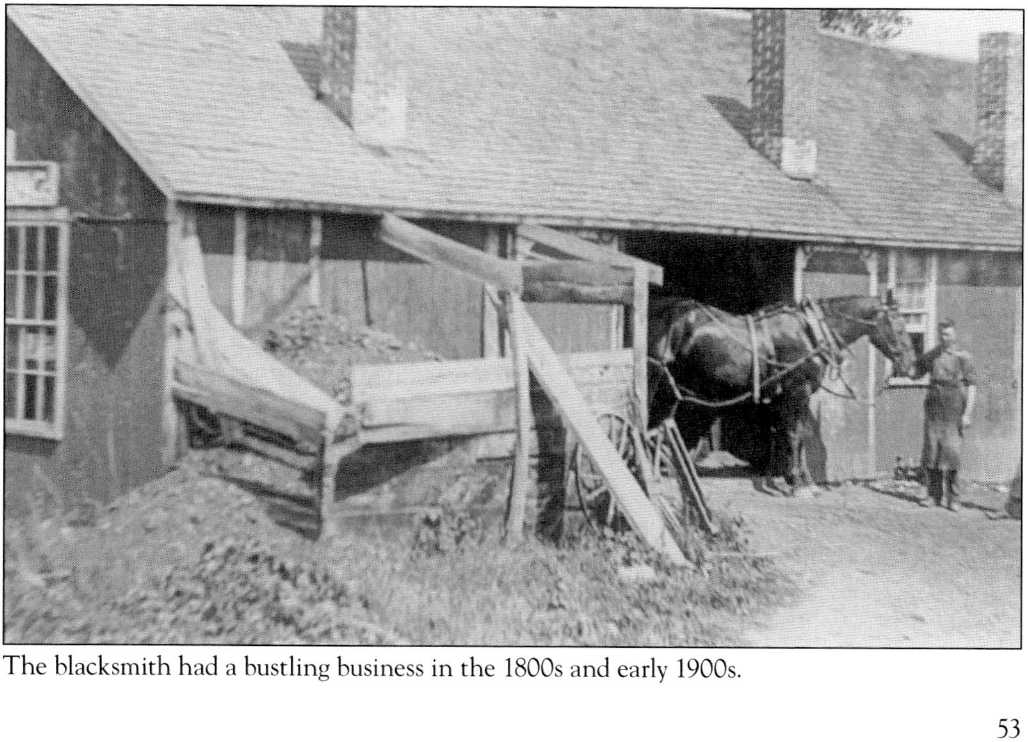

The blacksmith had a bustling business in the 1800s and early 1900s.

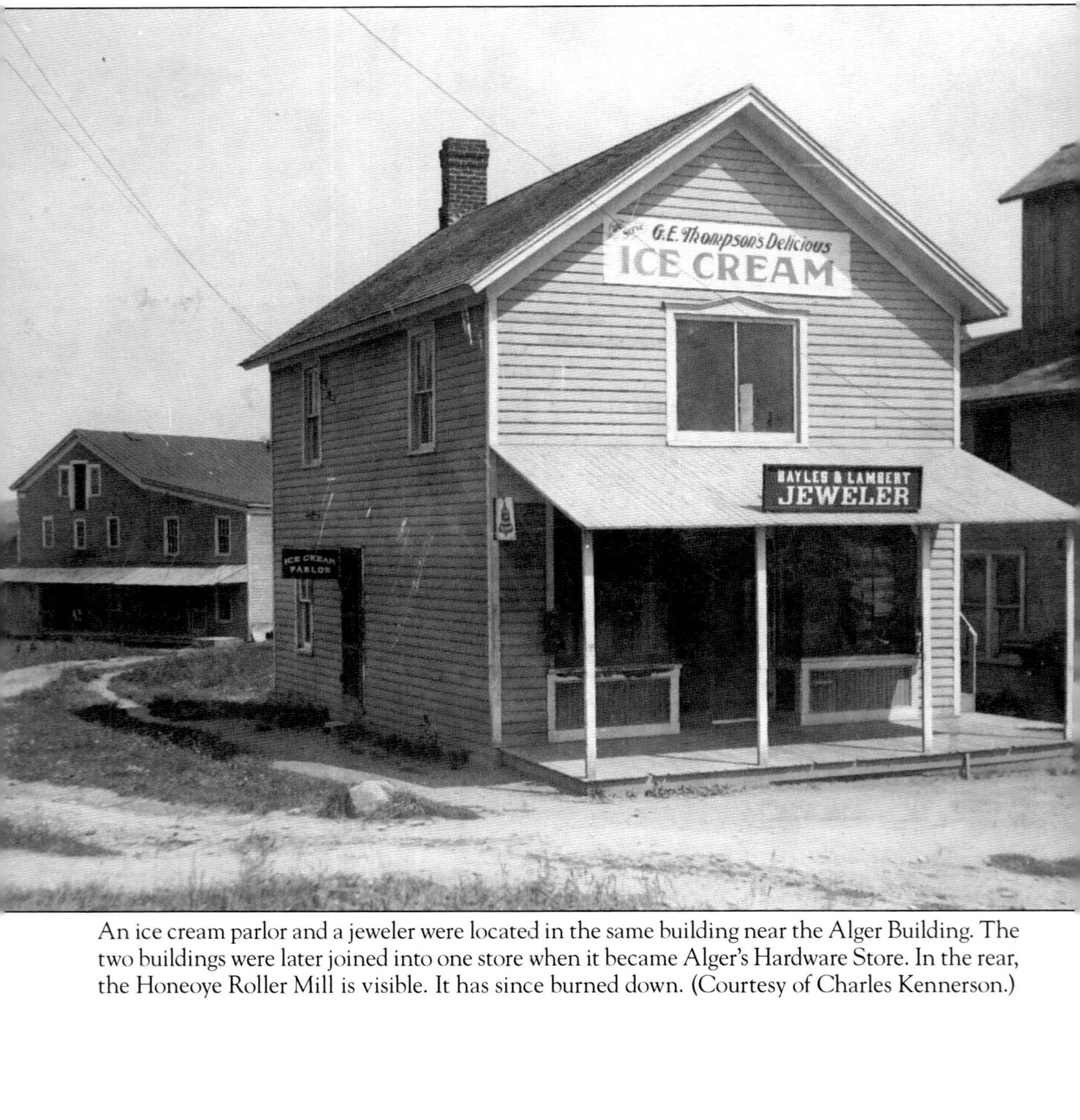

An ice cream parlor and a jeweler were located in the same building near the Alger Building. The two buildings were later joined into one store when it became Alger's Hardware Store. In the rear, the Honeoye Roller Mill is visible. It has since burned down. (Courtesy of Charles Kennerson.)

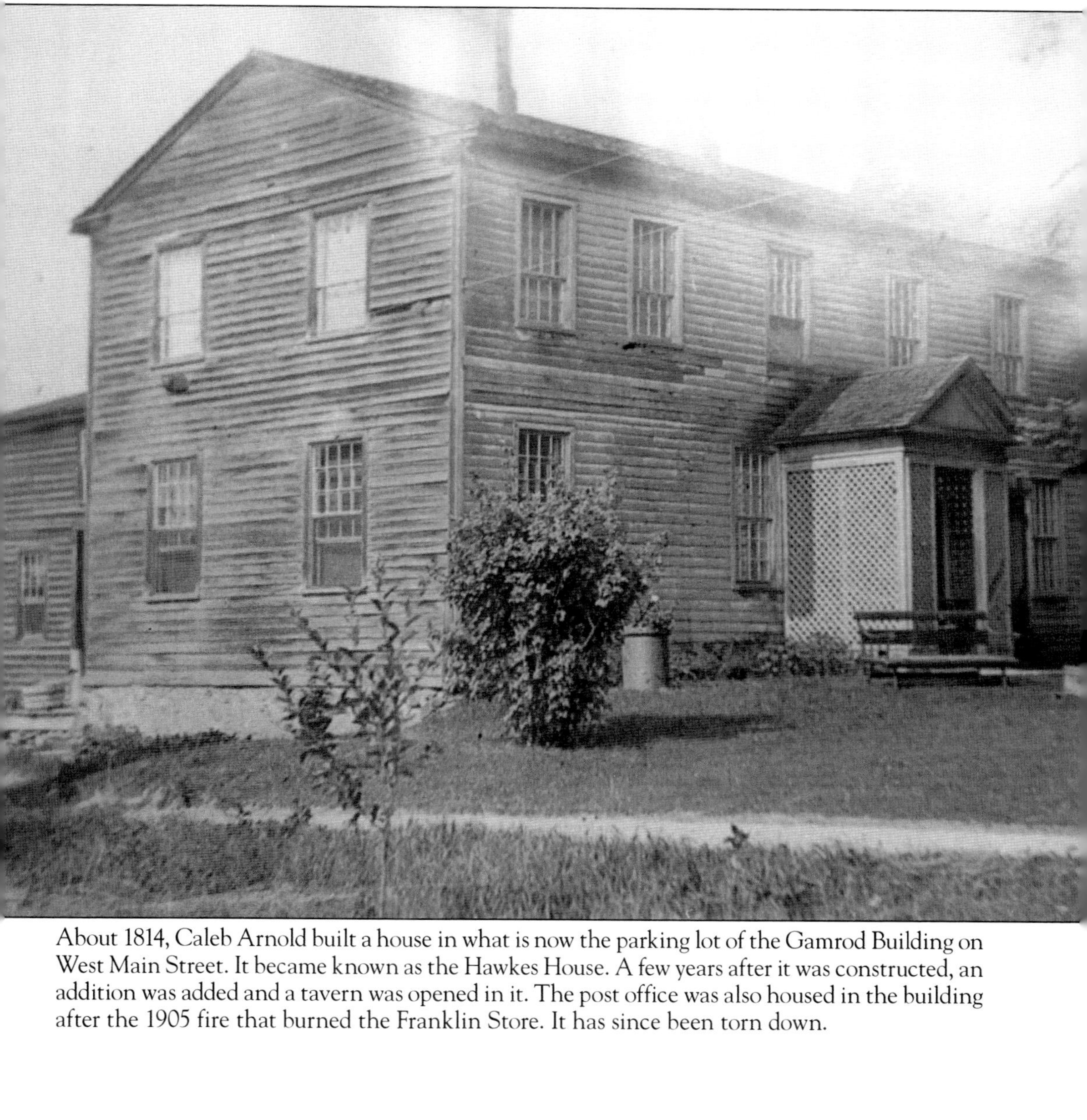

About 1814, Caleb Arnold built a house in what is now the parking lot of the Gamrod Building on West Main Street. It became known as the Hawkes House. A few years after it was constructed, an addition was added and a tavern was opened in it. The post office was also housed in the building after the 1905 fire that burned the Franklin Store. It has since been torn down.

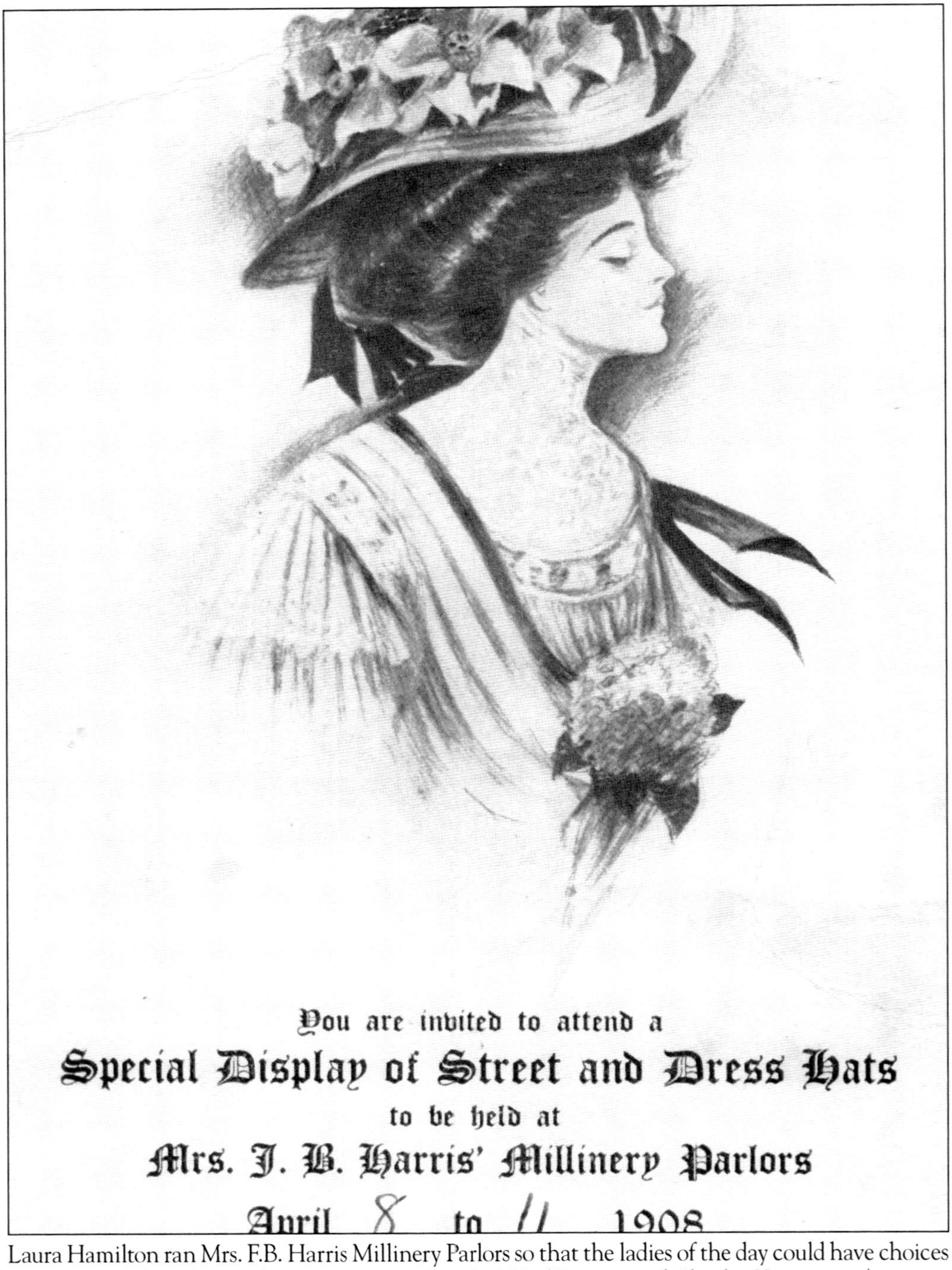

Laura Hamilton ran Mrs. F.B. Harris Millinery Parlors so that the ladies of the day could have choices of street and dress hats. This invitation is dated 1908. (Courtesy of Charles Kennerson.)

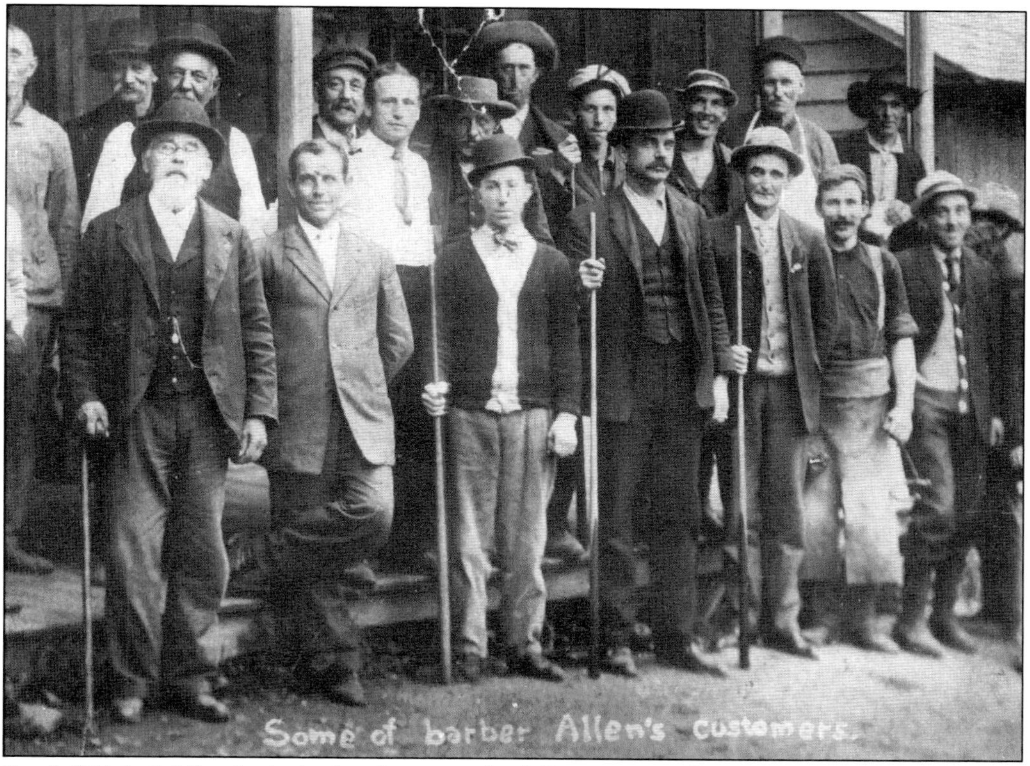

Frank "Dinky" Allen had a barbershop near Ace's Restaurant. These are some of his customers. Third from the left in the front row is John Burton, the undertaker.

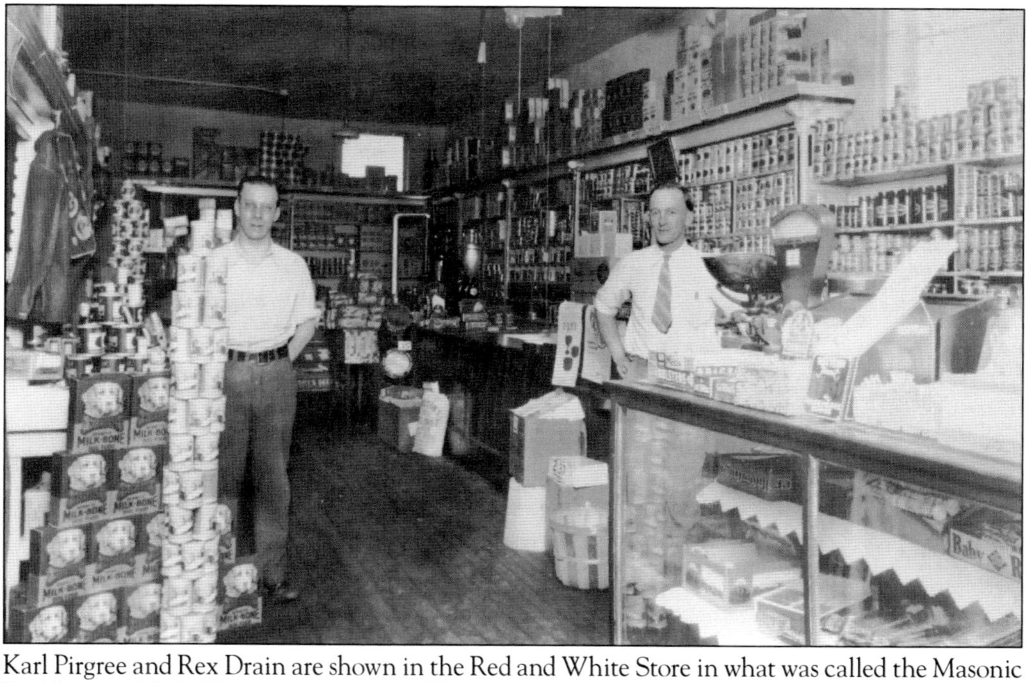

Karl Pirgree and Rex Drain are shown in the Red and White Store in what was called the Masonic Building in 1928. The store was rented by Pirgree and Drain along with Mortimer Clement. Clement peddled meat around the lake in a truck.

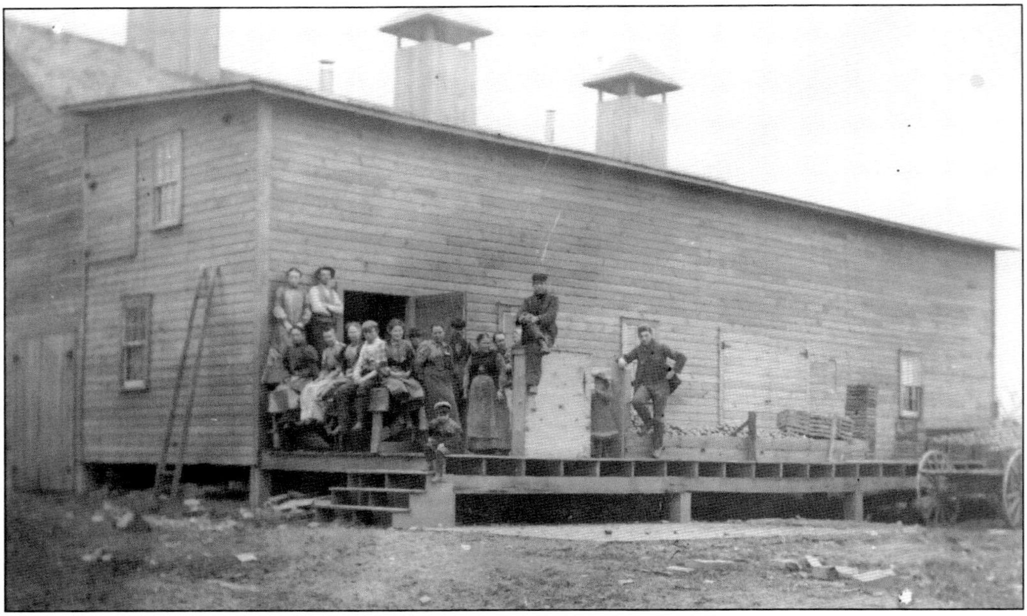

The Evaporator provided employment for some local women each fall. It was located on Briggs Street in Honeoye. The women would run machines that peeled apples. The apples would then be dried and sent in a Model T Ford to Bloomfield and then by train to Rochester and other locations.

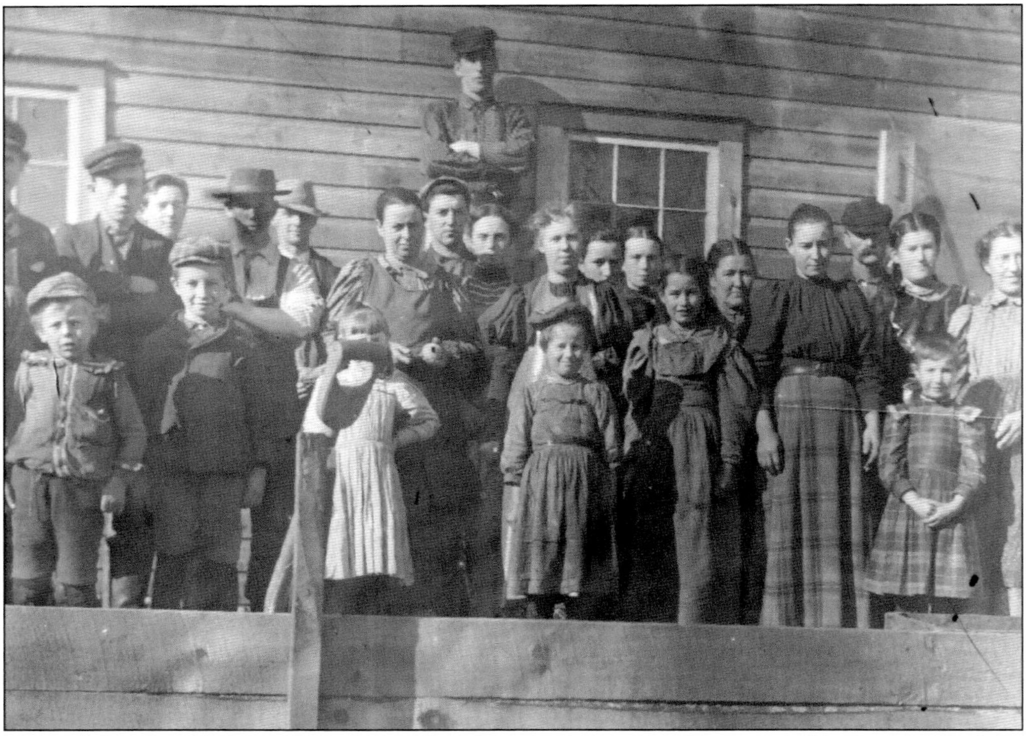

Jacob Cole owned the Evaporator Building on Briggs Street. Cole was in the south end of the building one day in 1920 when a fire broke out in the north end. He did not know the building was on fire until some neighbors who saw the blaze notified him. The cause was an overheated furnace. Cole had very little insurance coverage and did not rebuild after the fire.

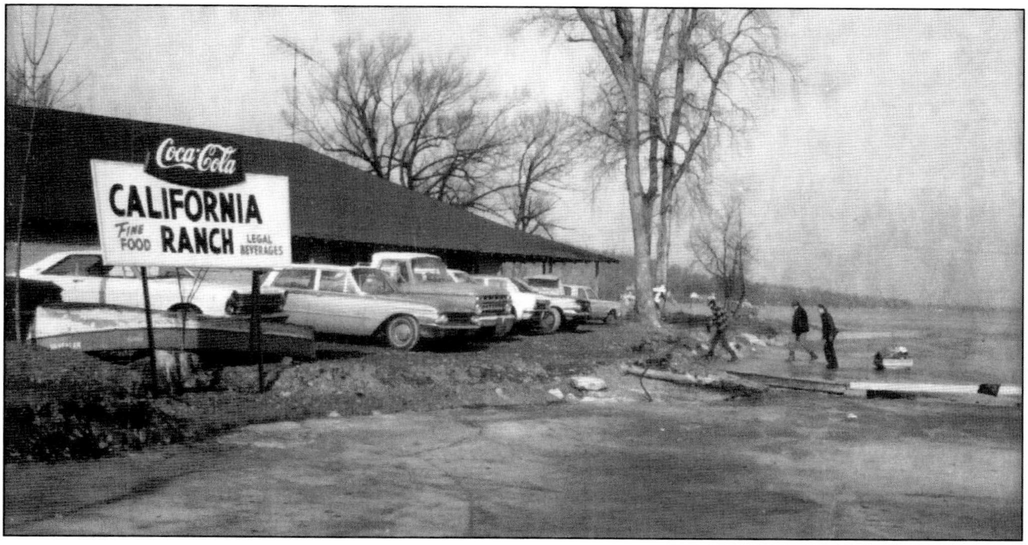

In 1884, Lewis Beam returned to Canadice following a long stay in California. He purchased property on West Lake Road and named it California Ranch. In 1928, Frank Burrett built an open-air dance pavilion on the property near the lake. It was later enlarged to be used for roller-skating. Later the building was enclosed, and a restaurant opened up. Since it was near the western shoreline, it was accessible by land or water. Burrett was originally from New York City. He had envisioned recreational development of the area. One of his projects was a nine-hole golf course, one of the first in Ontario County. The first tee was across the road from his house; the ninth was in the vicinity of 311 West Lake Road. It was well laid out, complete with a sprinkler system. Unfortunately the area was not ready for a golf course, and after two years with no use, it was plowed under.

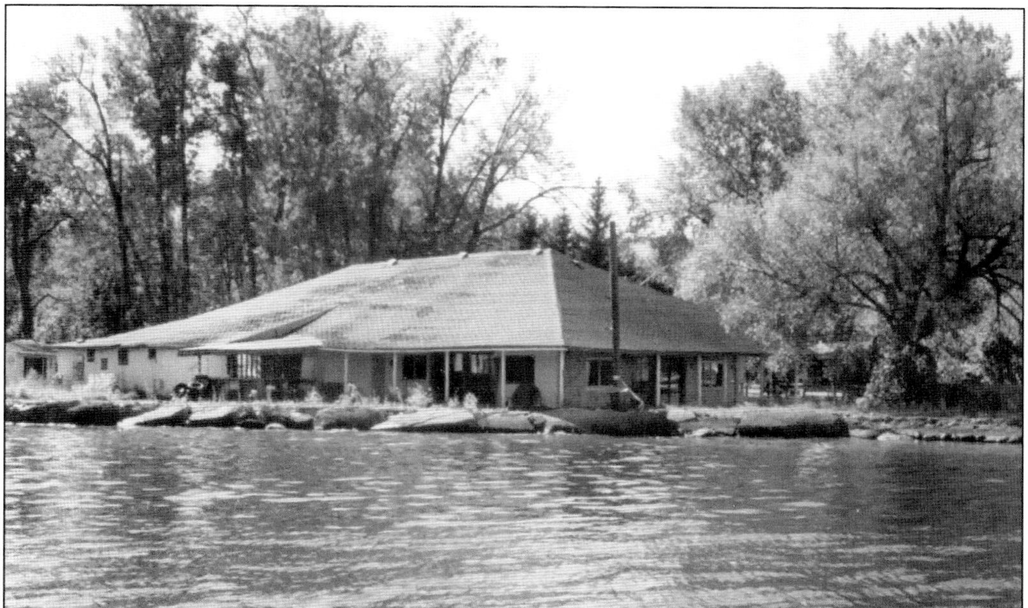

The California Ranch was a restaurant for many years under different owners. Today there is no sign of it, as it was torn down several years ago. A mobile home park sits on the surrounding land and the residents have access to Honeoye Lake at the shoreline.

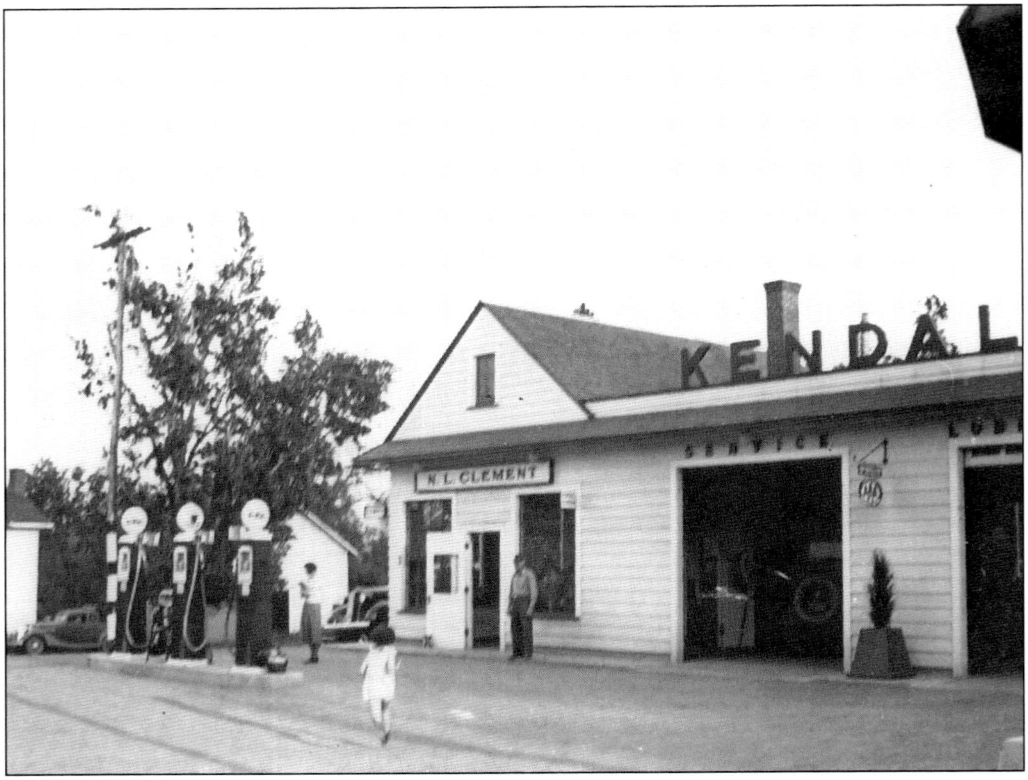

The Kendall Service Station opened as the first gas station on Main Street in Honeoye in 1935. It was built by Norris Clement on the site of the buildings destroyed by fire in 1930. It has been in continuous operation since then, under various owners. Eric Lang presently owns it as Bald Hill Automotive.

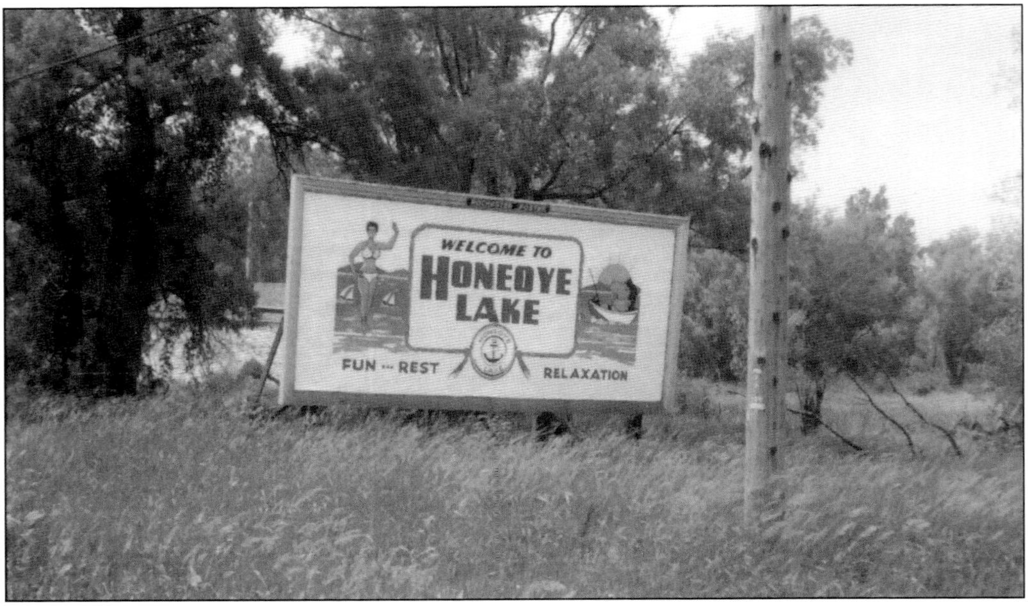

This billboard was erected in the 1960s, where Richmond Town Hall was to be built. The town hall was built in 1967 and was replaced in 2009 by a new building.

Five

PEOPLE

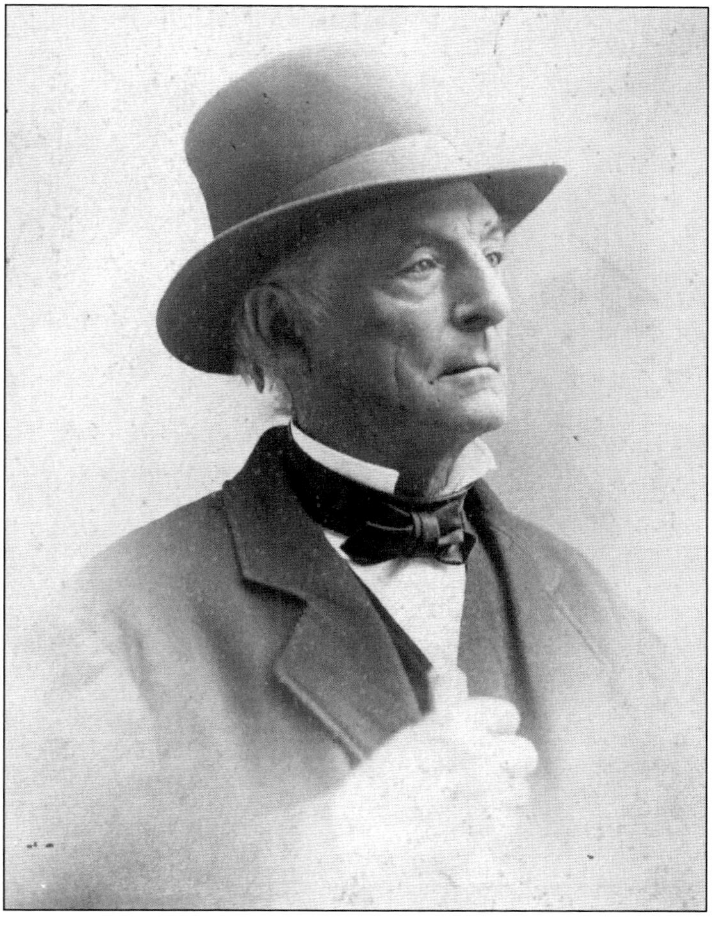

The Pitts family had an important impact on the settling of Richmond. This is a photograph of Gideon Pitts II. He was a staunch abolitionist and encouraged his daughter Helen in her political stance on abolition. He befriended Frederick Douglass in the 1840s and introduced her to him when she was still a child. However, he later disowned Helen for marrying Douglass and never spoke to her again.

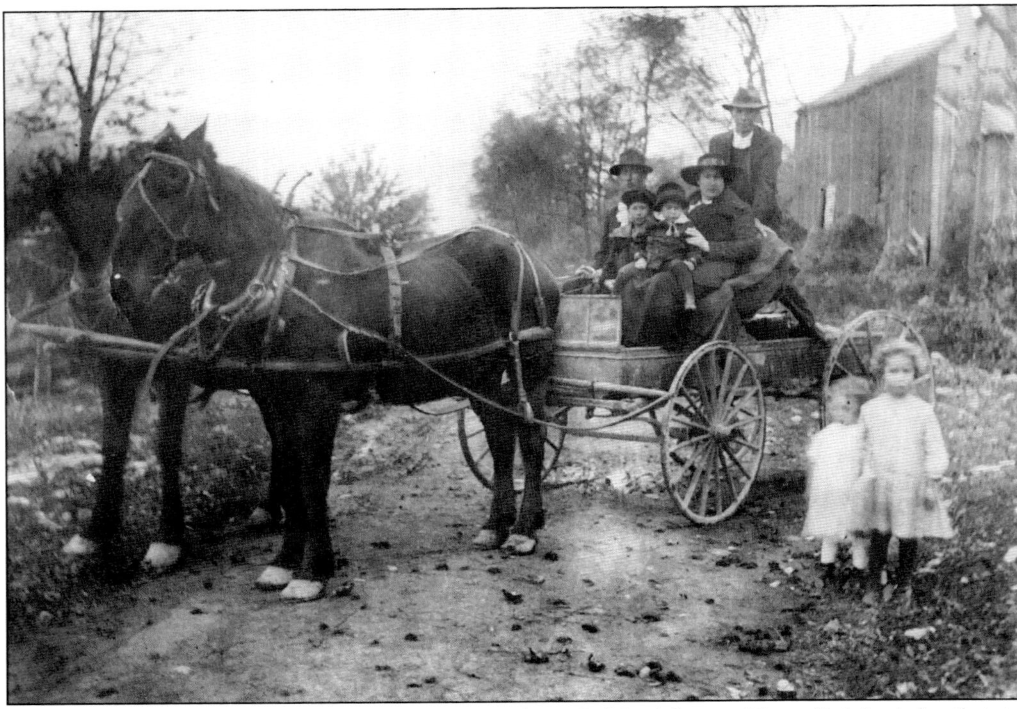

This photograph, dated 1918, was taken in front of Lew Belcher's home. Hattie Belcher's family is in the wagon. Lew Belcher's children are standing alongside the road. (Courtesy of Beverly Deats.)

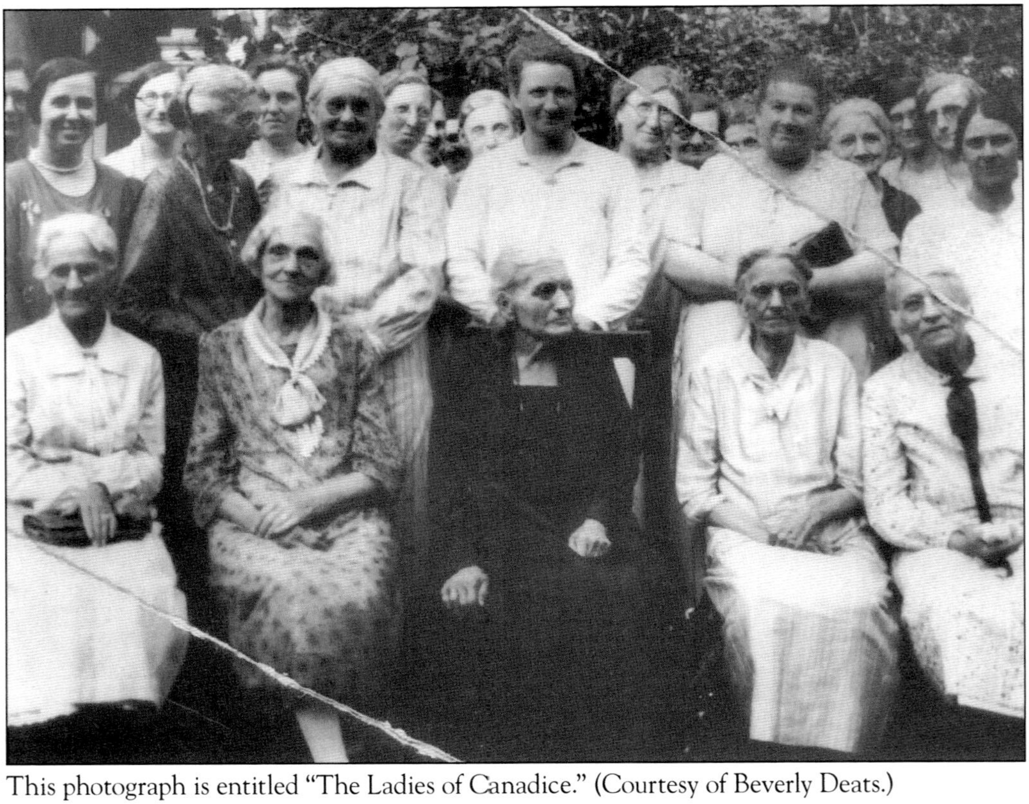

This photograph is entitled "The Ladies of Canadice." (Courtesy of Beverly Deats.)

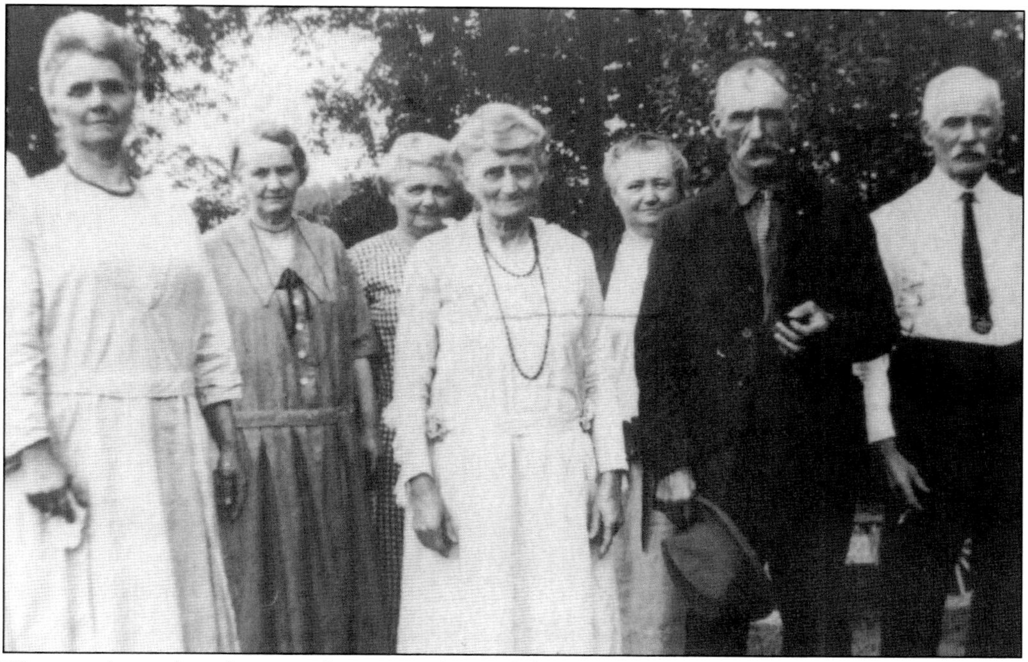

The people in this photograph are members of the Drain family. They are, from left to right, Belle McIlveen, Elizabeth Bentley, Martha Wood Fox, Jennie Kennedy, Katherine Bacon, Sam Drain, and Robert Drain.

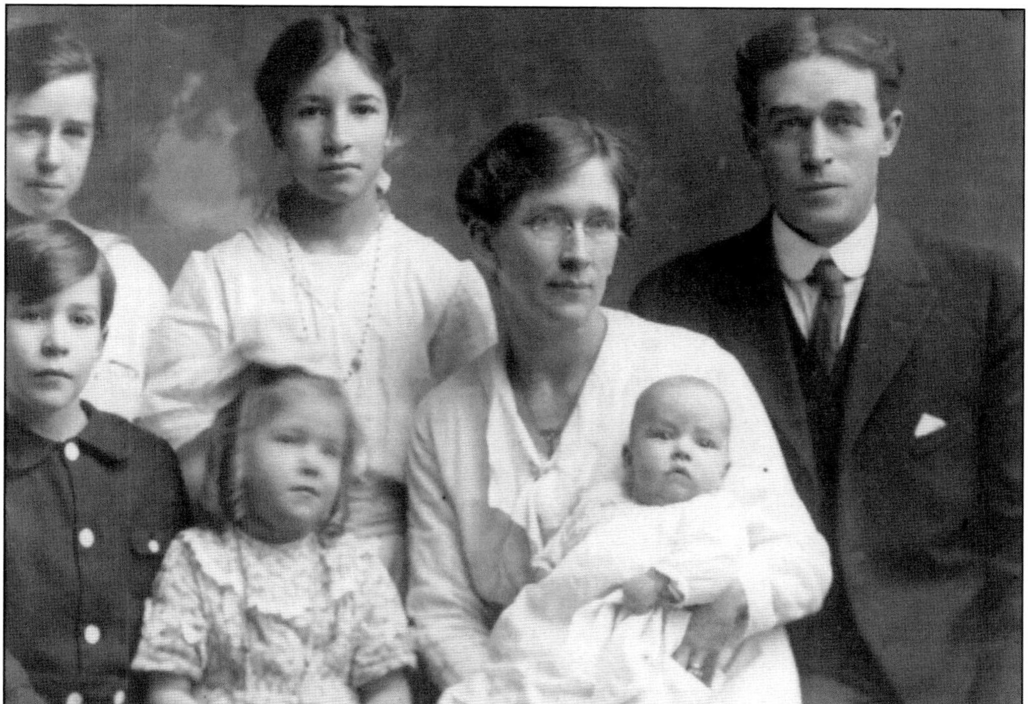

Pictured here is the family of George W. Deal. They are, from left to right, (first row) Asa Norget Deal, Caroline M. Deal, and George Wilson Deal; (second row) Elsie J. Deal, Emily M. Deal, Edith Norget Deal, and George Wolfe Deal.

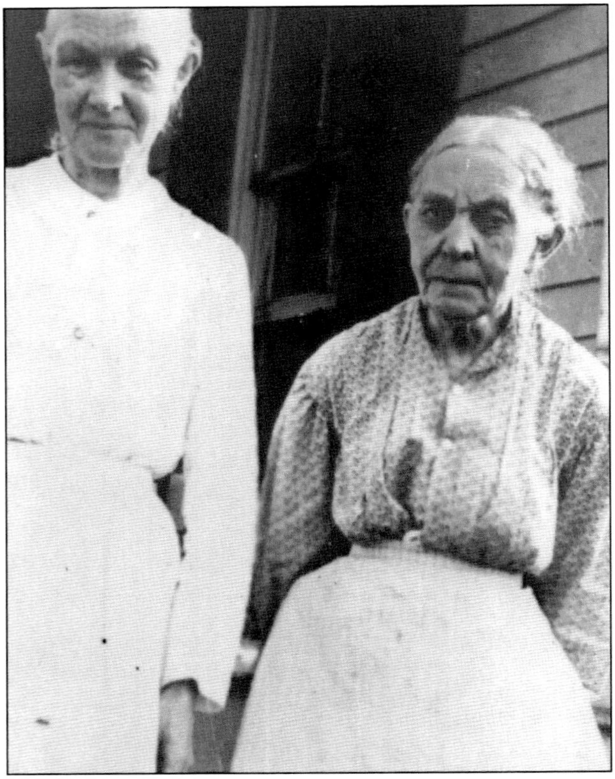

Ada Steele is on the left and Mary Norgate is on the right in this undated photograph. The Norgate family built a home on County Road 37.

The couple in this undated photograph is John and Mary (Steele) Norgate.

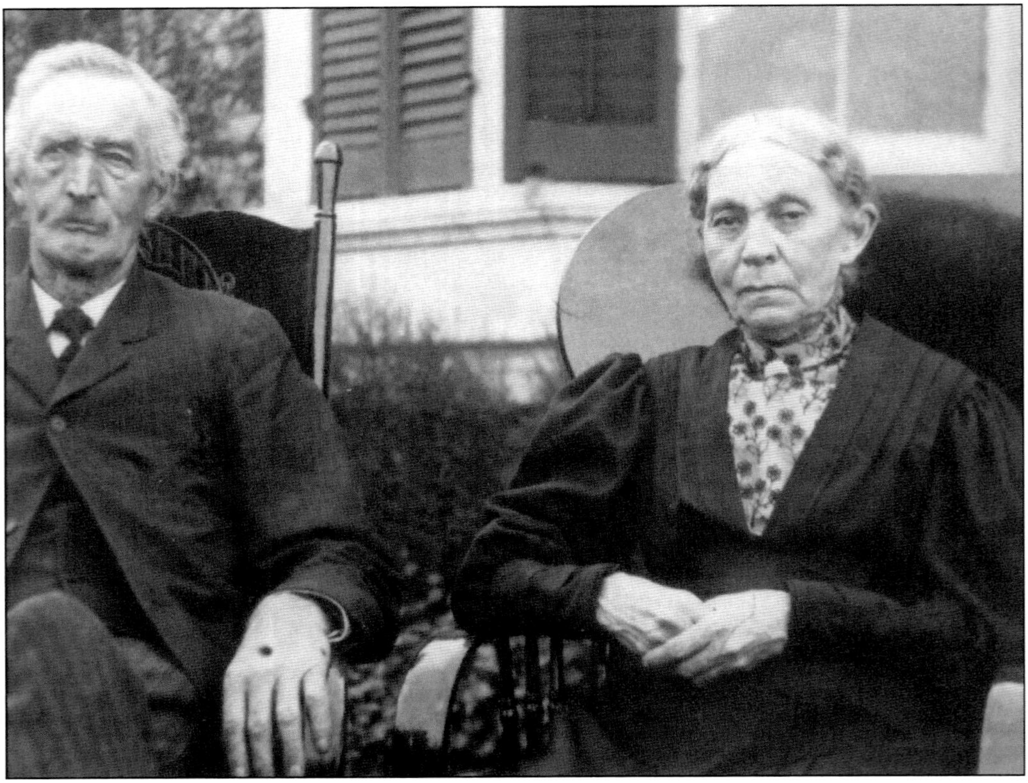

These two ladies are Mettie Plimpton and Marie Rakies, pictured in 1940.

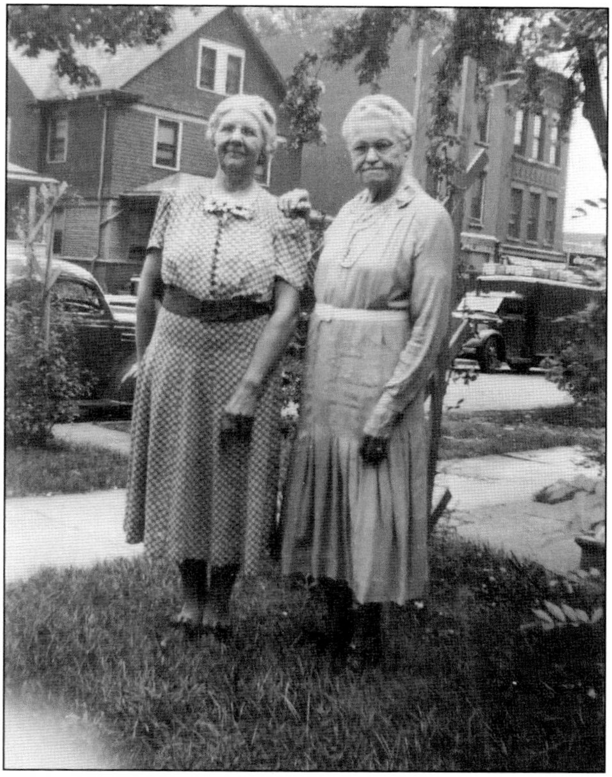

In this 1955 photograph are, from left to right, Georgia Fox, Anna Jerome, Effie Cochrane, Martha Fox, Susie Francis, and Ethel Clement. Georgia Fox was one of the women who made a chain down Main Street to the creek when the Franklin Building burned in 1905. She also recalled that a barn and house nearby burned down. The post office also burned, but most of its contents were removed from the building safely.

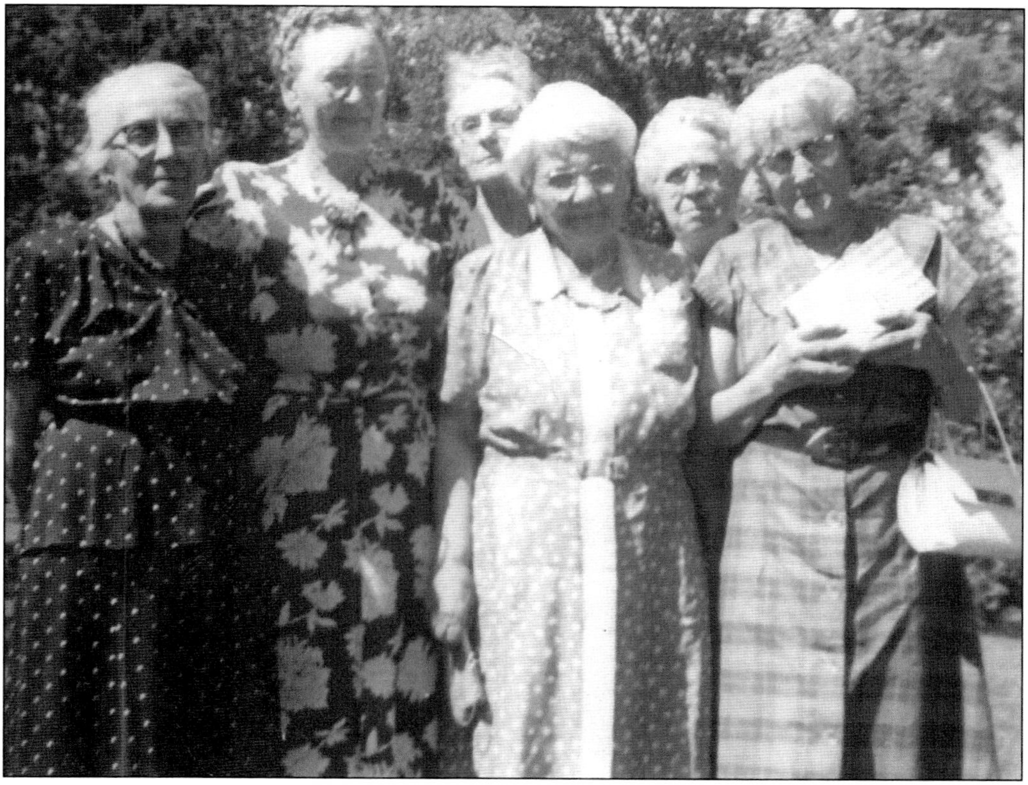

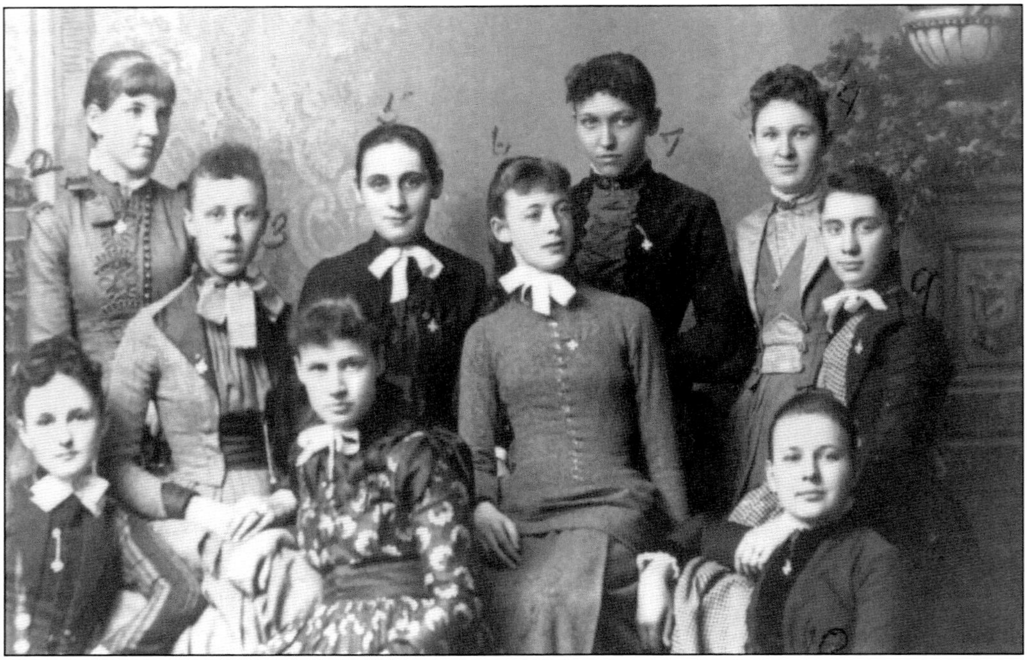

In this undated family portrait are, from left to right, (first row) Nellie Hawkes, Kitty Reed, Alice Reed, and Maude Wilbur; (second row) Millie Stevens, Minnie Deyo, Nellie Ashley, Lizzie Bartlett, Mettie Beach, and Jessie Smith.

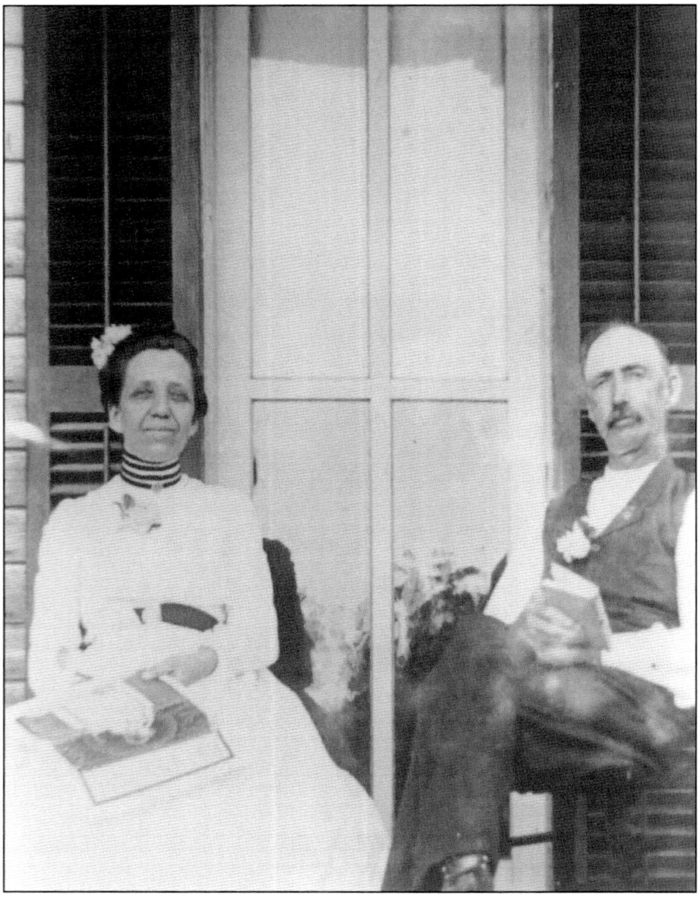

This undated photograph shows Felicia (Phillips) Wallace and her husband.

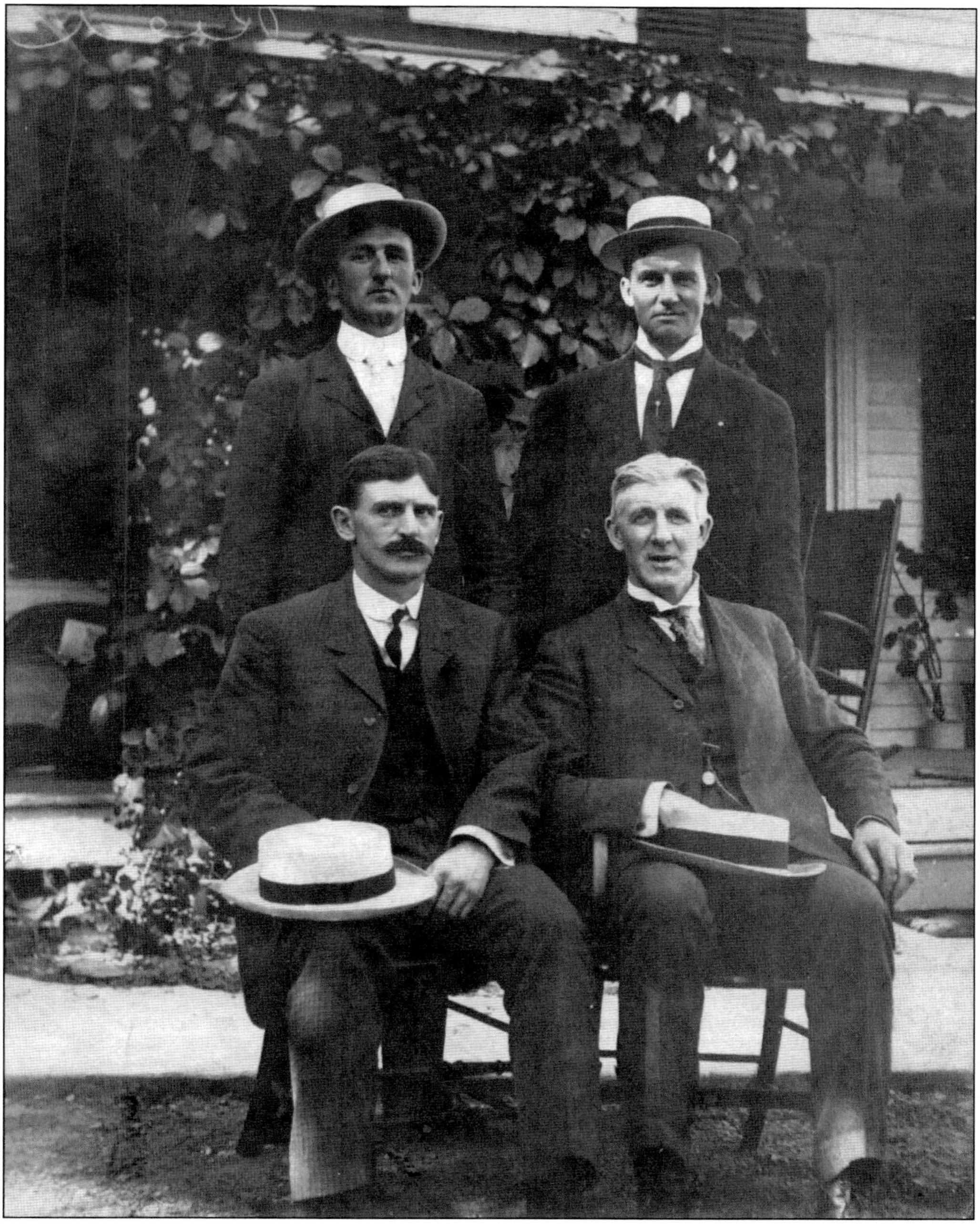

The gentlemen in this undated photograph are all members of the Reed family. They are, from left to right, (first row) Harry and Fred; (second row) Roy and Murry.

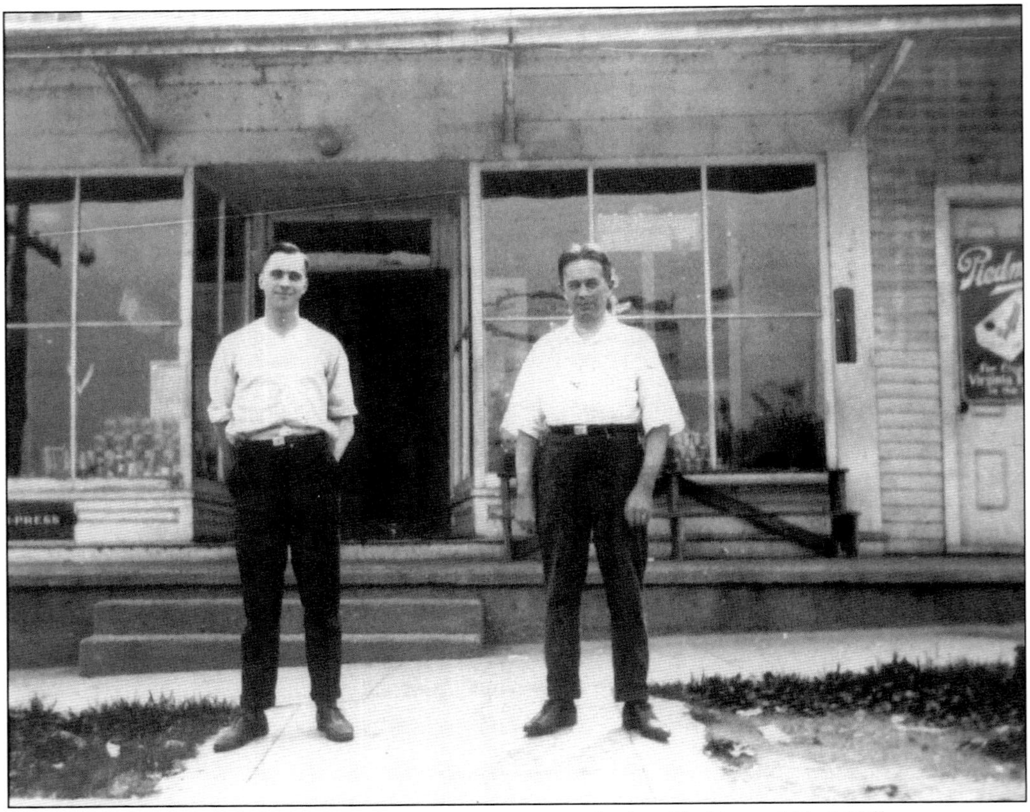

Arthur Treble and Ned Gilbert are shown in front of Gilbert's Store in 1925 on Main Street in Honeoye.

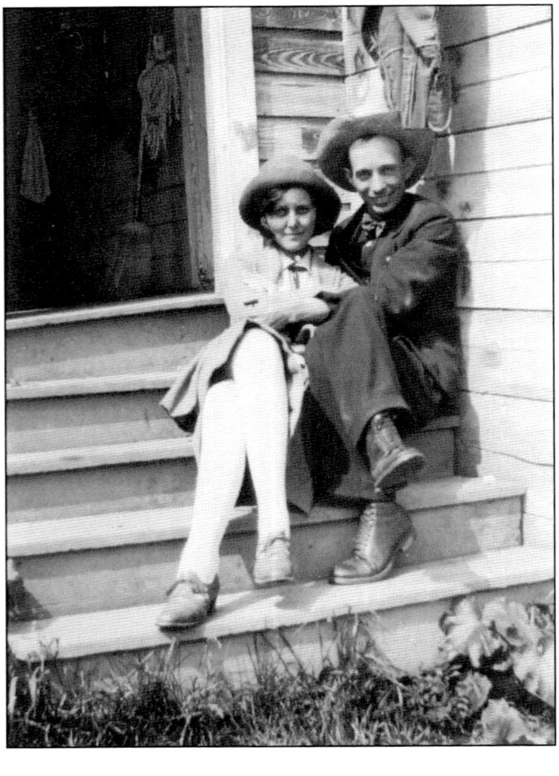

Catherine (Burton) Portnow and Clarence Bennett pose in this undated photograph. Catherine was one of John Burton's daughters who grew up living in the family's undertaker building.

Clarence Bennett is seated in front of Gilbert's Store on Main Street in Honeoye.

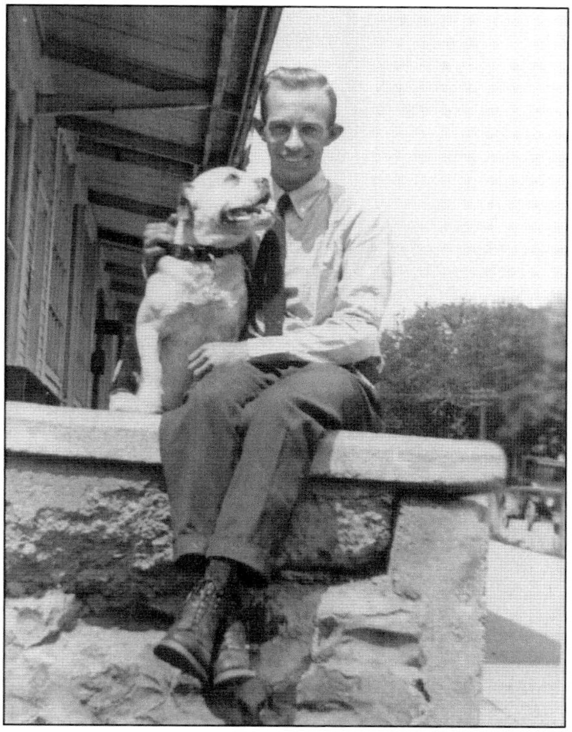

Munson and Georgia Daniels are shown in this 1964 photograph. Munson was the last of the blacksmiths to shoe horses in Richmond. His shop was east of the hamlet on Route 20A. He worked for Dan Menihan for five years to learn the trade and purchased the business from him in 1920. He retired from blacksmithing in 1945.

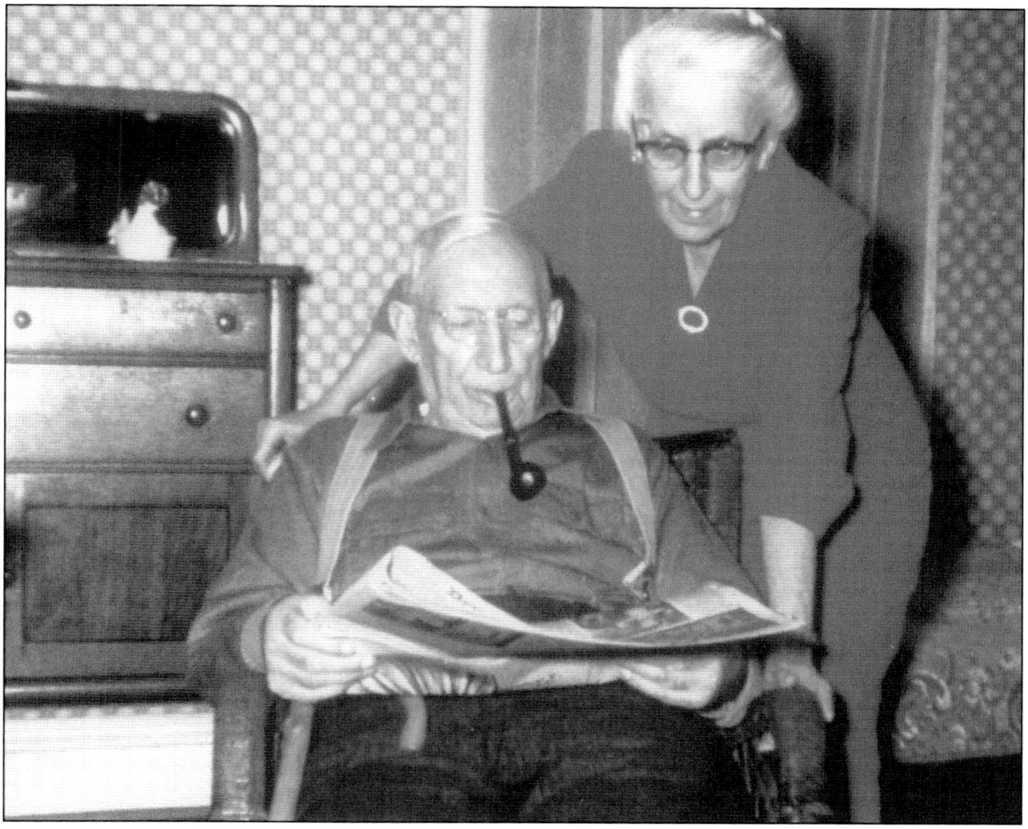

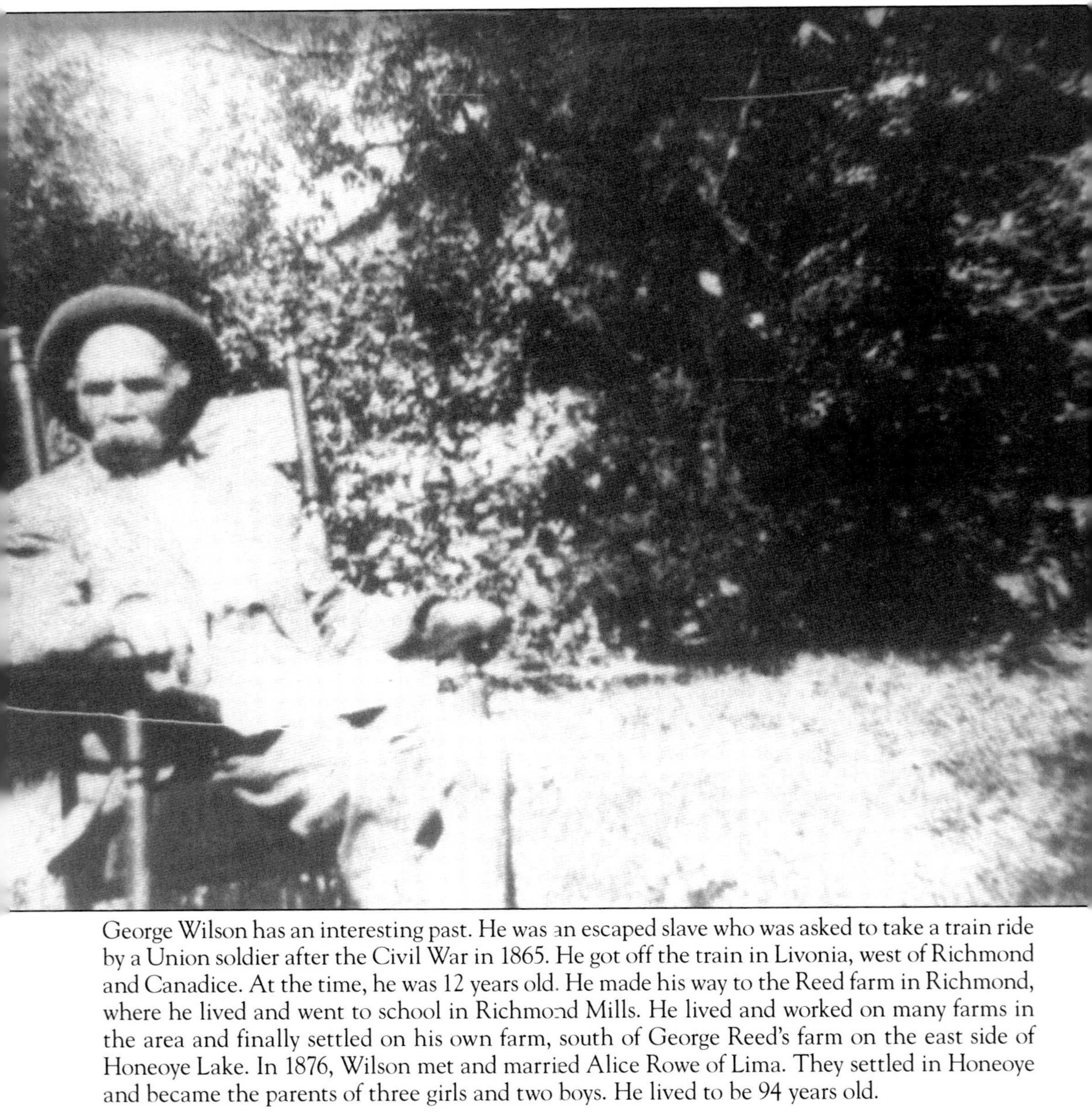

George Wilson has an interesting past. He was an escaped slave who was asked to take a train ride by a Union soldier after the Civil War in 1865. He got off the train in Livonia, west of Richmond and Canadice. At the time, he was 12 years old. He made his way to the Reed farm in Richmond, where he lived and went to school in Richmond Mills. He lived and worked on many farms in the area and finally settled on his own farm, south of George Reed's farm on the east side of Honeoye Lake. In 1876, Wilson met and married Alice Rowe of Lima. They settled in Honeoye and became the parents of three girls and two boys. He lived to be 94 years old.

This is Mabel Cronin at the age of one year. She is the grandmother of local resident Linda Guffey. (Courtesy of Linda Guffey.)

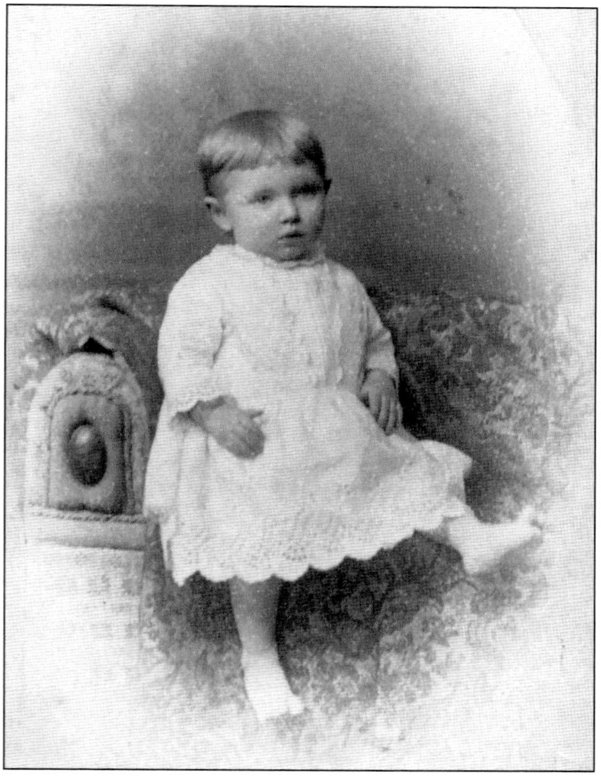

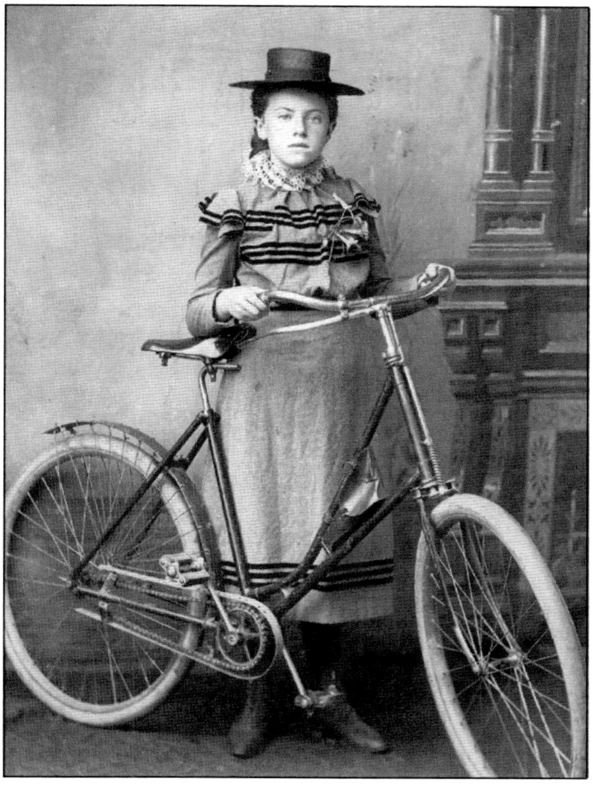

This is Mabel Cronin at the age of 12. (Courtesy of Linda Guffey.)

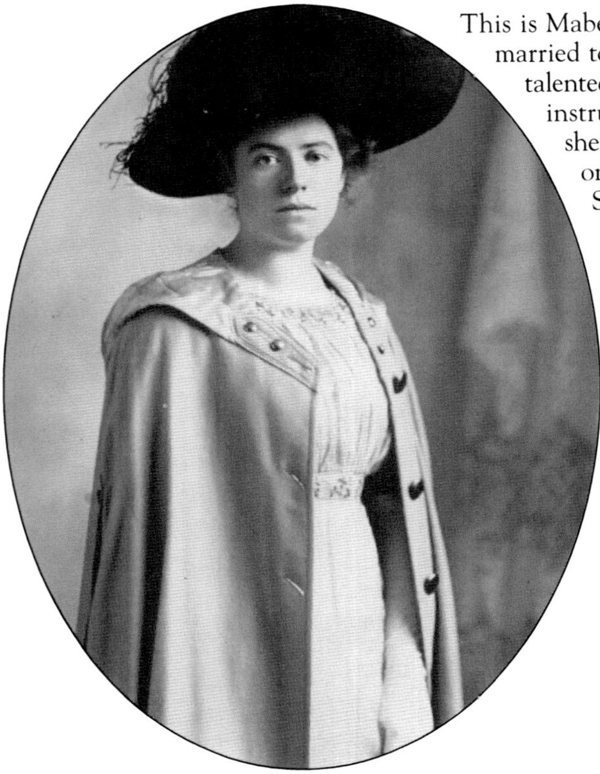

This is Mabel (Cronin) Colt as an adult. She was married to Leonard Colt. She was an extremely talented musician who could play many musical instruments. After graduating from college, she taught in Rochester and was eventually on the faculty at the Genesee Wesleyan Seminary in Lima, which is now known as Elim Bible Institute. She died in 1929. (Courtesy of Linda Guffey.)

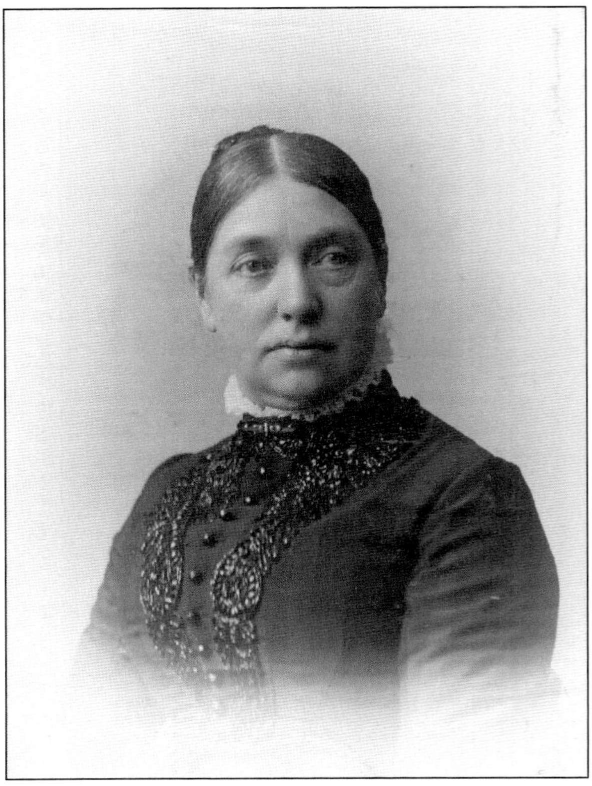

This is an undated photograph of Mandy Franklin of Honeoye. Mandy, or "Ma" as she was called, worked at the family business, which was the Franklin Cash Store. "Cash" was not always the way that business was done, as bartering was common in the early 1900s.

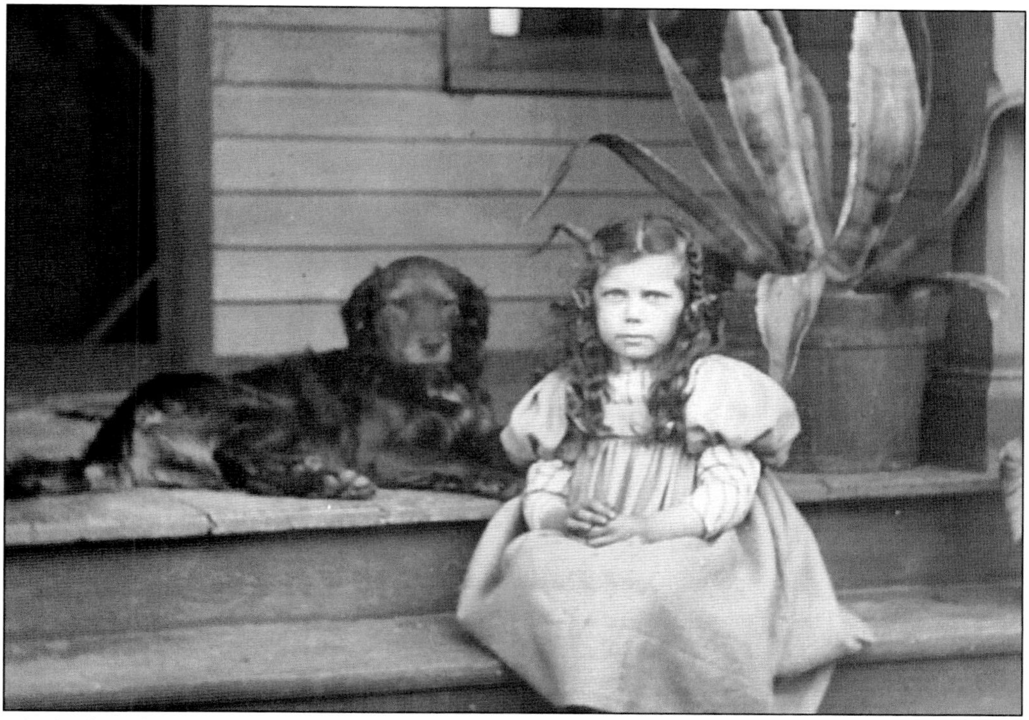

The little girl with the dog in this undated photograph is Rachel Stilwell, granddaughter of Ma Franklin of Honeoye.

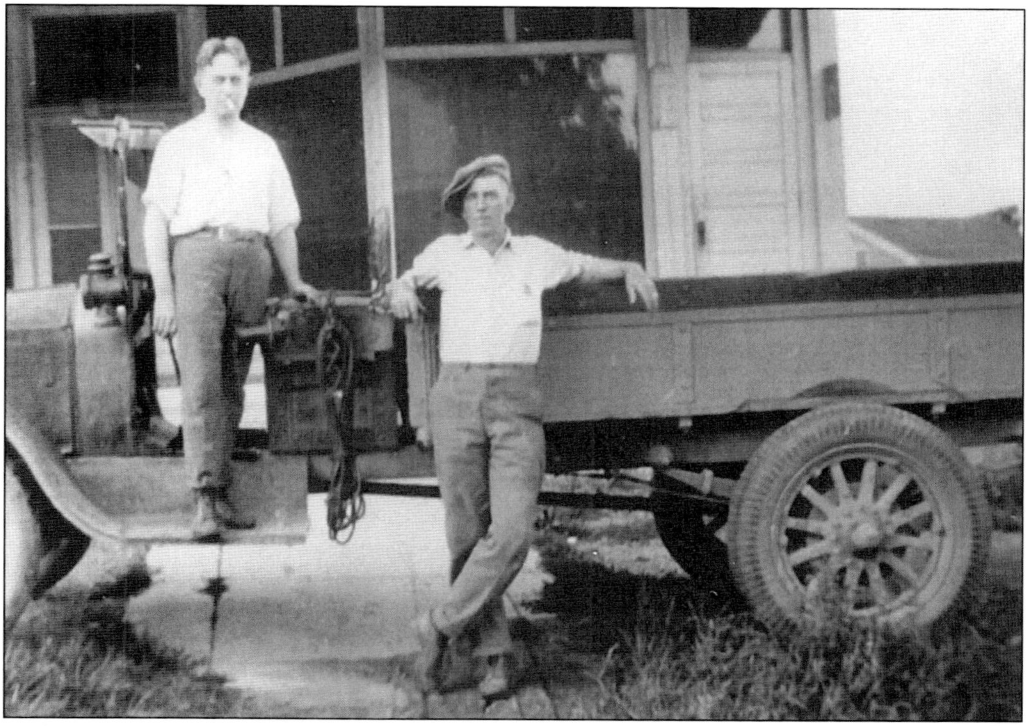

Ned Gilbert and Bill Morrow are posing in front of the Franklin Cash Store on Main Street in Honeoye.

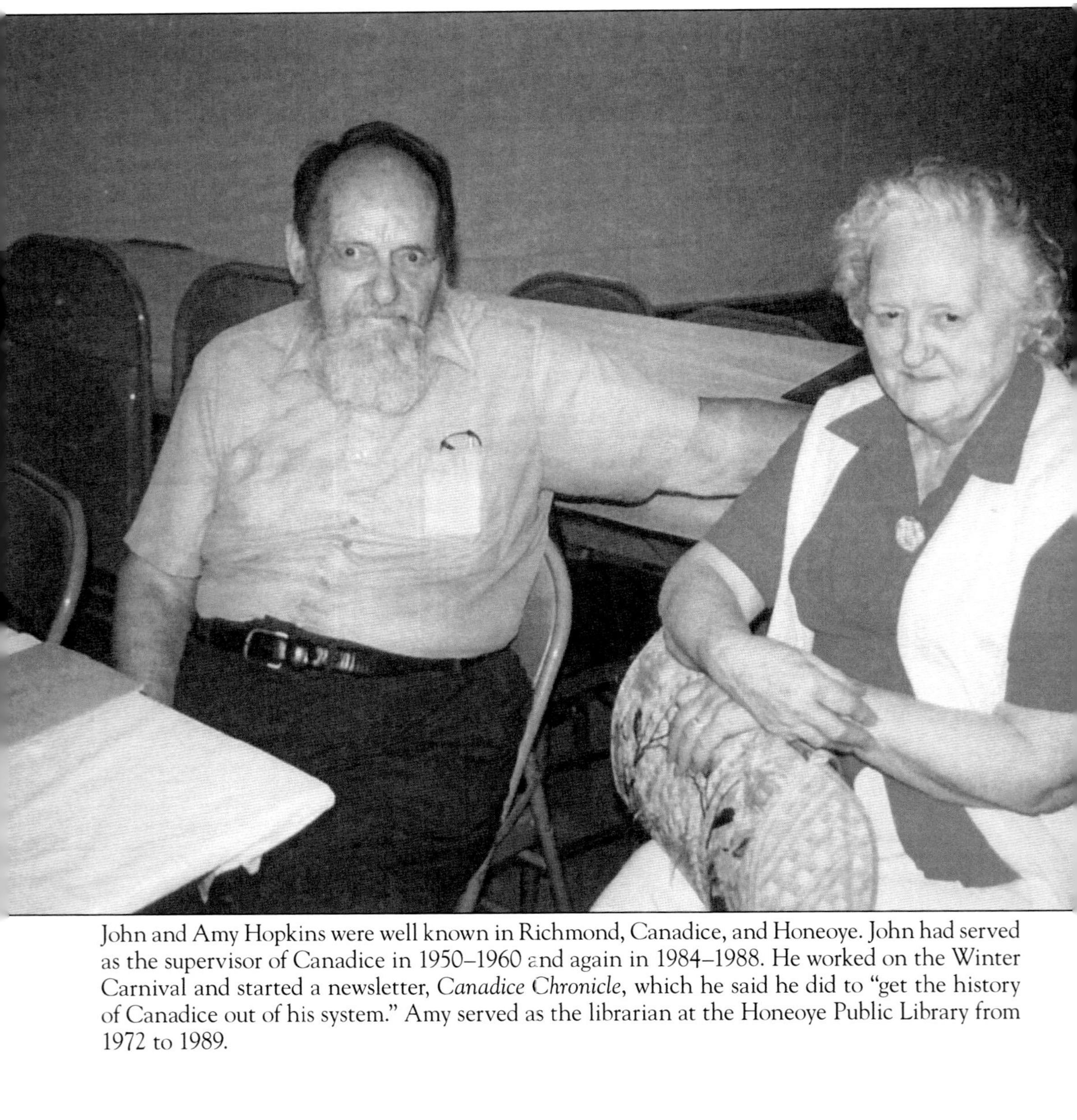

John and Amy Hopkins were well known in Richmond, Canadice, and Honeoye. John had served as the supervisor of Canadice in 1950–1960 and again in 1984–1988. He worked on the Winter Carnival and started a newsletter, *Canadice Chronicle*, which he said he did to "get the history of Canadice out of his system." Amy served as the librarian at the Honeoye Public Library from 1972 to 1989.

Six

Churches and Cemeteries

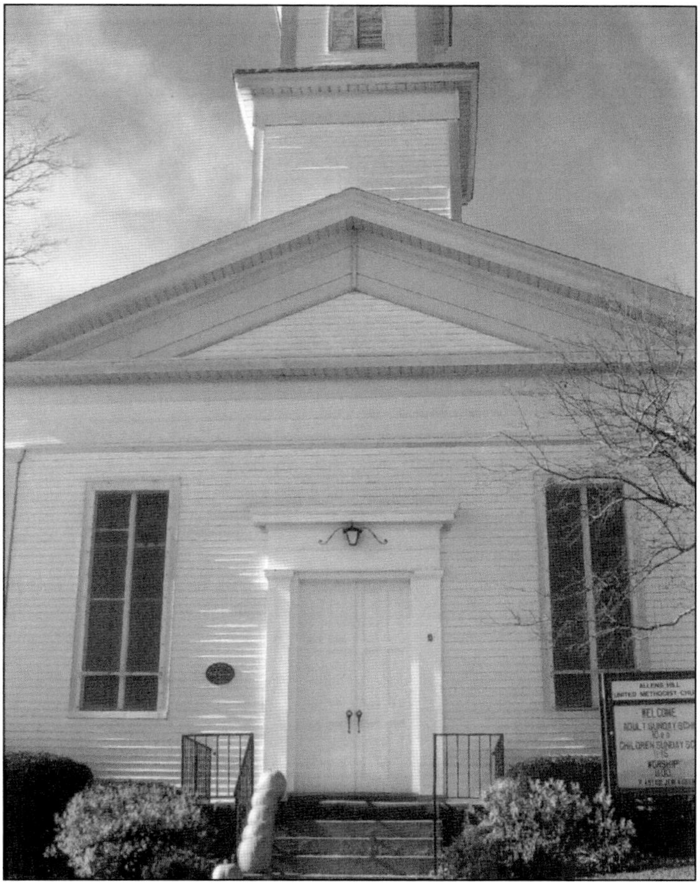

The Allens Hill Methodist Church was completed and dedicated in 1861. The bell on the church was imported from England. It was one of the two churches on Allens Hill when the hamlet was thriving. Today it remains as the only church in that area.

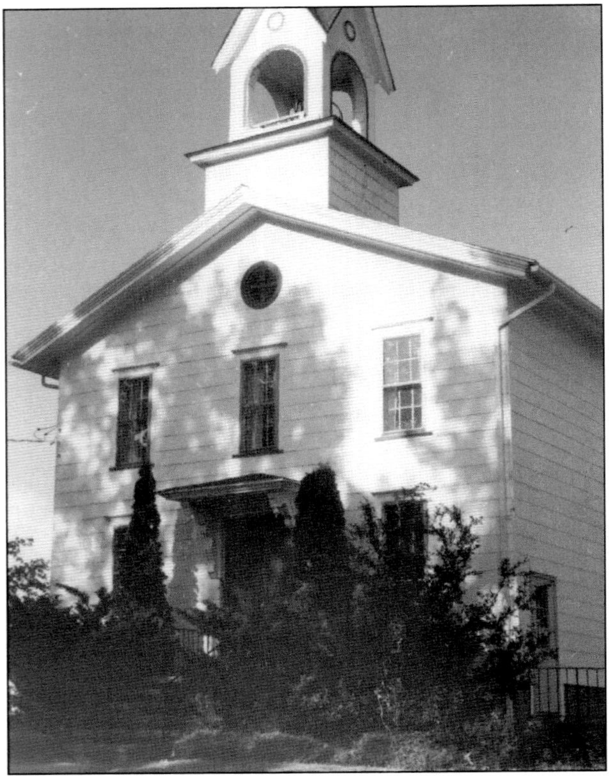

The Canadice Methodist Church was built in 1834 at a cost of $1,050. It has been enlarged, and a modern kitchen and heating have been added. It sits high on the hill at Canadice Corners, next to the cemetery that is the resting place for many residents who have passed.

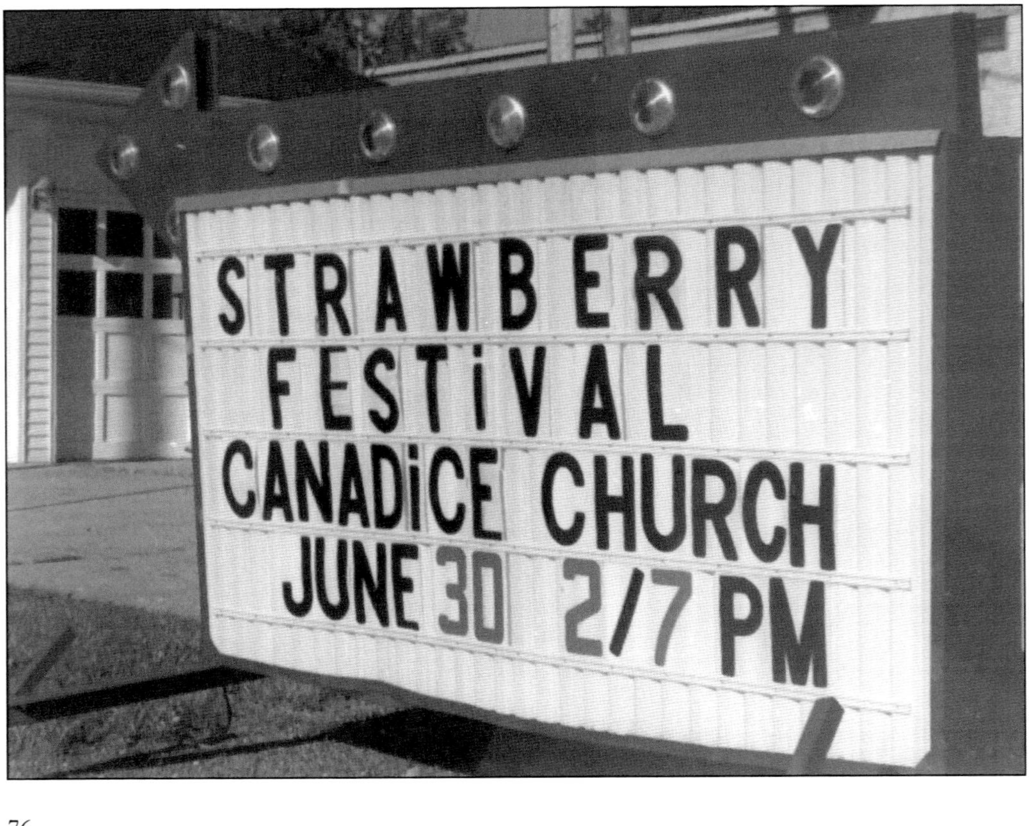

The Canadice Methodist Church is known for its annual Strawberry Festival, held at the end of June for well over 100 years. A family-style dinner is served in the church basement, followed by strawberry shortcake for dessert.

The Faith Bible Church, west of Honeoye, had its beginnings in 1968. Ground was broken for a building in 1972. The church was dedicated in 1973 with 105 people present. John Karle had donated the land, and the men of the church did much work on Saturdays under Karle's direction.

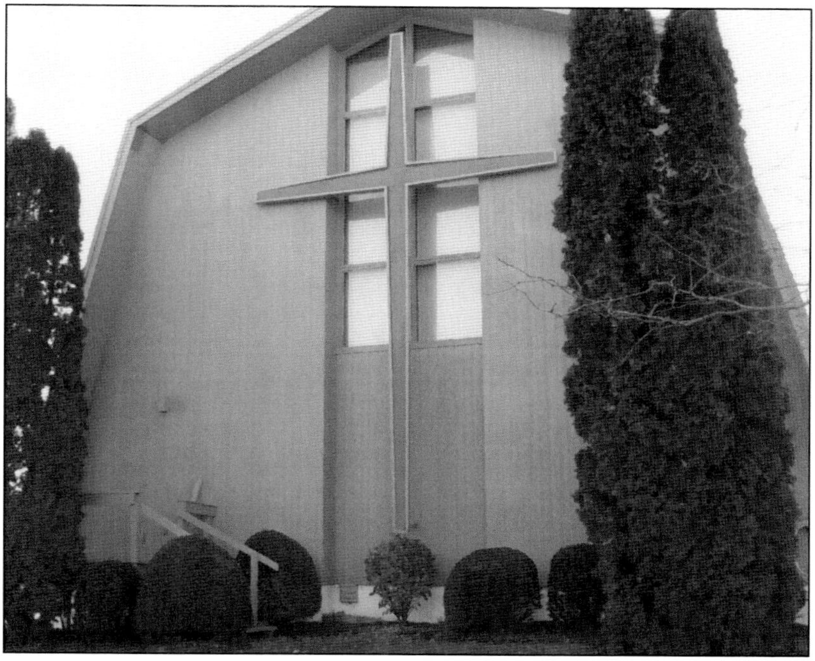

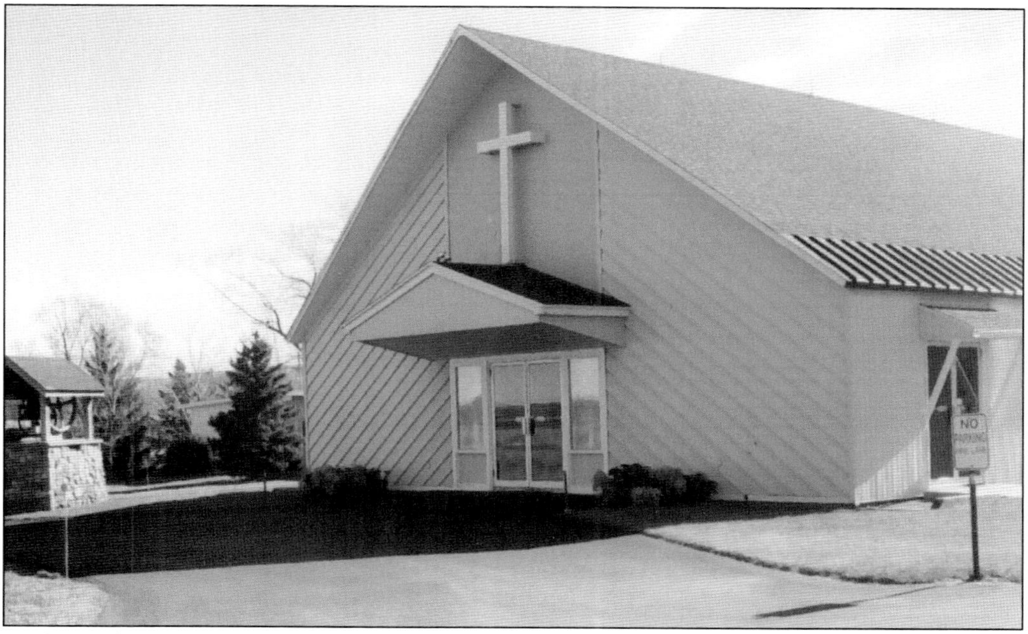

In the mid-1800s, there was an exodus of families from Ireland, and several families came to western New York. Honeoye, at that time, had no Catholic church. The closest churches were in East Bloomfield and Lima. Transportation was an issue—either a family would have to walk, or, if they could afford a horse, use a buggy to get to church. In 1874, land was purchased on West Main Street in Honeoye, and a church was built in 1875–1876. As the number of parishioners increased and the summer influx grew, the church was strained. Finally in 1956, five acres of land was purchased on the corner of Main Street and County Road 37. A new St. Mary's was constructed at a cost of $63,000. A large parking area is adjacent to the church. The former wooden structure on Main Street has been converted to apartments.

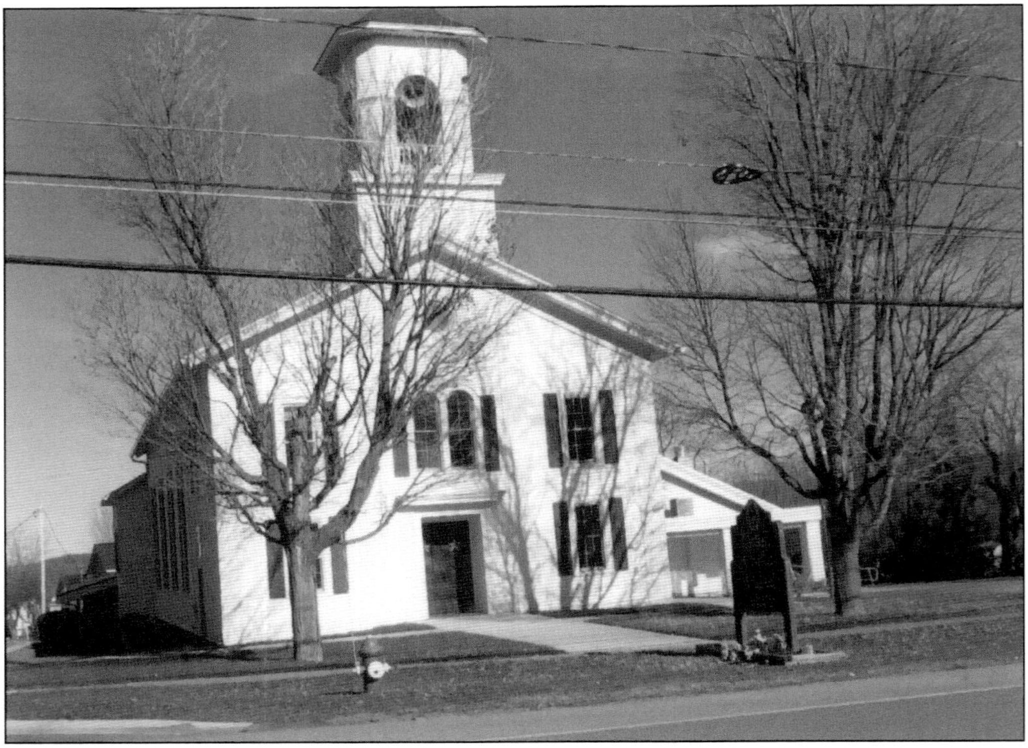

Rev. Cyrus Pitts organized the United Church of Christ in 1854. In 1861, the present church was built on Main Street in Honeoye. Until 1862, the pastor serving this church also served the Richmond Center Church. Frederick Douglass spoke at the Honeoye church when he would visit the Pitts family. Professor F.B. Short played the church organ for 25 years. In 1869, a vestibule, balcony, and church tower were added. The parlor, basement dining room, and kitchen were added in 1897. A traditional family-style turkey dinner has been served for many years every election day in November.

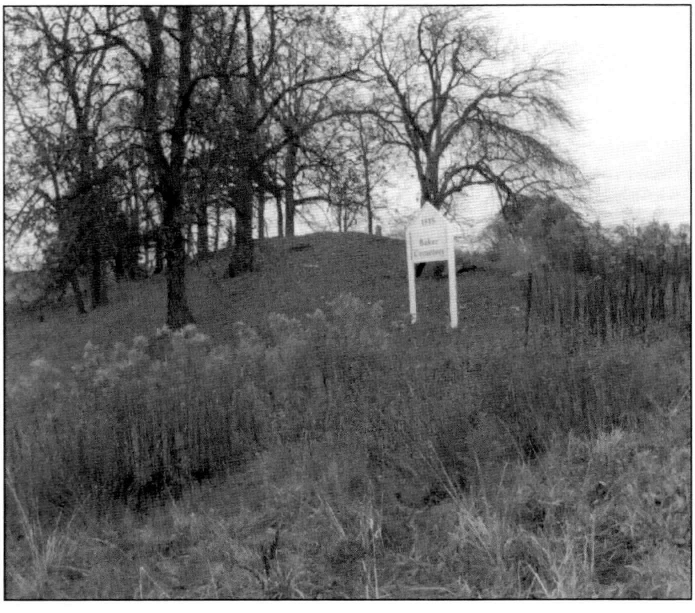

Baker Cemetery sits on a knoll, high behind the Abbey Road schoolhouse. It is the resting place for many of the area's early settlers. It can be reached by using the right-of-way pathway up to the hillside. Dr. David Crooks, an early physician in the area, and his family are buried there. Herb Knight was a volunteer caretaker of the cemetery. A plaque has been placed near his shovel and wheelbarrow, which he left up against a fence when he last visited the cemetery.

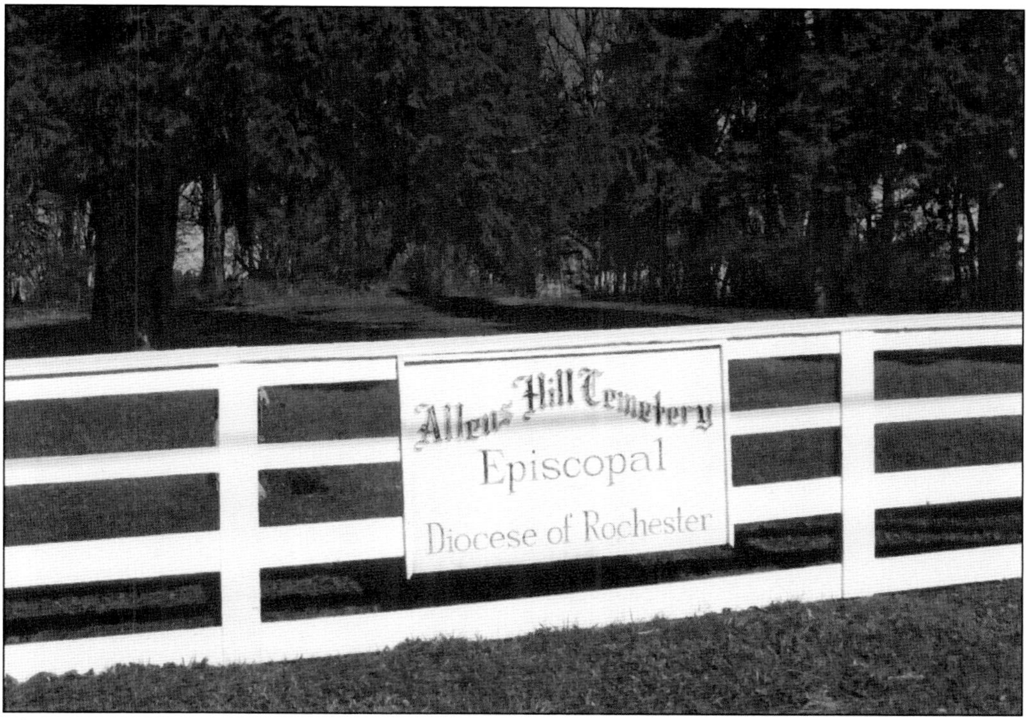

The Episcopal Cemetery remains in its original location on Allens Hill. However, the church is no longer there, having been struck by lightning in the 1920s and not rebuilt.

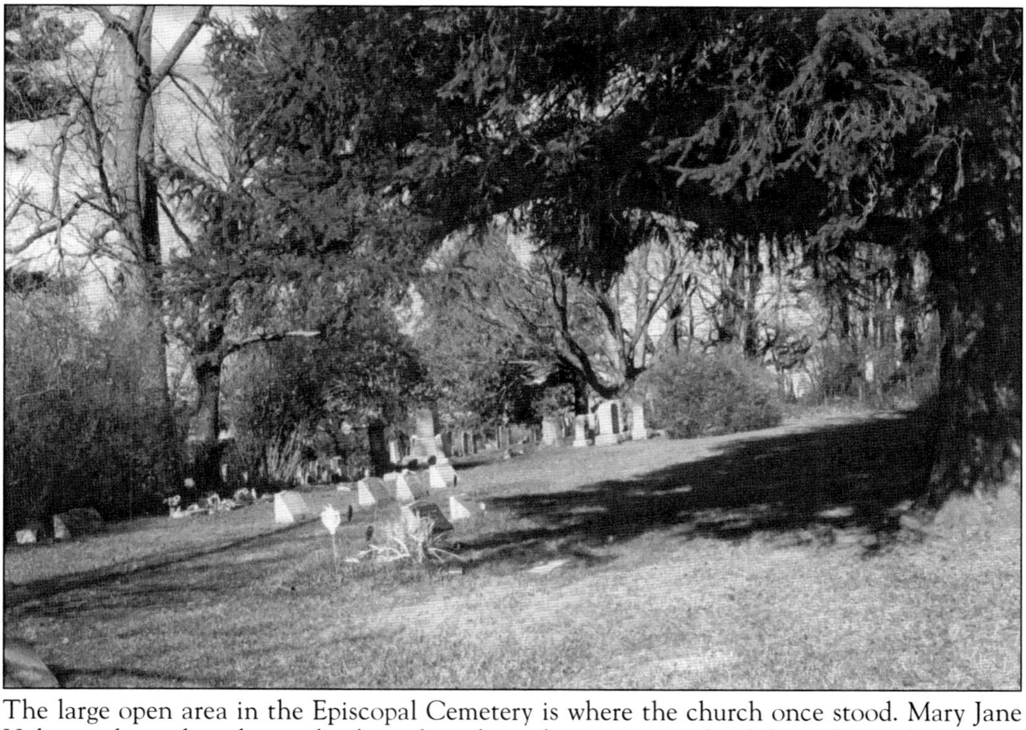
The large open area in the Episcopal Cemetery is where the church once stood. Mary Jane Holmes, who authored many books and taught at the one-room school down the road and ran a girl's private school, was married in the church.

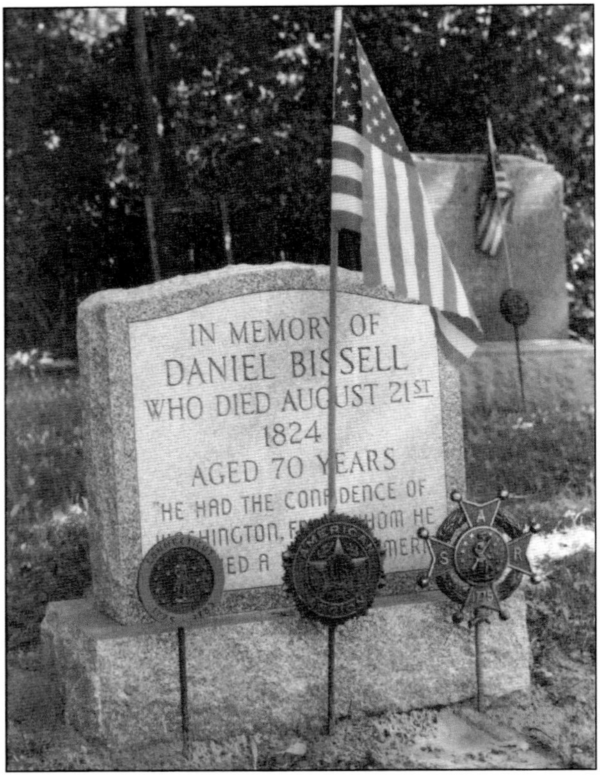

Daniel Bissell, (1754–1824) was a soldier and a spy under Gen. George Washington during the Revolutionary War. He was ordered to pose as a deserter and go behind enemy lines. He joined the British Army for 13 months, memorizing everything he was able to before making his way back to friendly territory. Washington awarded him the Badge of Military Merit in 1783, the precursor to the Purple Heart. It was destroyed in a fire at the Bissell home in 1813. Edmund Nighan led a drive to have the Bissell stone replaced with a new one issued by the US government. The original stone is in the Richmond Historical Museum. Daniel Bissell had six sons, all of them named Daniel with different middle names.

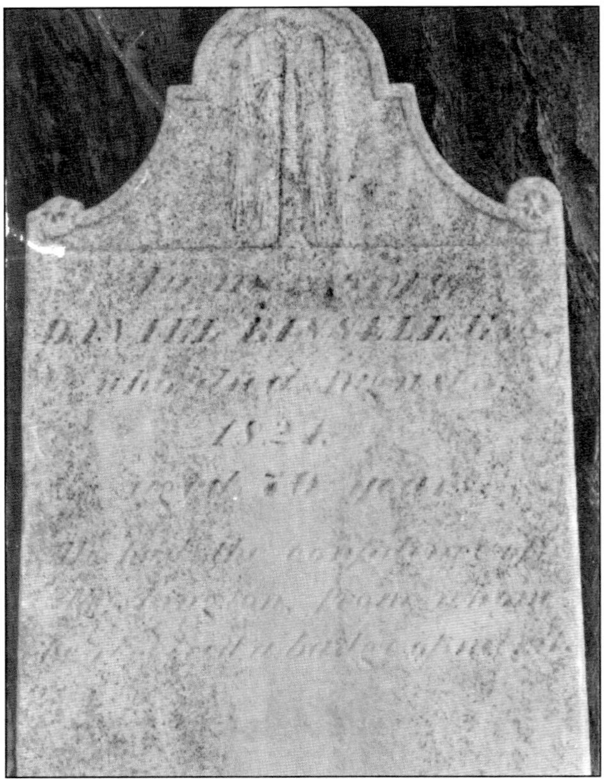

The original stone for Daniel Bissell is shown here. It shows the wear and tear of weathering over the many years it was on his grave.

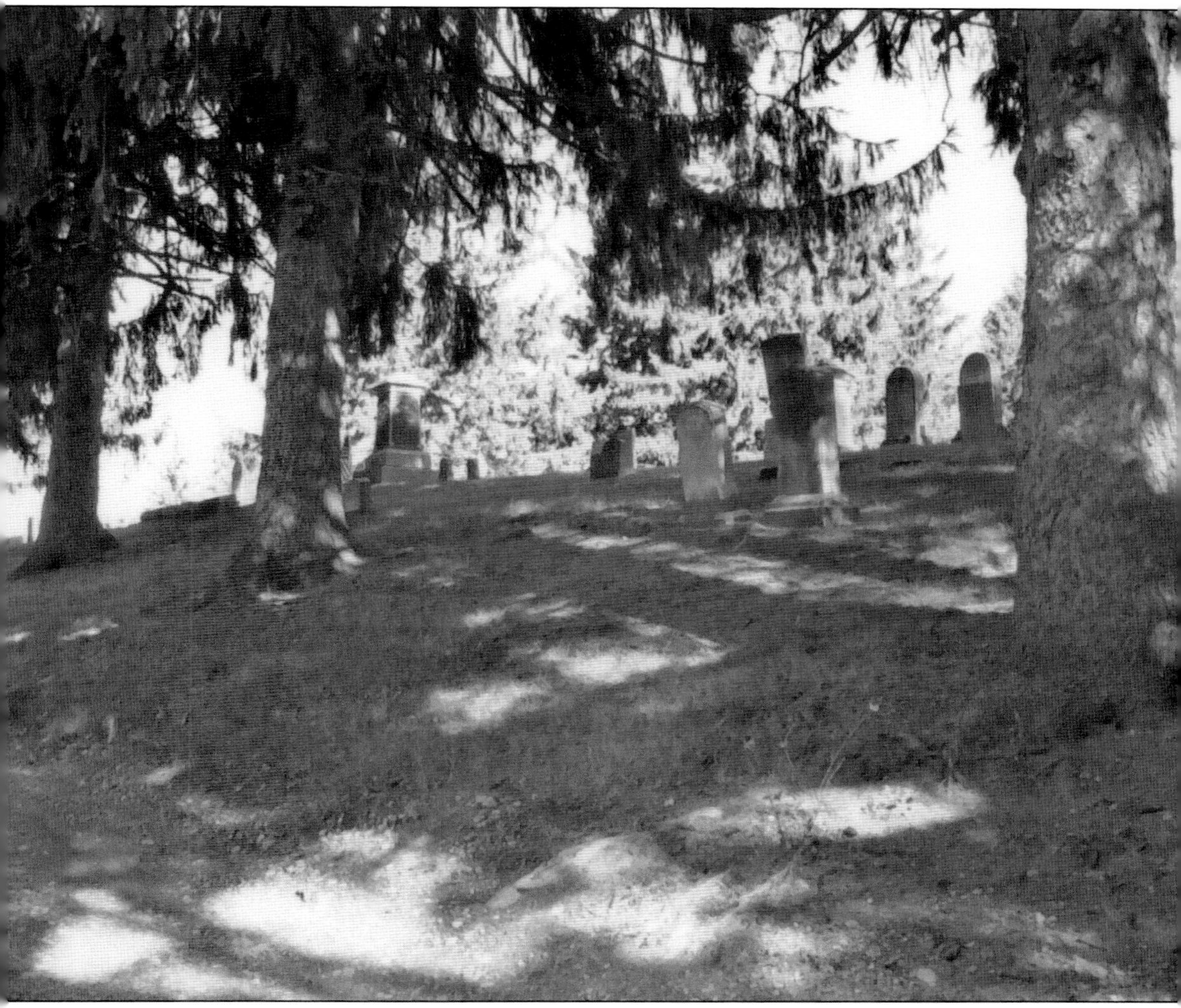

Lakeview Cemetery is in a beautiful location off West Lake Road on a rolling hillside. It is still used for many local burials. It also was a place that early people used for burials, and Native American graves were found in the area.

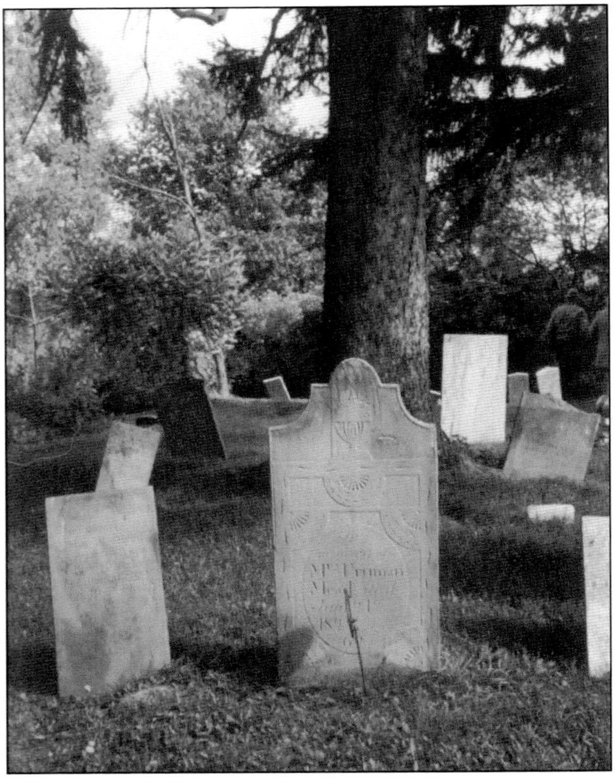

Dennison's Corners Cemetery is about a half-mile north of the intersection of Shetler and Larned Roads in the northwest section of Richmond. It contains the graves of many of the earliest residents of that area.

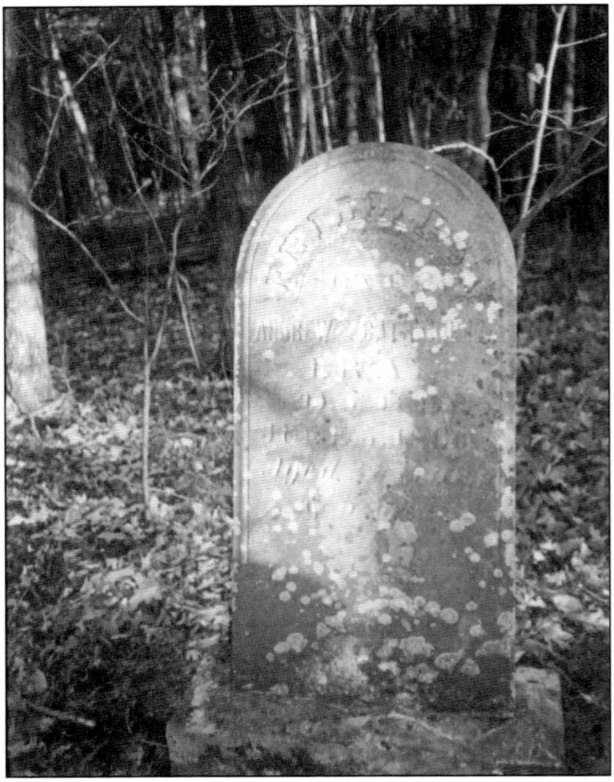

The Hamilton/Bray Cemetery is difficult to get to, and permission is required to cross the private property. Many of the stones are lying on the ground, now illegible. A Revolutionary War soldier, William Lane, is buried there.

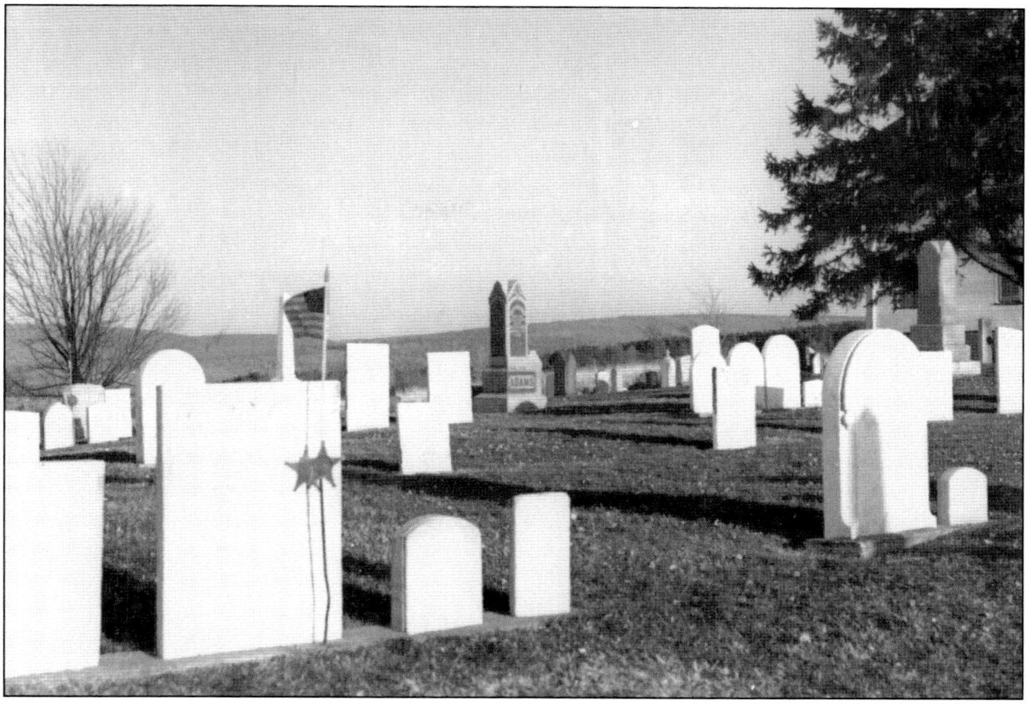

Canadice Corners Cemetery is located next to the Canadice Methodist Church. It contains the graves of many of the early settlers of the area and is still in use.

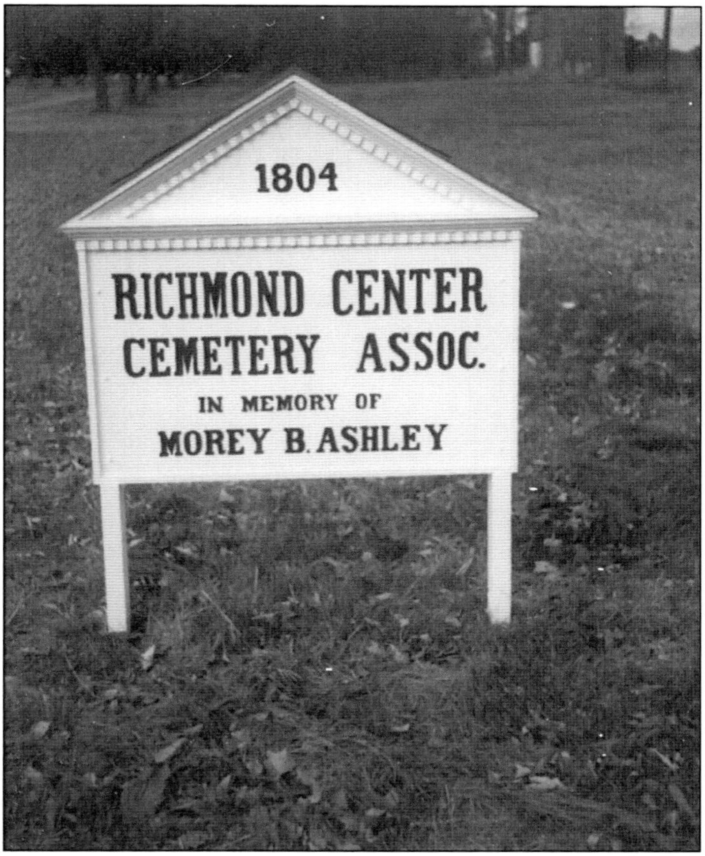

Richmond Center Cemetery is sometimes referred to as the Reed Cemetery, probably because many of the Reed family are buried there, including their black servant Jane Lebanon. It is located back from the road off of County Road 37 near the corner of Ashley Road.

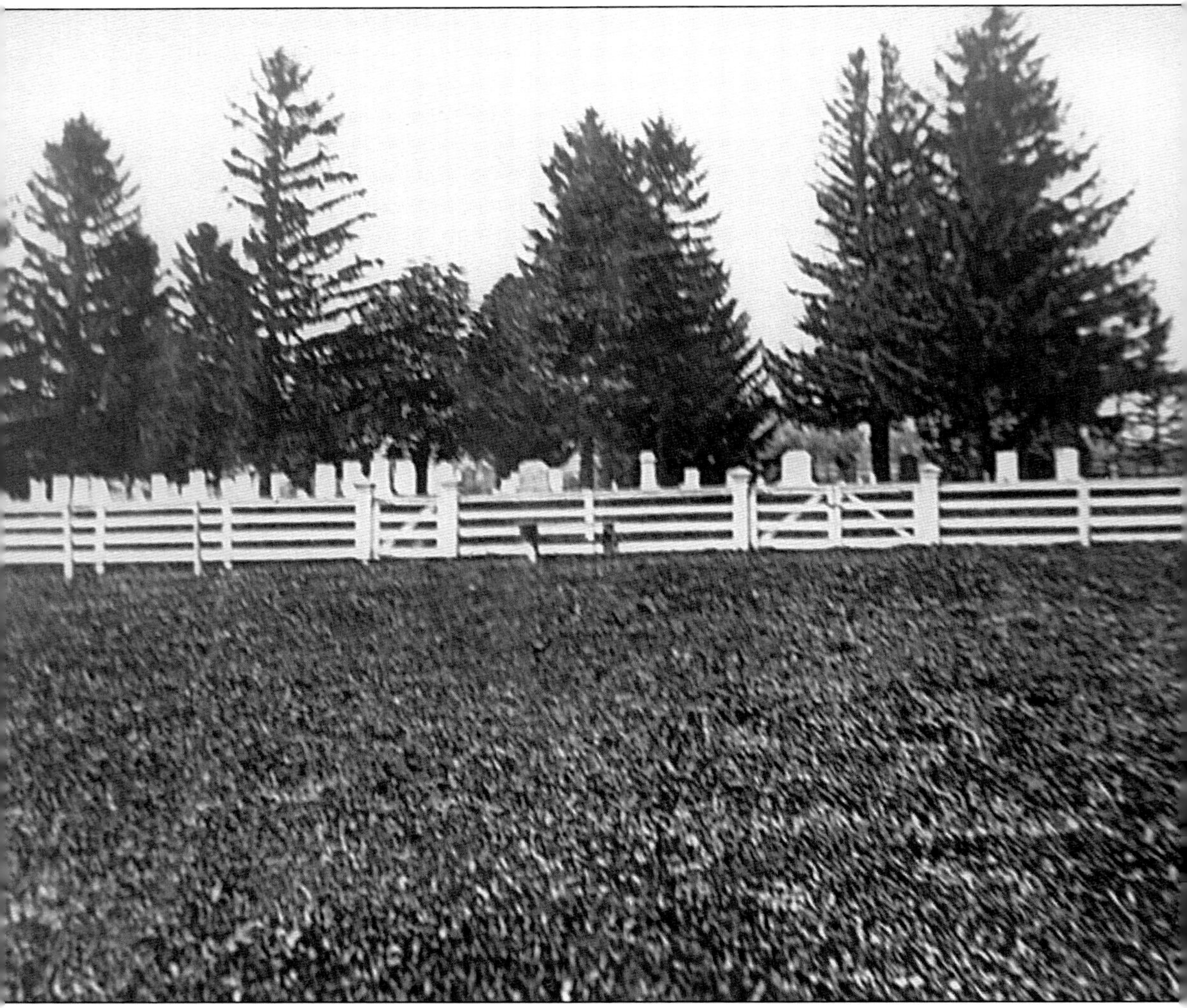

The fence for Richmond Center Cemetery was built in the early 1900s. It is still in good repair and makes a pleasant entryway into the cemetery. Many of Richmond's early settlers are buried there.

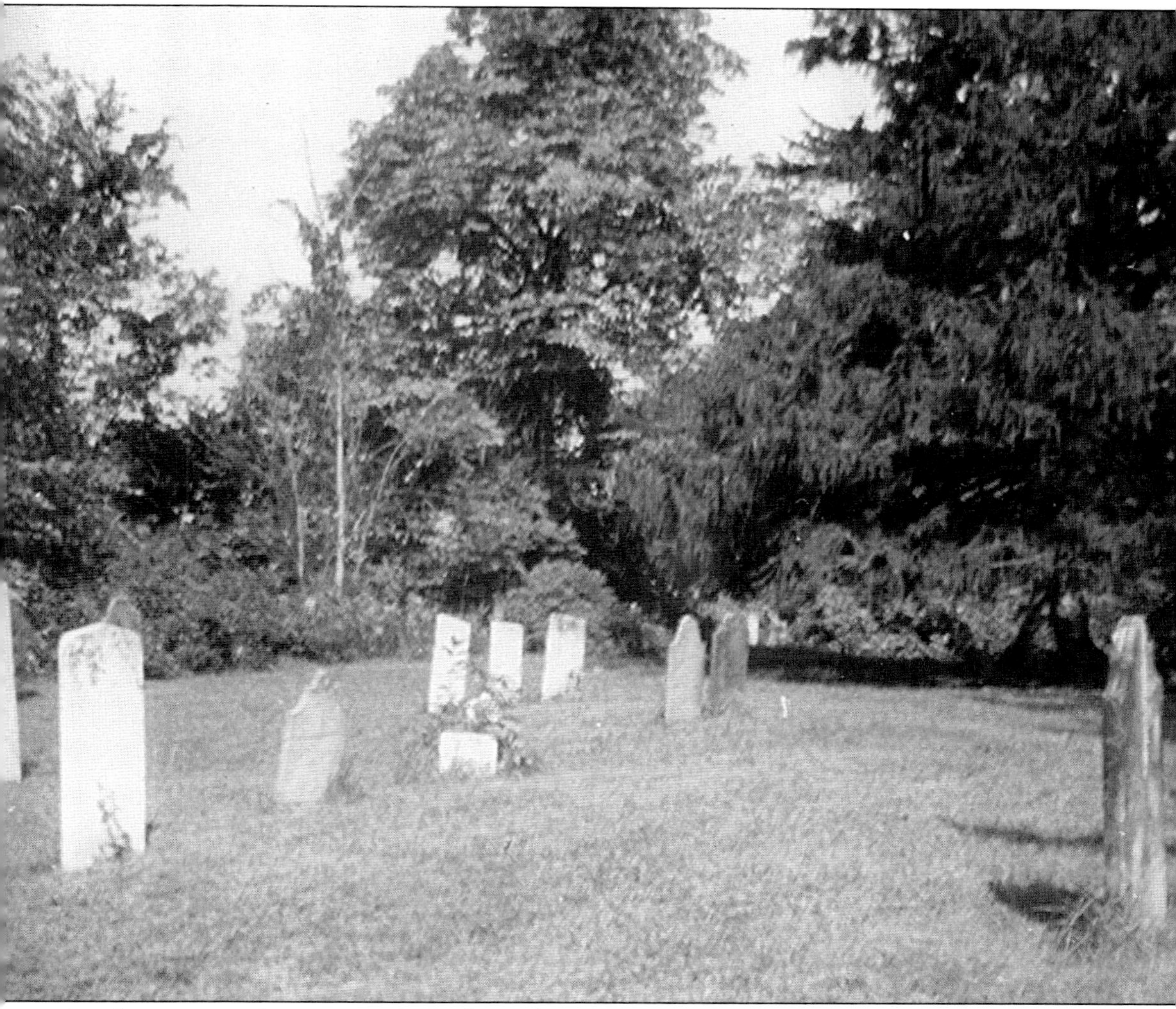

A cedar post is under a tree in the Richmond Center Cemetery. It is thought to be marking the grave of an escaped slave, but no one knows its origin for sure. Some people have thought it was for Jane Lebanon of the Reed family, but her grave is marked with her name on a stone in the same row as the rest of the Reed family.

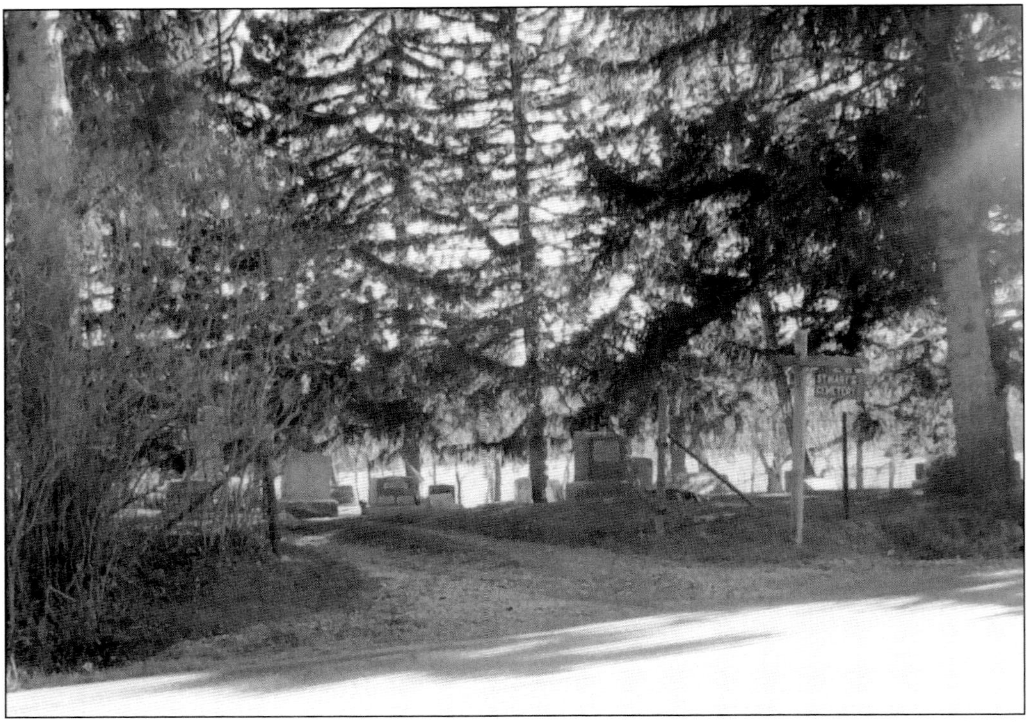

St. Mary's Cemetery is the community's Catholic cemetery. It is located behind St. Mary's Church at the intersection of Briggs Street and County Road 37.

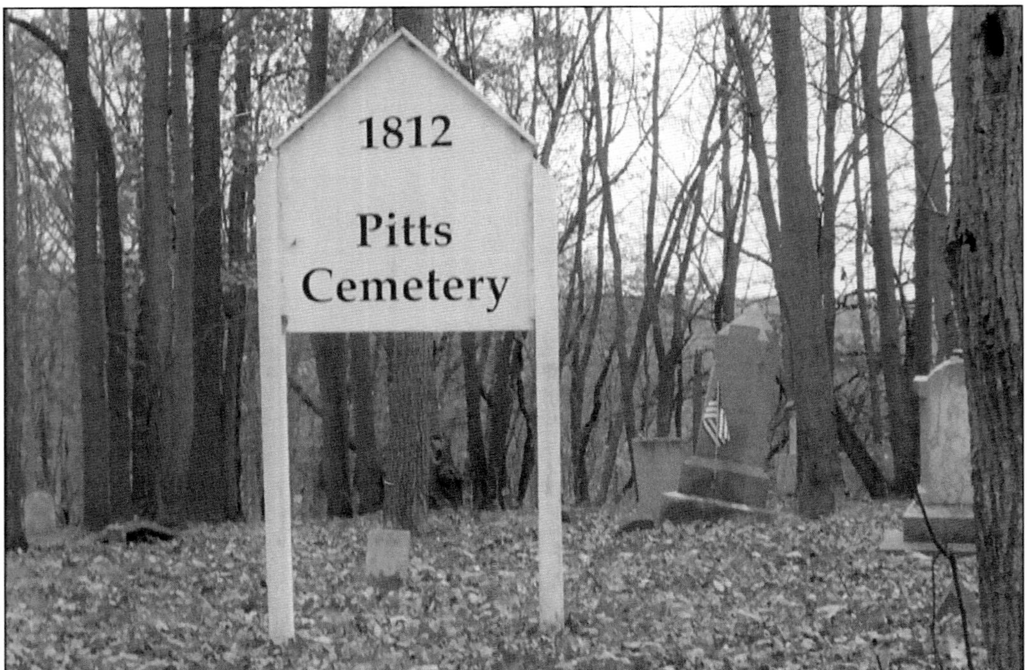

The Pitts Cemetery sits high on a hill off of Grandview Drive in Honeoye. It is now considered an abandoned cemetery. Many of the graves are of early settlers, but many graves have been exhumed and the bodies buried in Lakeview Cemetery.

Seven

Houses and Barns

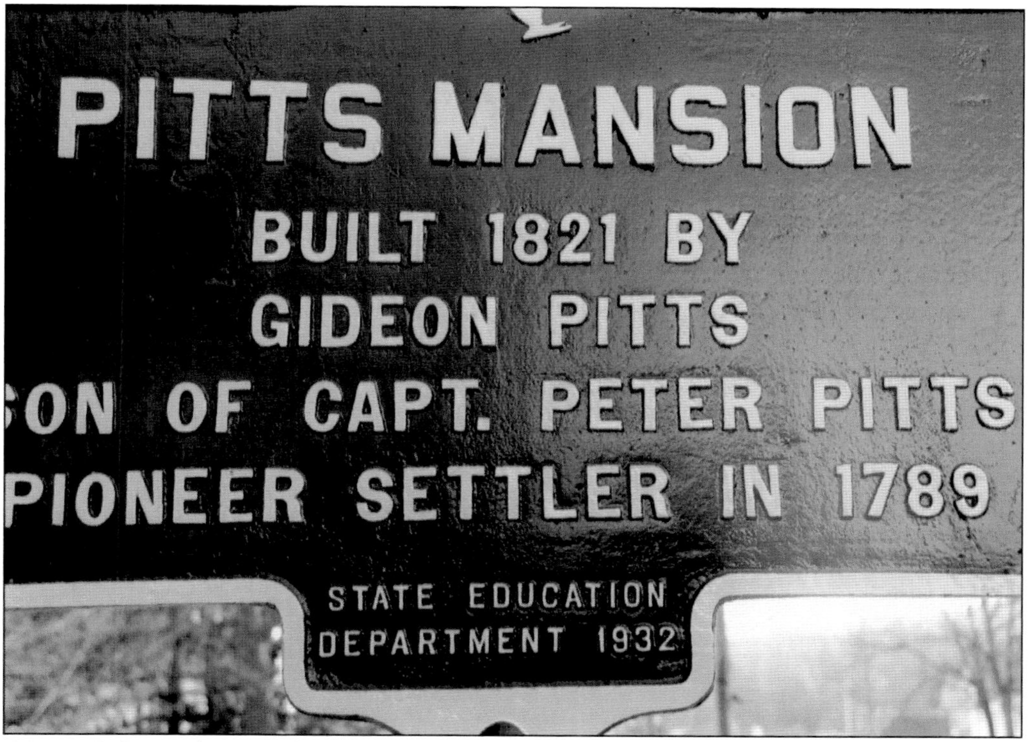

A New York state historical marker is in front of the Pitts Mansion, marking the home that was built in 1821 by Gideon Pitts.

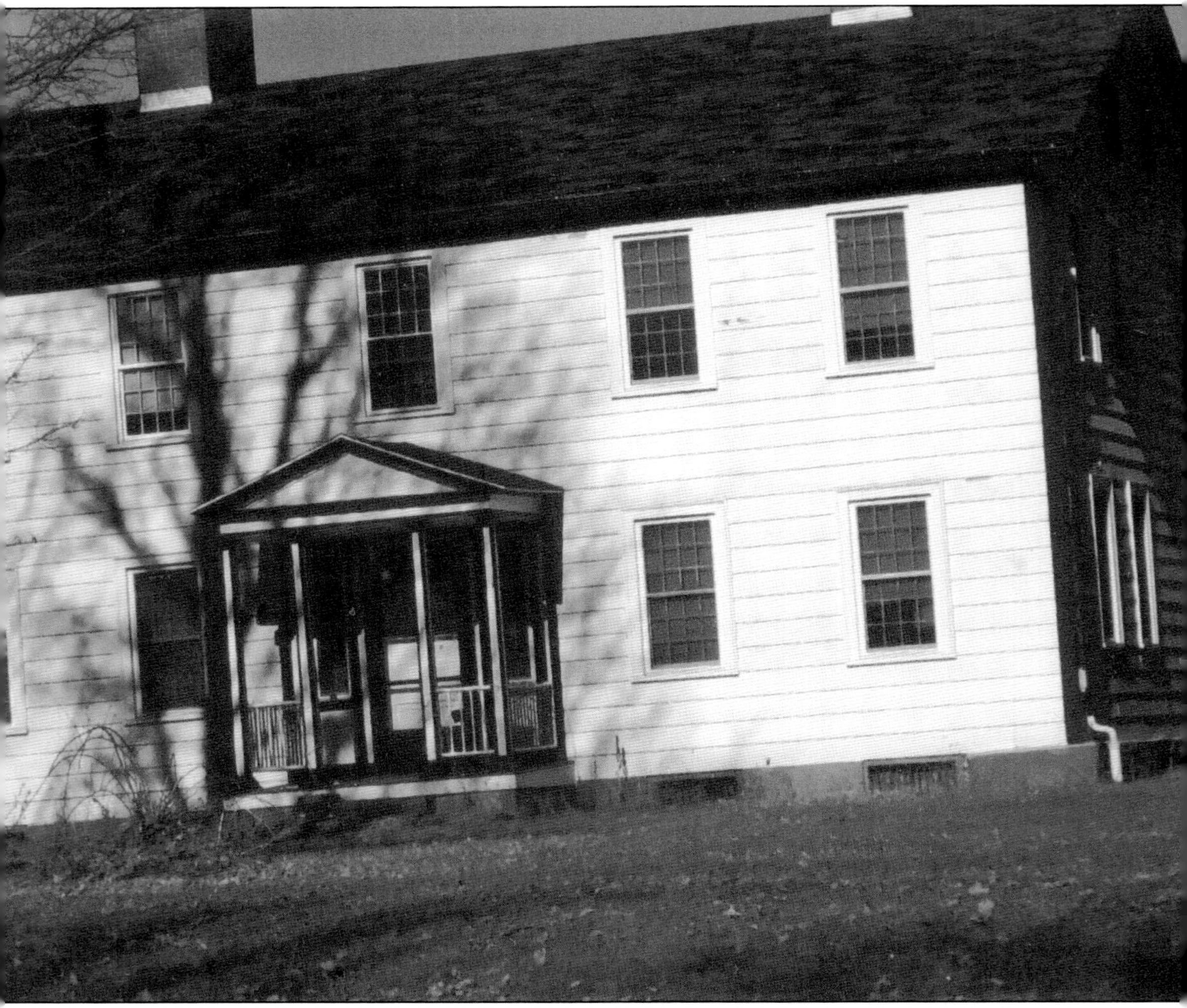

The Pitts Mansion is well known as a station on the Underground Railroad for escaping slaves. The basement no longer contains the false wall for hiding slaves, and the house is now a private home.

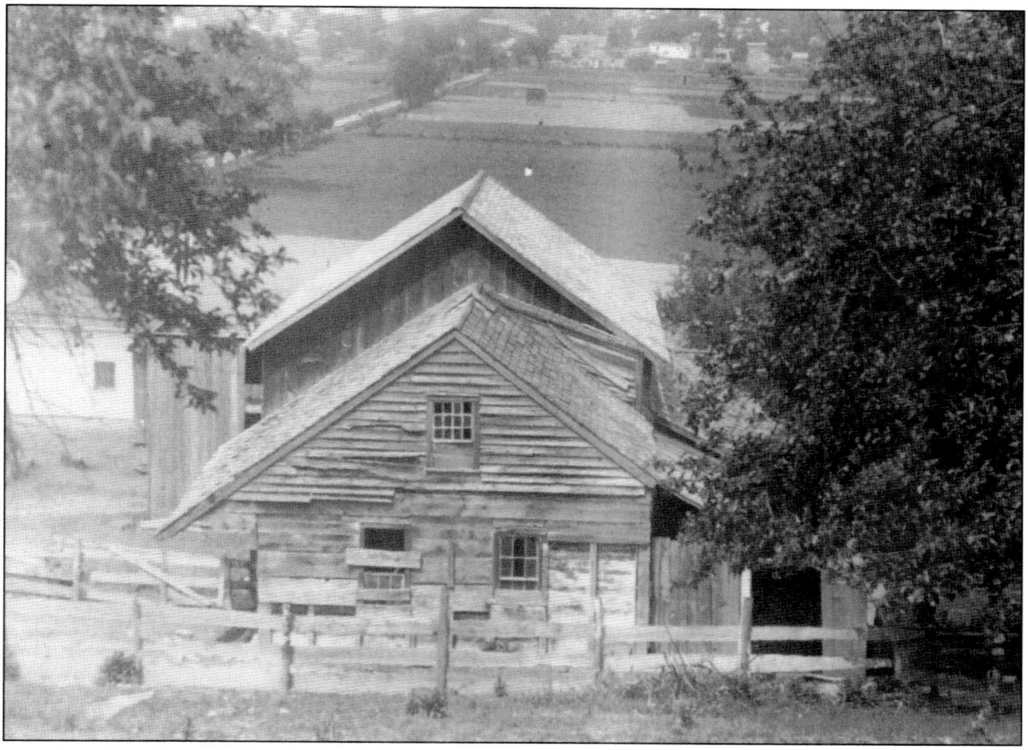

Peter Pitts's cabin was built near the intersection of Grandview Drive and Allens Hill Road.

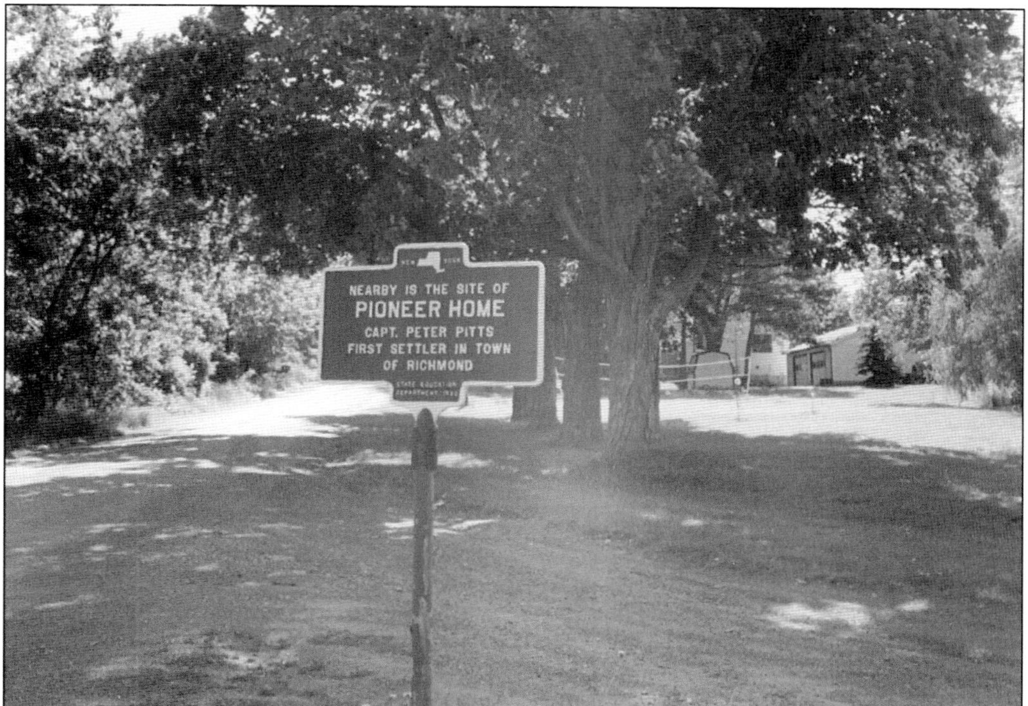

A New York state historical marker was placed near the location of the first log cabin in Richmond.

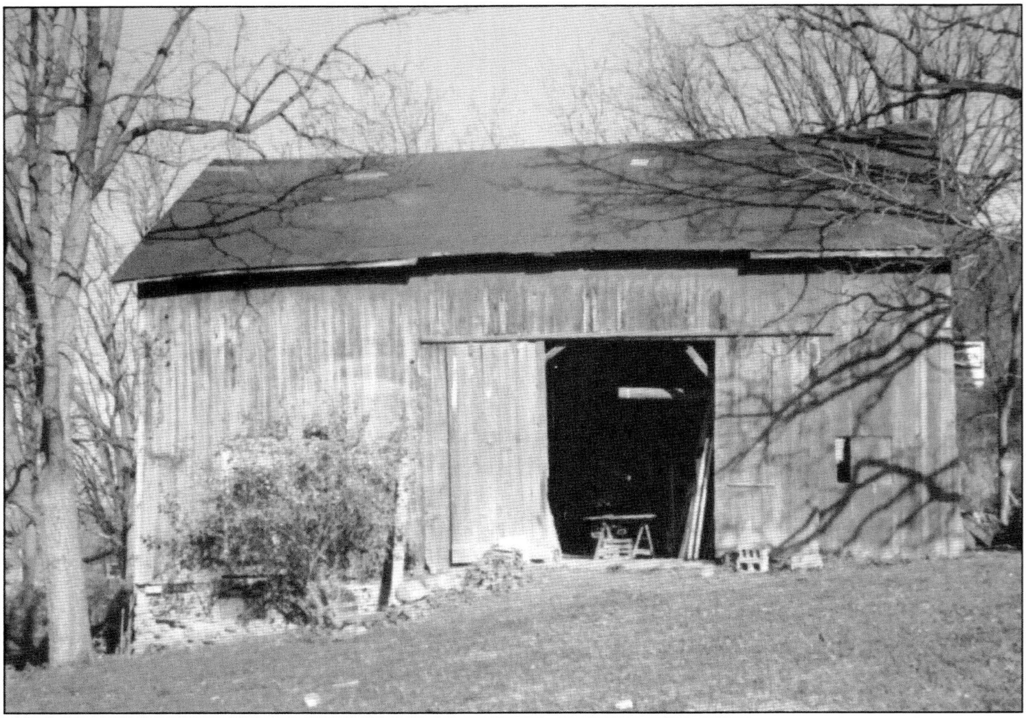

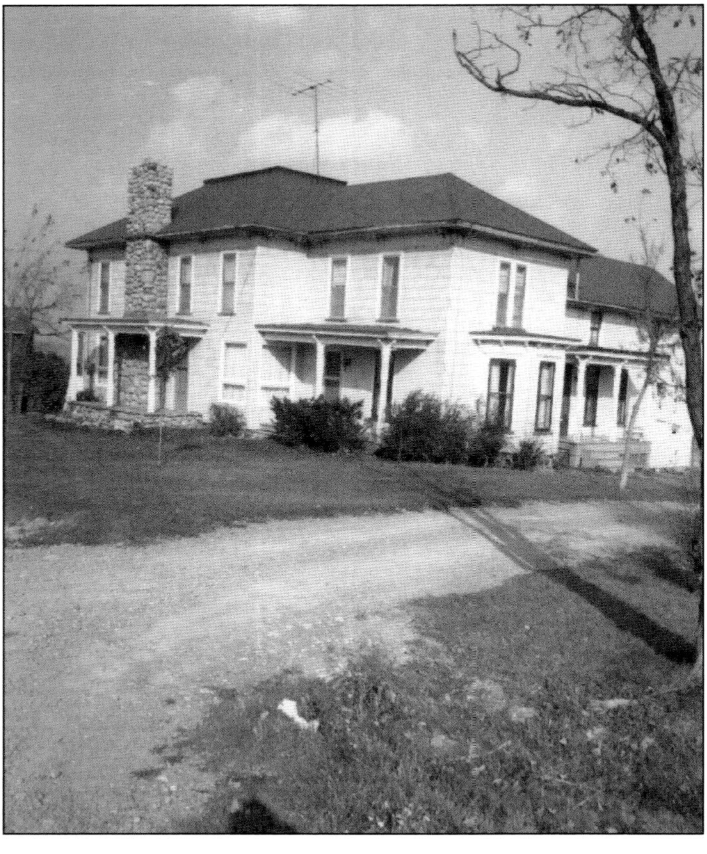

This is a photograph of the barn that was behind the first house in Richmond. Part of the original barn may have been used to build the barn that now stands in the same location.

The Mastin House on County Road 37 is one of the grand old houses built in Richmond. The date of the photograph is 1963.

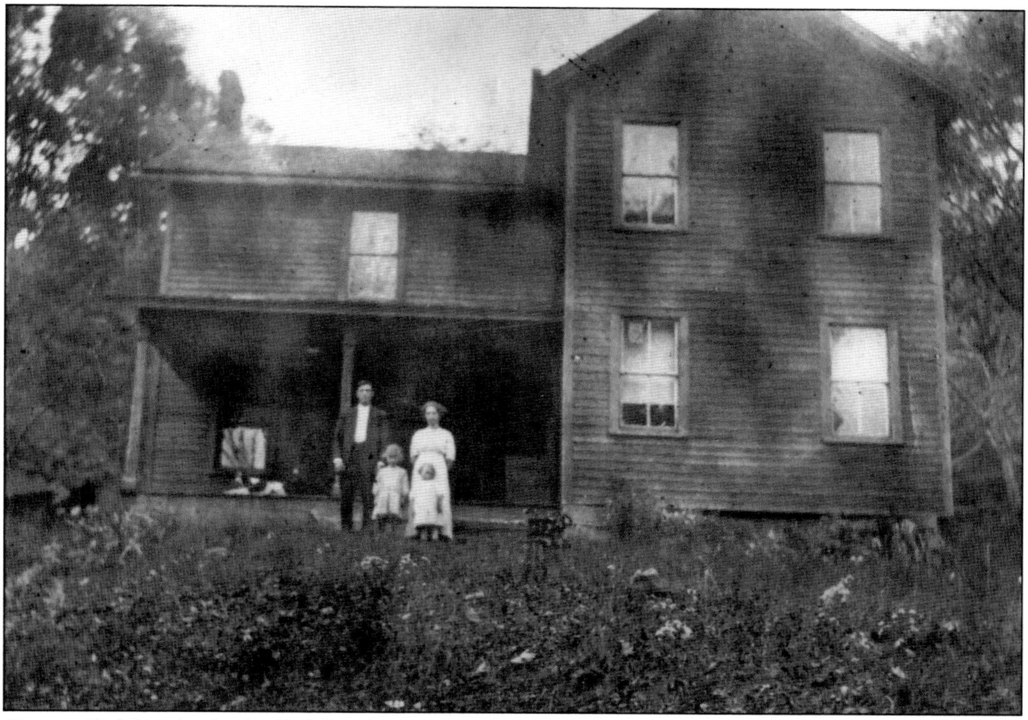

George Belcher built the Belcher home on West Lake Road in Canadice. The picture is dated 1918. (Courtesy of Beverly Deats.)

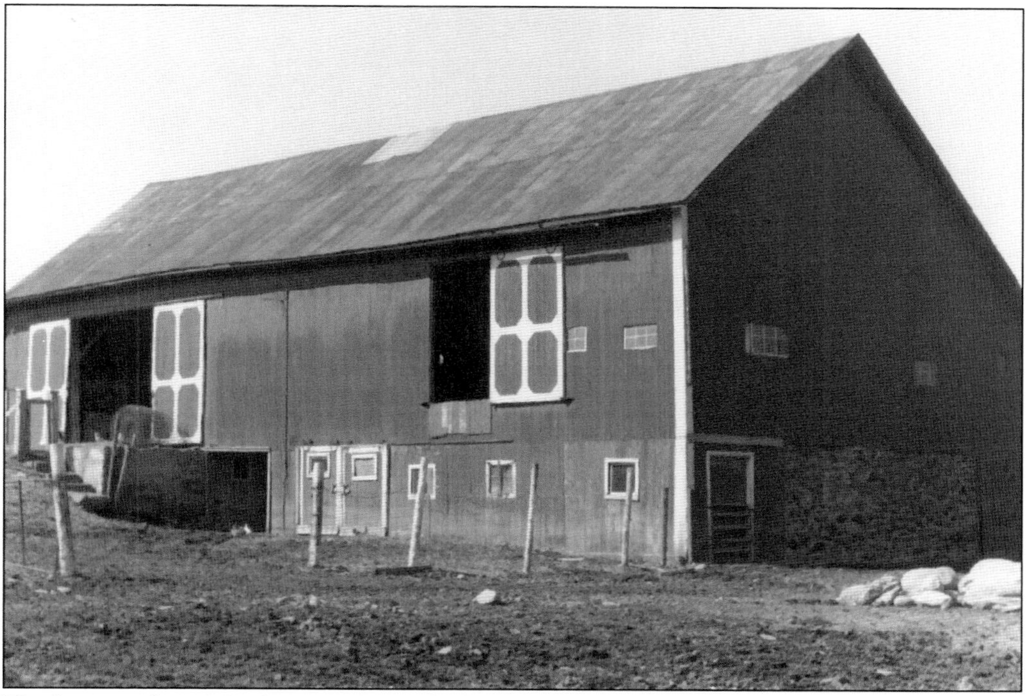

The barn in this 1960 photograph was built on the Herbert Treble farm on East Lake Road in Honeoye. Farmers would sometimes order small barn models from companies out of town, and then have local contractors build a similar life-sized barn.

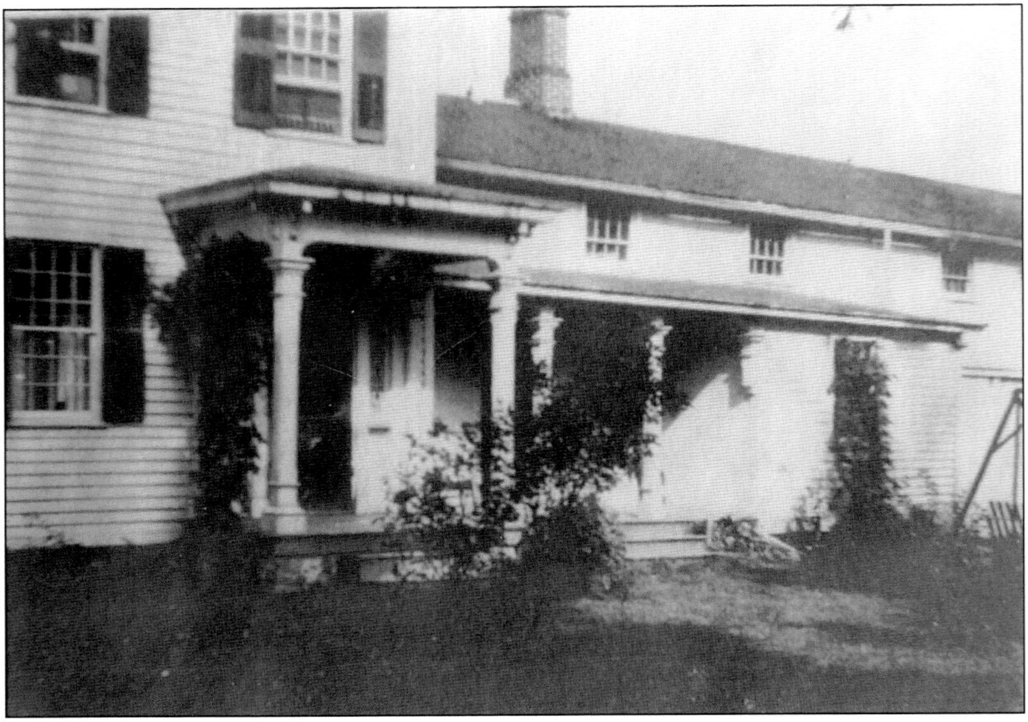

This is the William Pitts homestead on Allens Hill Road. The home was built around 1790 and still has many of its original features. William Pitts married three times and died in 1815.

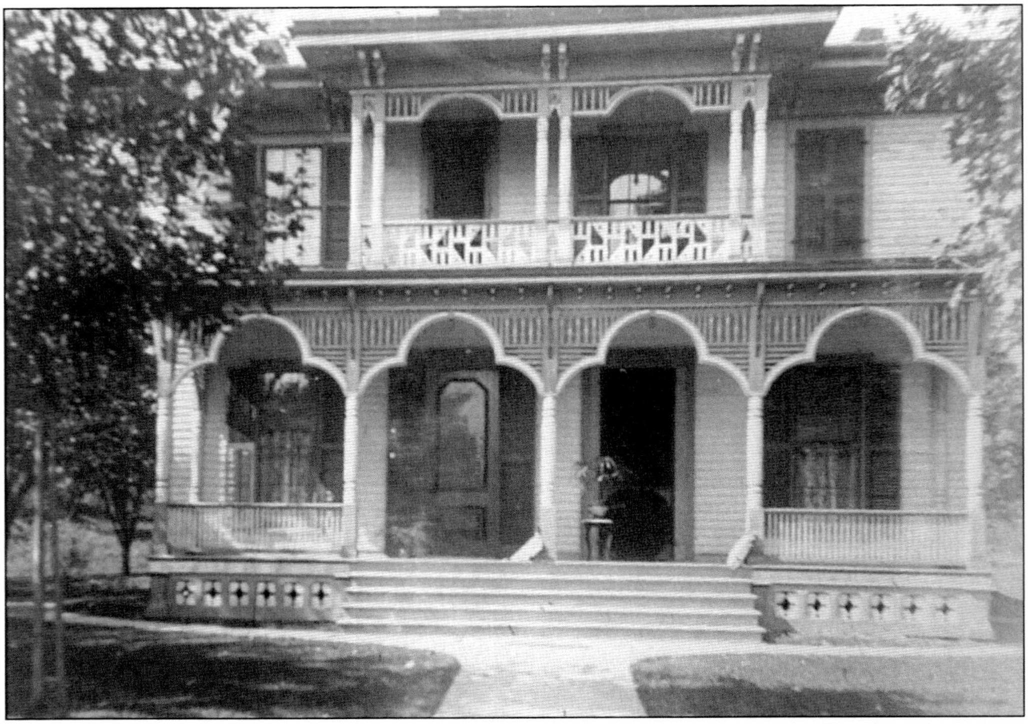

This house is the one built on the California Ranch property on West Lake Road in Canadice. The house still looks very much as it did in the early 1900s.

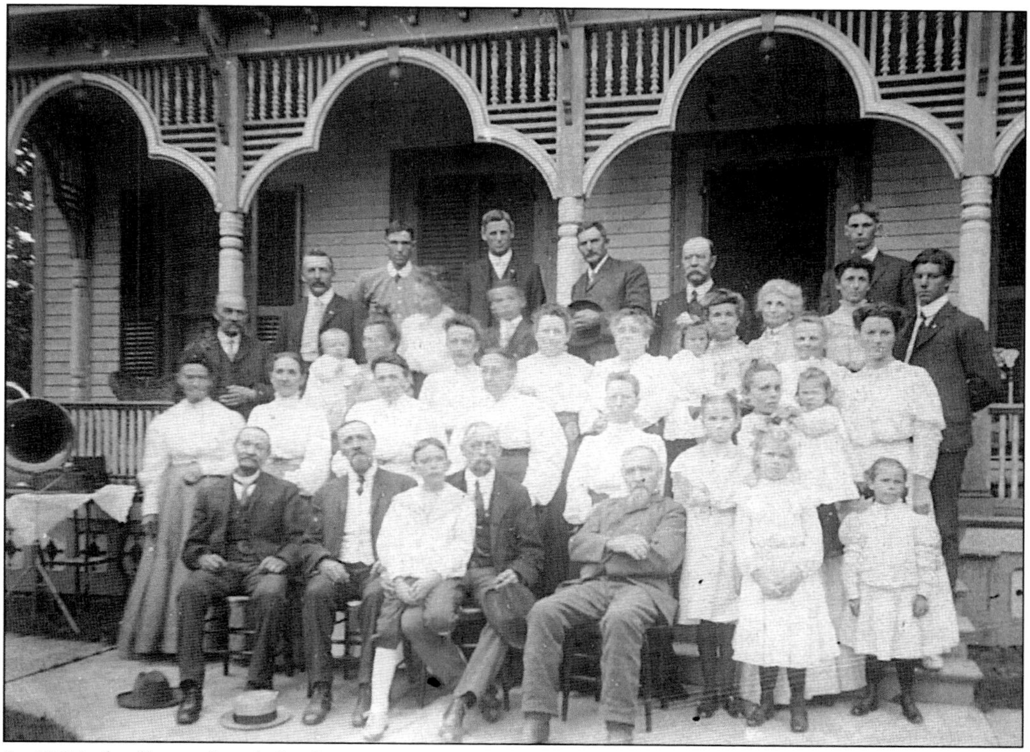

In 1907, the Beam family had a reunion at the California Ranch in Canadice.

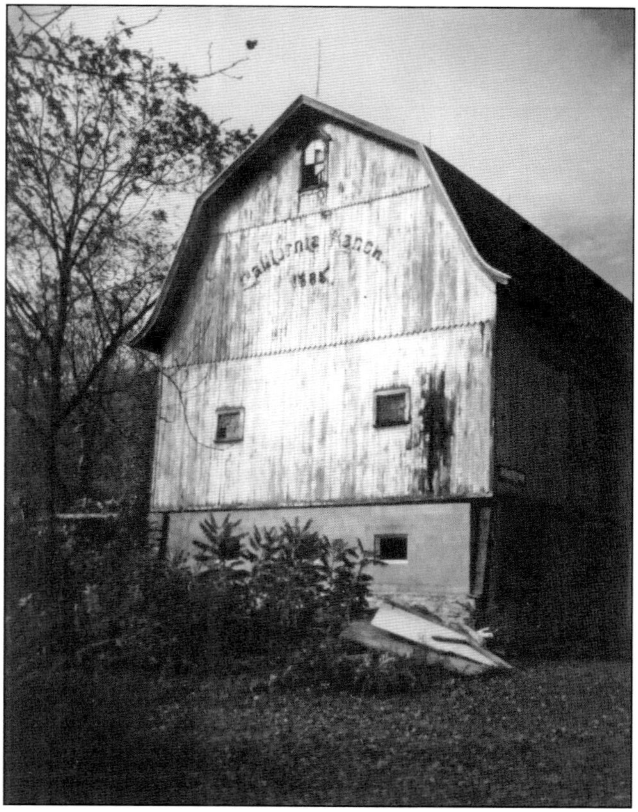

The barn on the Beam property still has the date of 1885 showing on it.

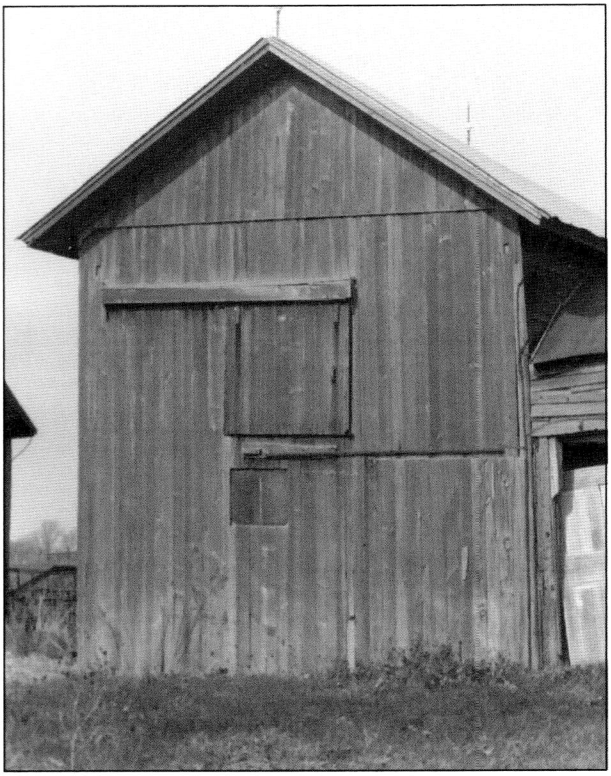

This barn was built in Dennison's Corners. The barn is believed to have kept the horses that pulled the stagecoaches, as it is located on the stagecoach route from Canandaigua to points west. It is near the Dennison's Corners Tavern.

The Pest House is shown when it was under construction on the west end of Briggs Street in Honeoye. It was built as a place for victims of the smallpox outbreaks that were starting to occur in the area. Only one husband and wife occupied the Pest House while the wife nursed her husband back to health. After 18 days, the county Board of Health allowed them to leave and return home. The building was empty for many years until someone bought it to move and live in. After it was no longer being used, it was torn down.

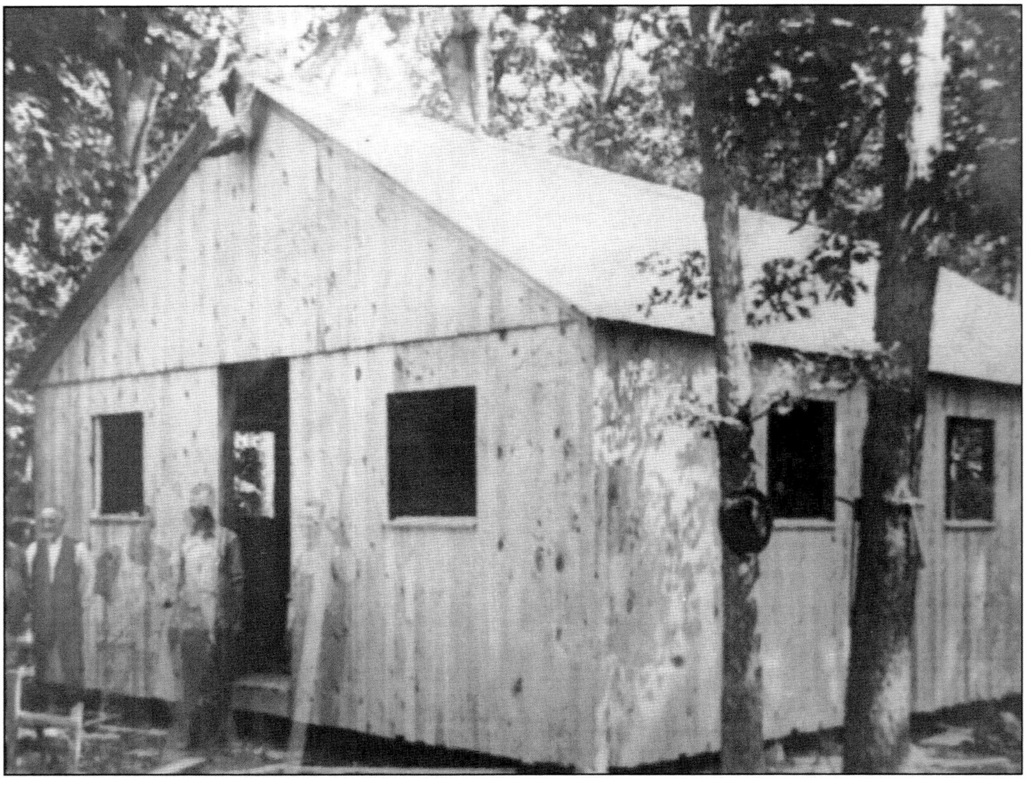

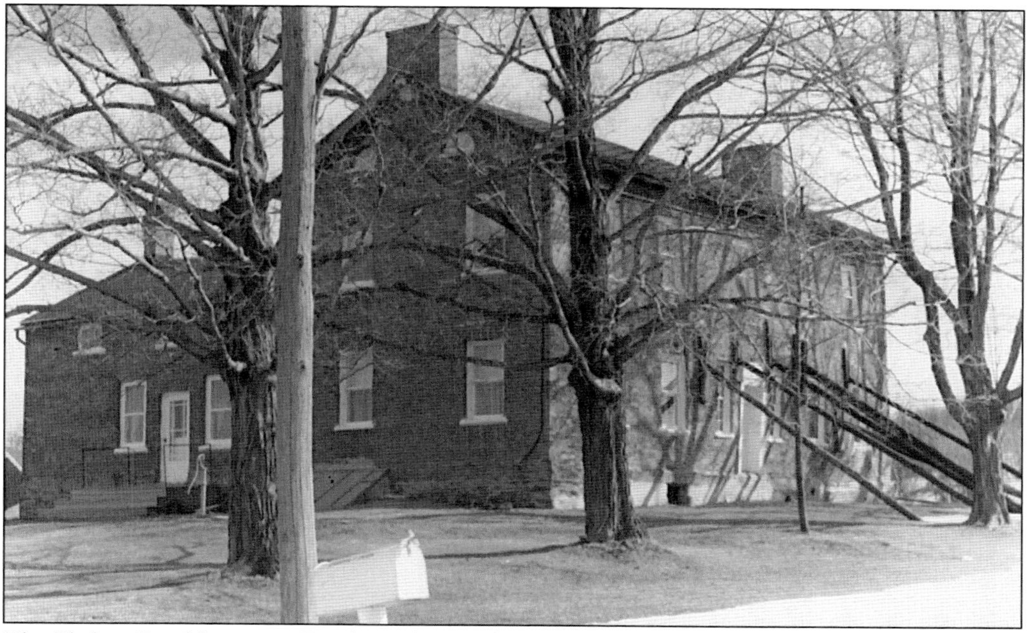

The Philipp Reed house on Reed Road in Richmond was the first brick house to be built in the town. In 1803, the house was constructed at a cost of $400. The bricks were made from clay found across the road. With the front wall constructed with a thickness of three bricks, it started bowing outward and had to be supported for many years. Some thought it was built on quicksand and others thought it was because the front wall was sitting on small, round stones that had shifted.

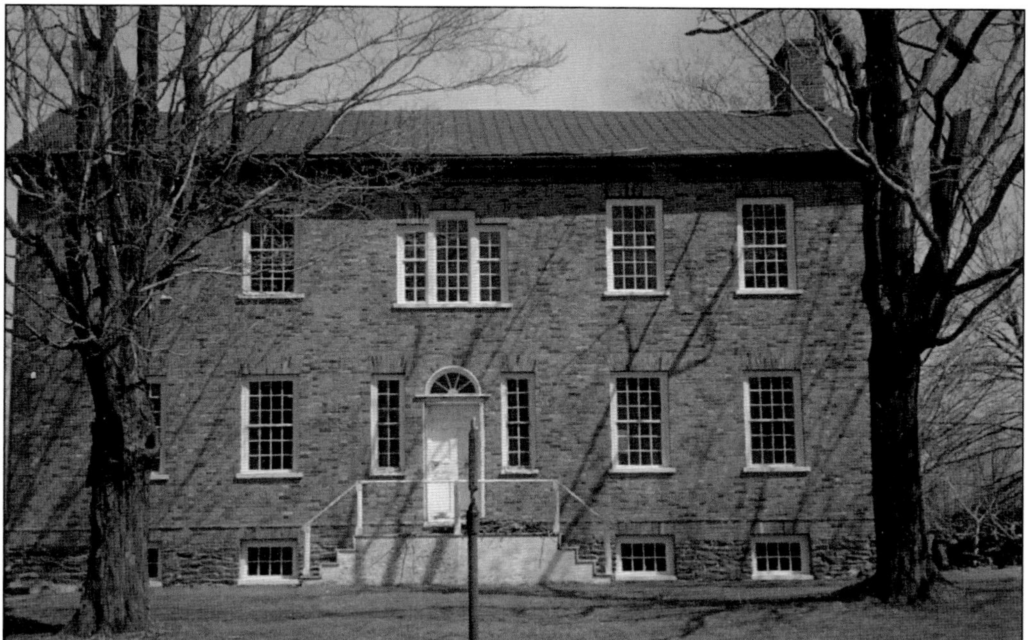

Eventually Horace Lethbridge had the wall restored so it could stand upright without support. He put in much time and effort over the 40 years that he resided in the home, restoring it to its original beauty and usefulness. Lethbridge died in 2008.

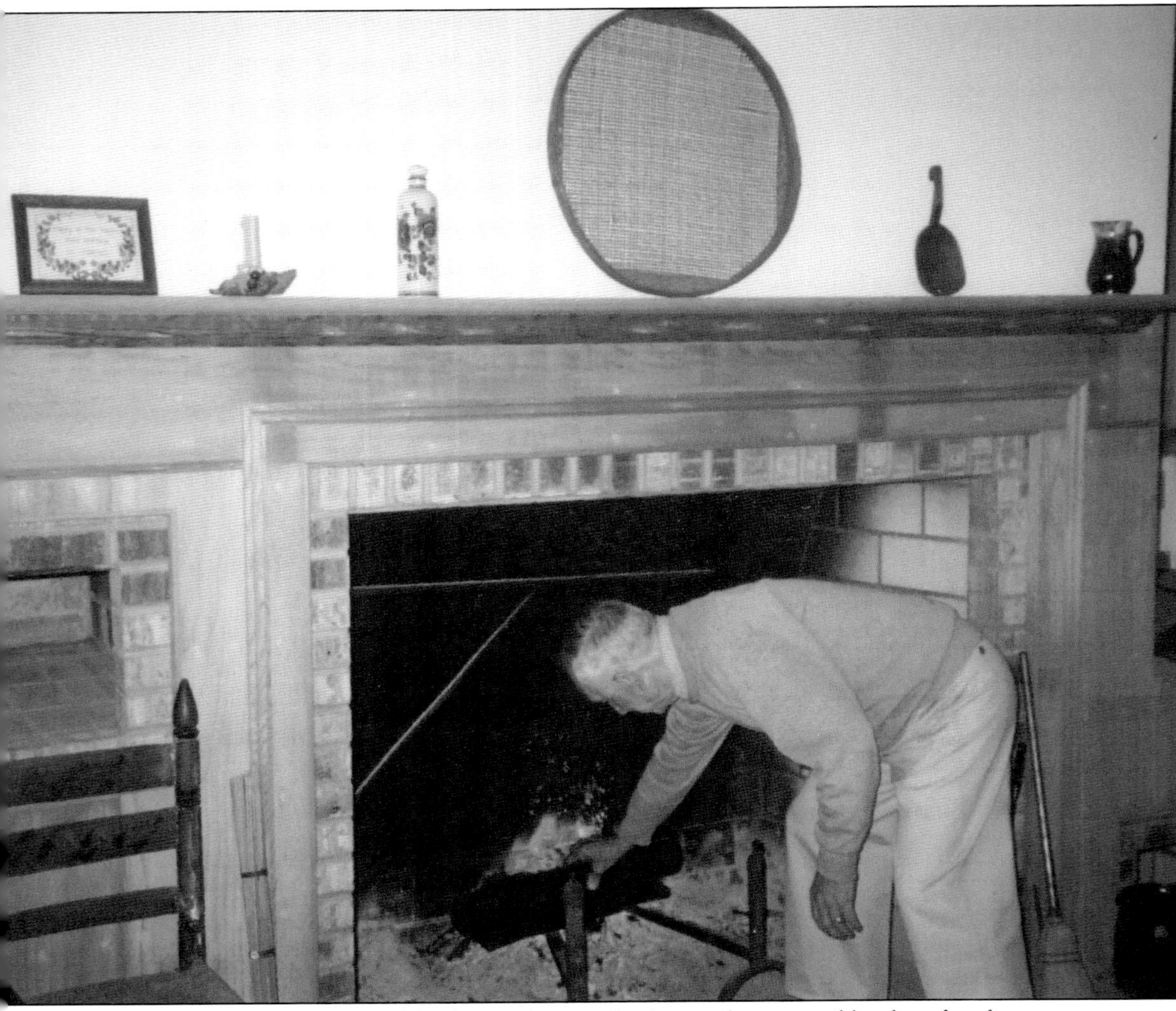

This photograph shows Lethbridge tending to the fire in the restored kitchen fireplace.

Eight

Fire Department

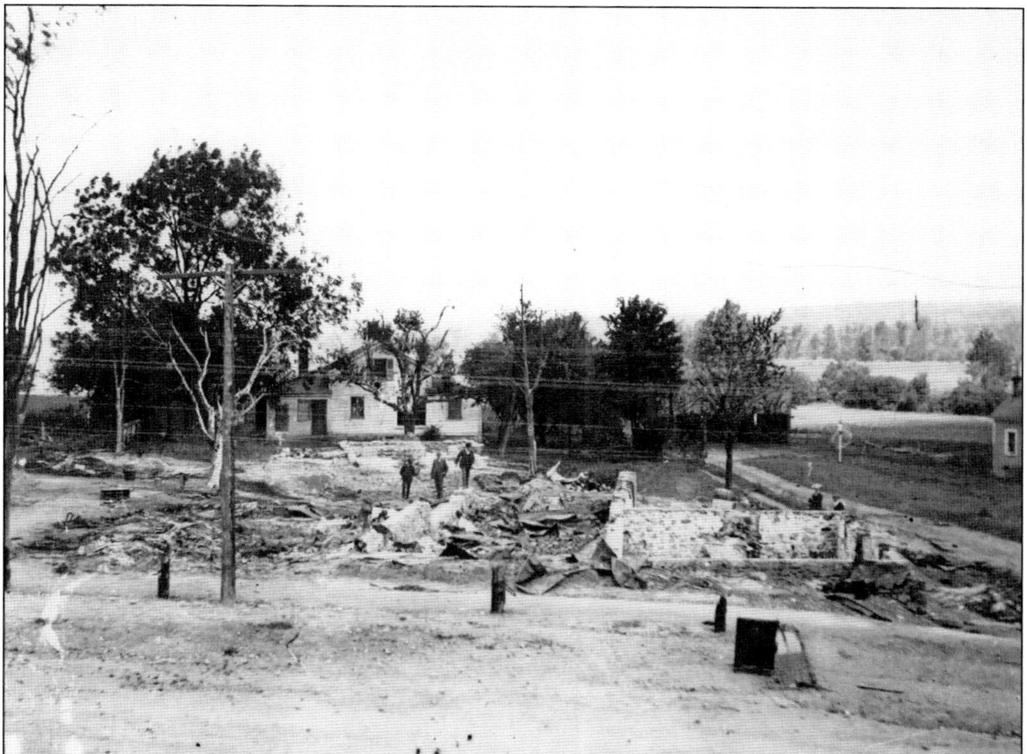

The Franklin Block fire occurred in 1905. Church bells rang to alert residents, who brought water from the creek. The area was a total loss, as nearby buildings were also lost in the blaze.

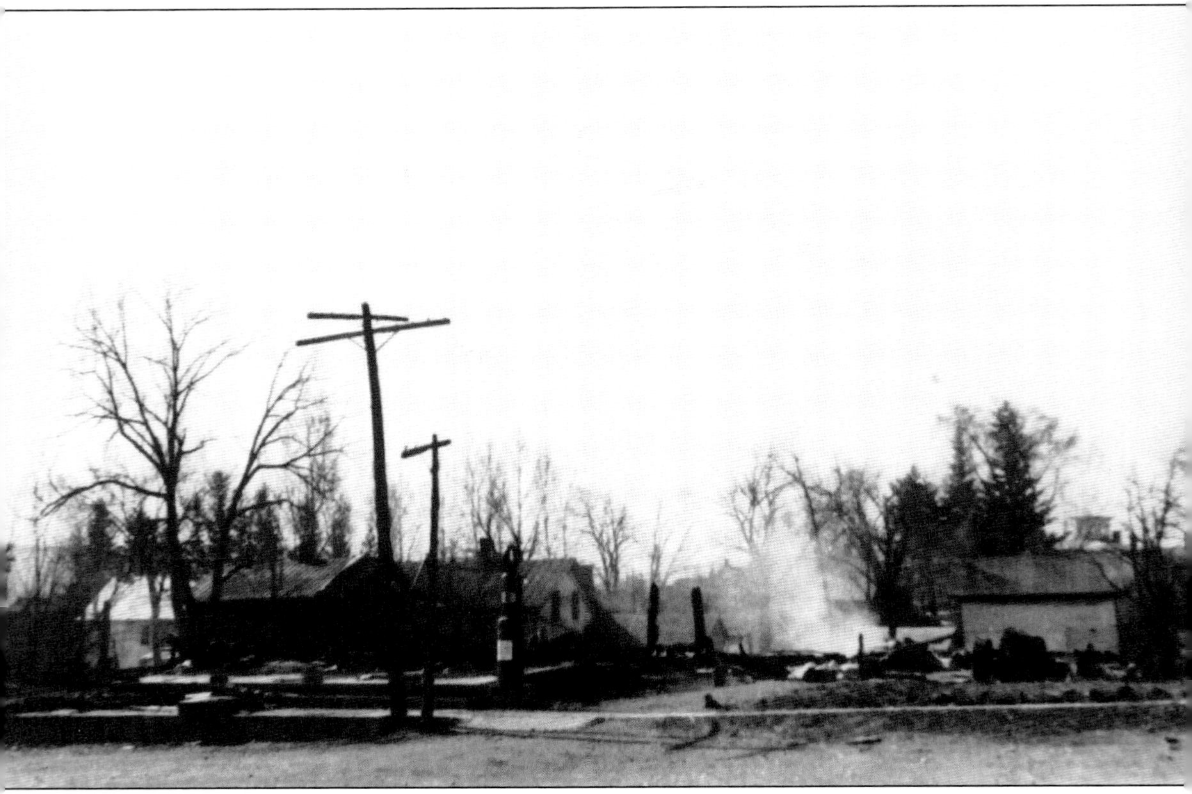

The Gilbert Store fire destroyed several businesses—the lack of a local fire department was a major detriment. Fires were also occurring on the east side of the lake from carelessly tossed cigarettes, as automobile traffic increased. In 1935, the Richmond Town Board was petitioned by local citizens to establish the Richmond Fire District. The idea did not get approved by New York state, which felt the community was not large enough to support its own fire department. It was necessary to get 51 percent of the residents to sign for establishing the district. The town board offered the leaders of the petition a bond of $7,000 to cover the cost of a firehouse and a truck.

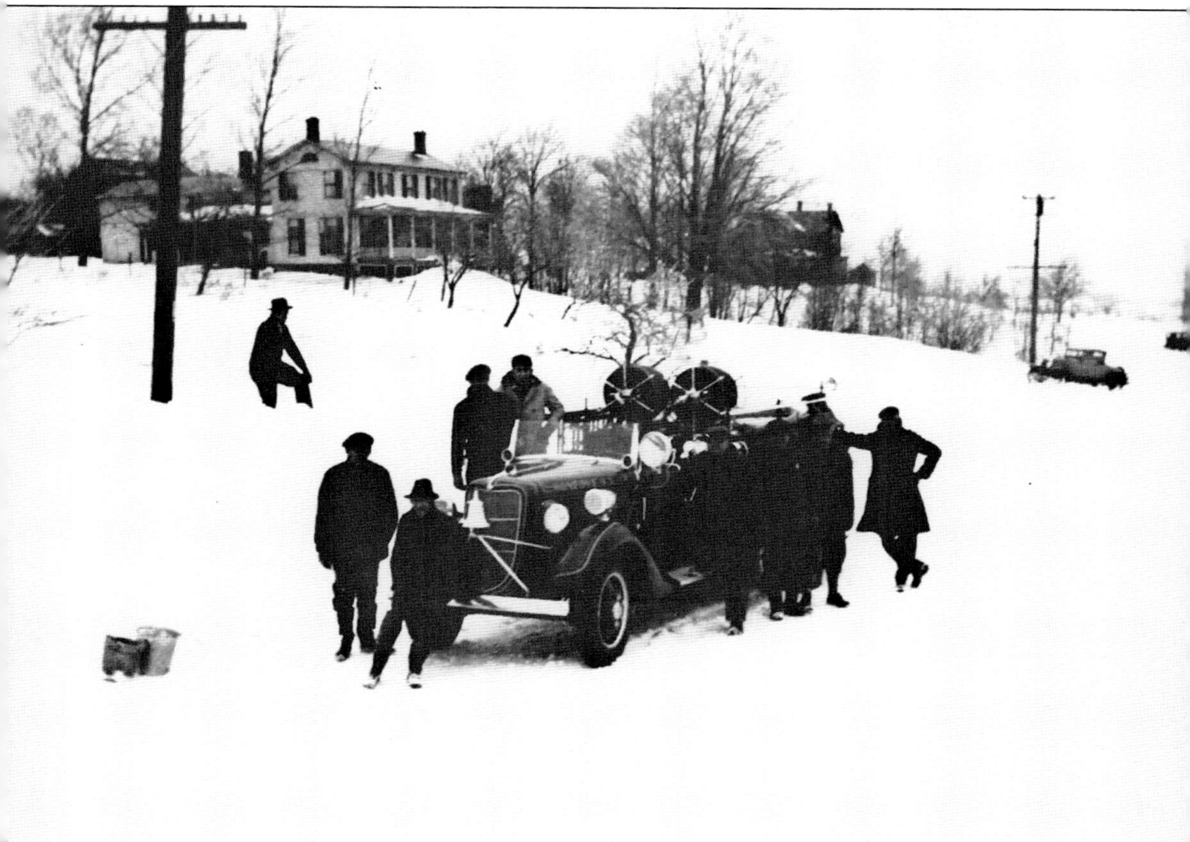

The first fire for the new fire department was at the Lawrence Grouse home on the Stevens farm. The new truck was outfitted with equipment from the Buffalo company of Ralph R. Young who was a cottager on the west side of Honeoye Lake in Canadice.

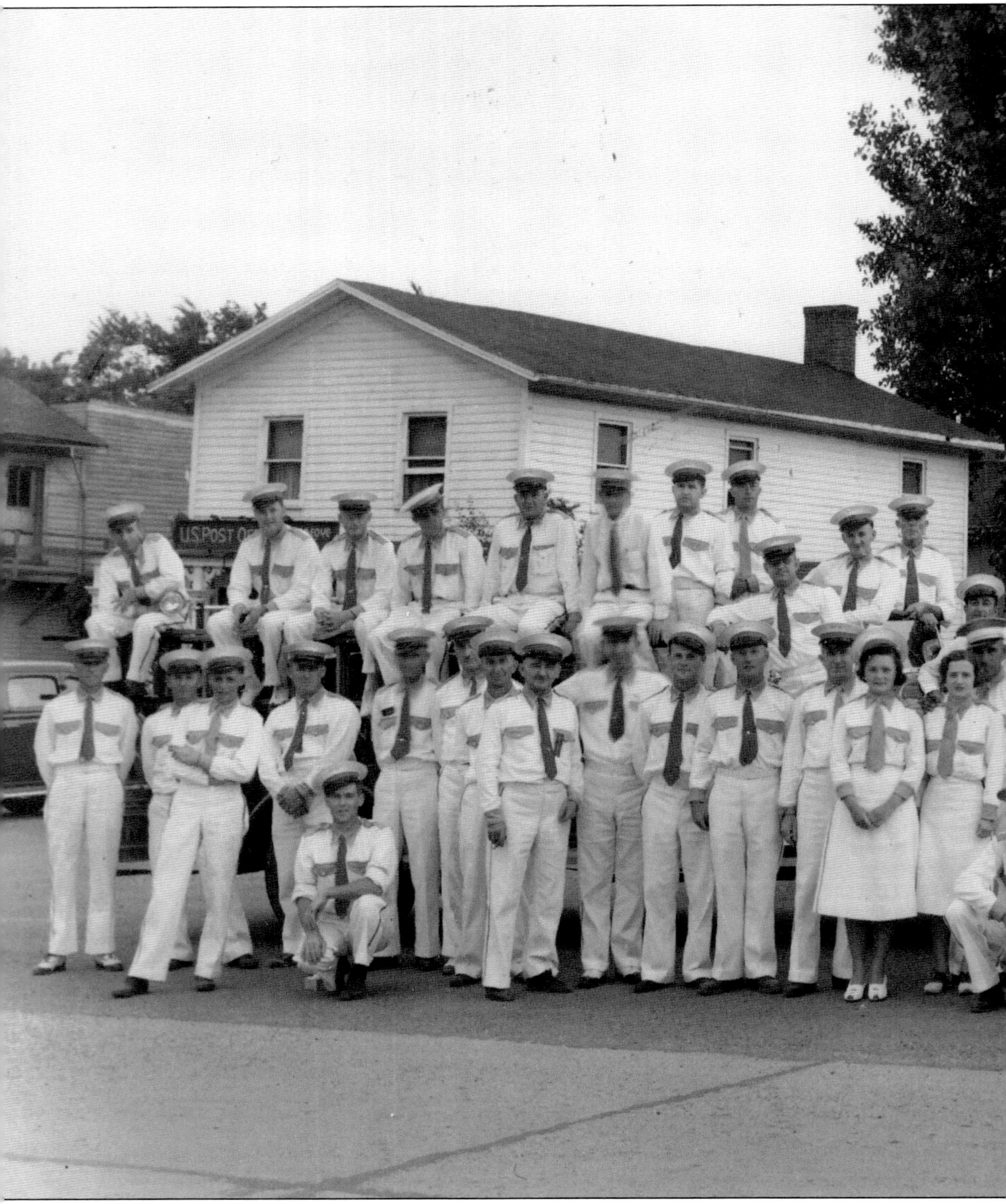

The members of the 1938–1939 Richmond Fire Department are, from left to right, (first row) Coral Wells, Emory Fox, Tom Keyes, Burton Deuel, Clarence Becker, Wells Blackmer, Charles Grouse, Norris Clement, Mike Coyne, William Boyd, James Ace, Clarence Hicks, Gertrude Potter, Virginia Hicks, Herman Wood, George Bartlett, Ralph Bacon, Lewis Ward, John Simpson, Clarence Ryan, Laurence Grouse, Harland Boardman, Andrew Hathorne, John Specksgoor, and

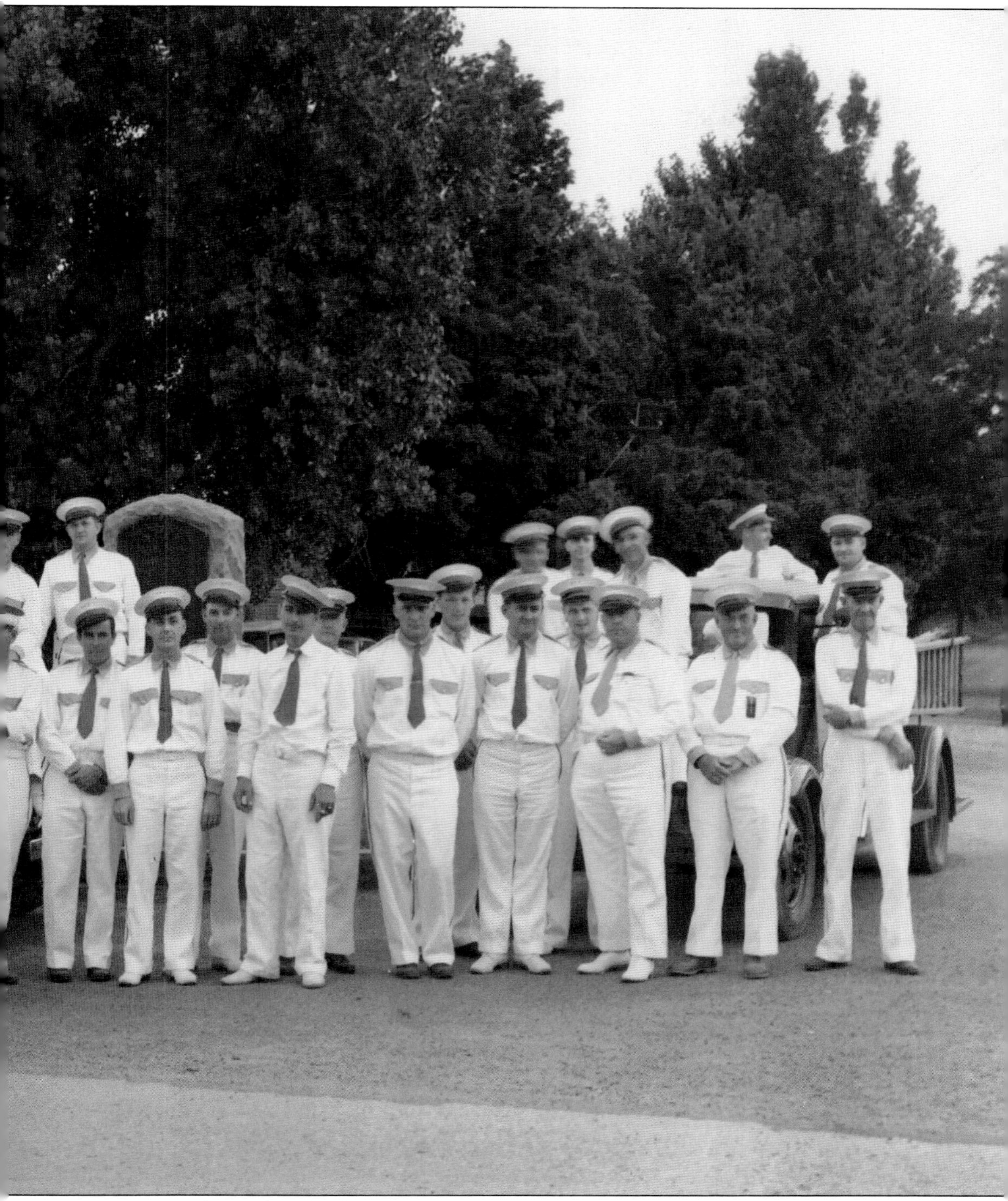

James Morrow; (second row) Clarence Bennett, Willliam Kirkbright, Clinton Sears, Charles Blackmer, Olin Brown, Sam Boyd, Elmer Ace, John Reed, Peter Baart, Rex Drain, John Boyd, Donald Hamilton, Levan Ashley, Furman Huff, Wheeler Reed, Ray Frances, Harold Ace, Sam Potter, Arthur Tremble, Arthur Bentley, and Jesse Plain.

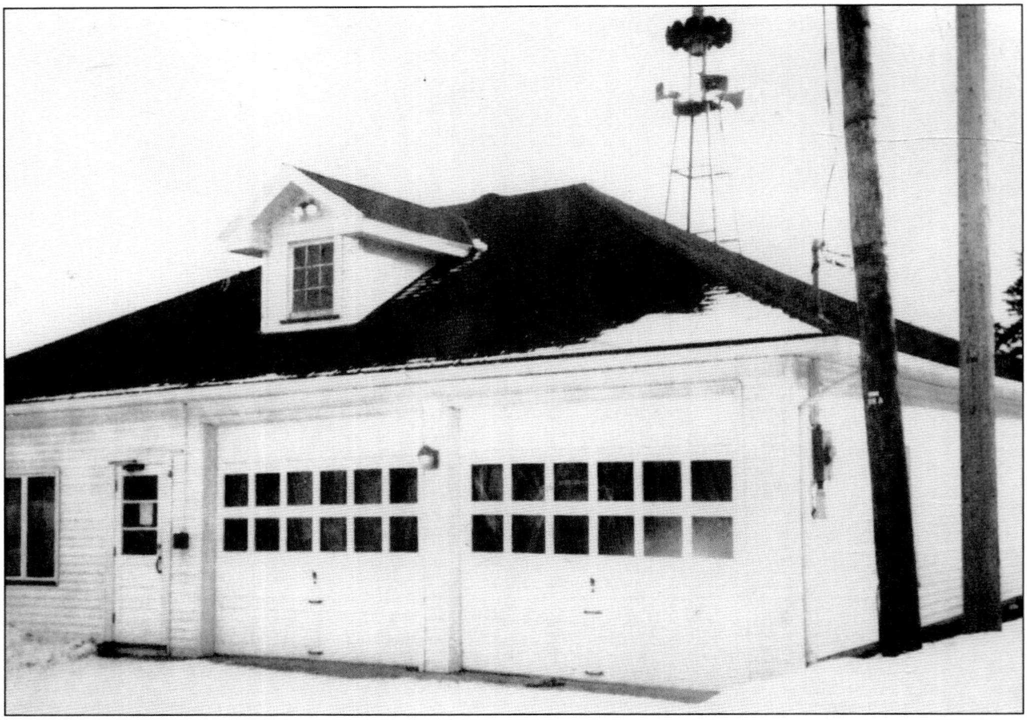

This is the old firehouse, located on Main Street in Honeoye. It has now been converted to a meeting and community activity building.

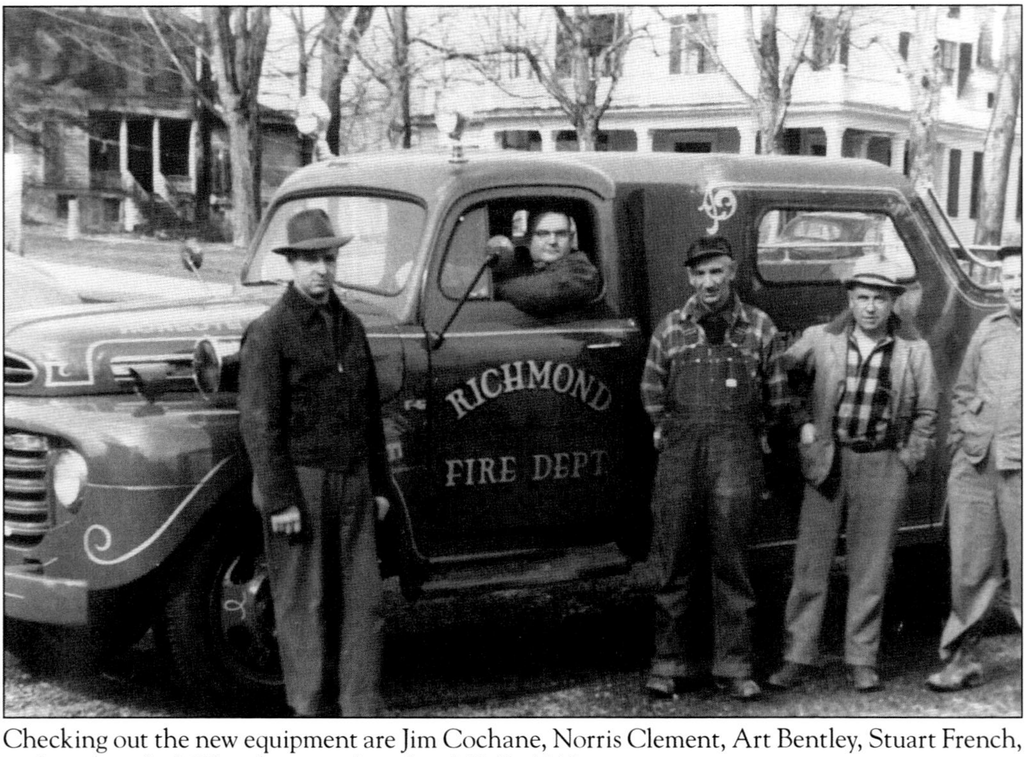

Checking out the new equipment are Jim Cochane, Norris Clement, Art Bentley, Stuart French, and unidentified. The photograph is dated 1948–1949.

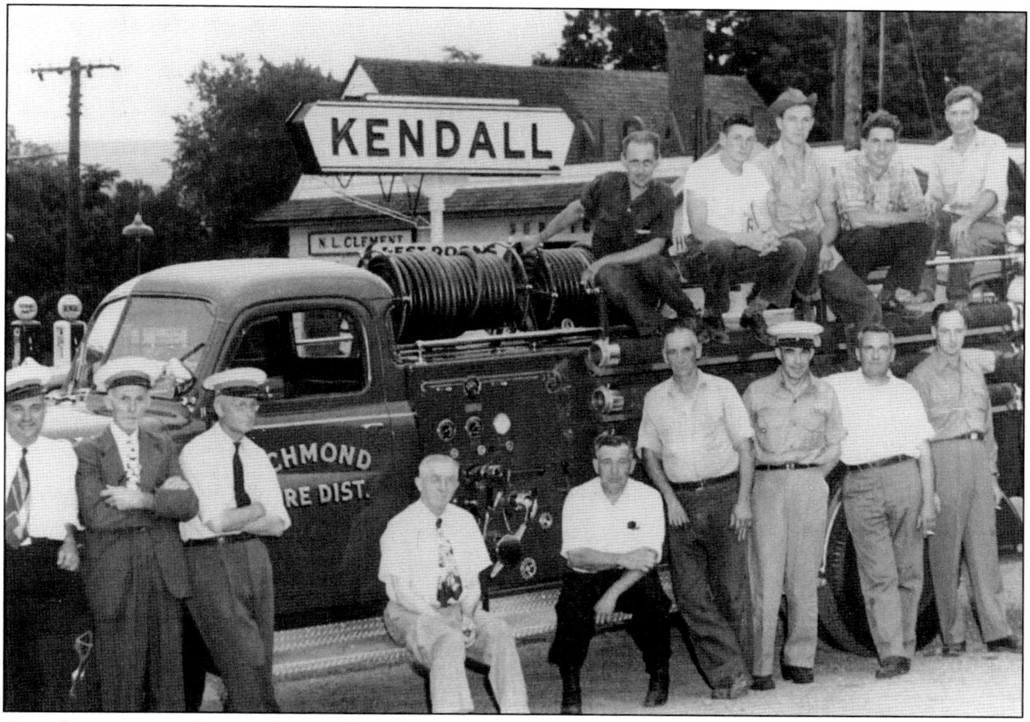

Another new truck was obtained, and several members of the fire department are posing by it.

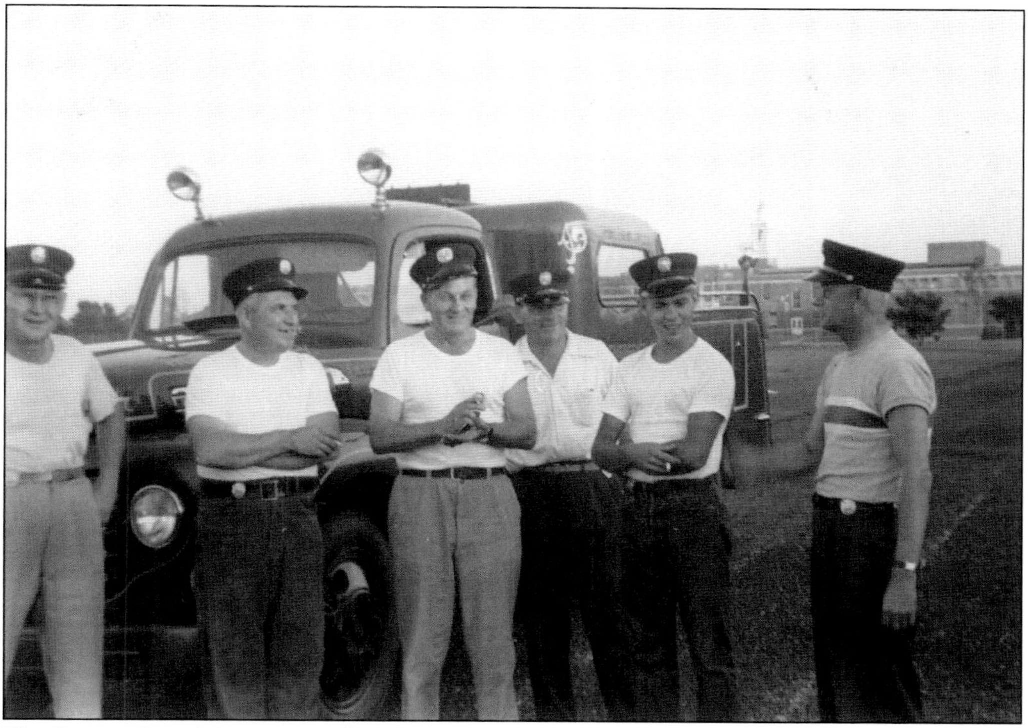
The Rescue Squad demonstrated at the State Fire School in Old Forge, New York, in 1954. The participants were Clint Sears, Carl May, George Schnurr, Sam Potter, Stu French, and Frank Rice.

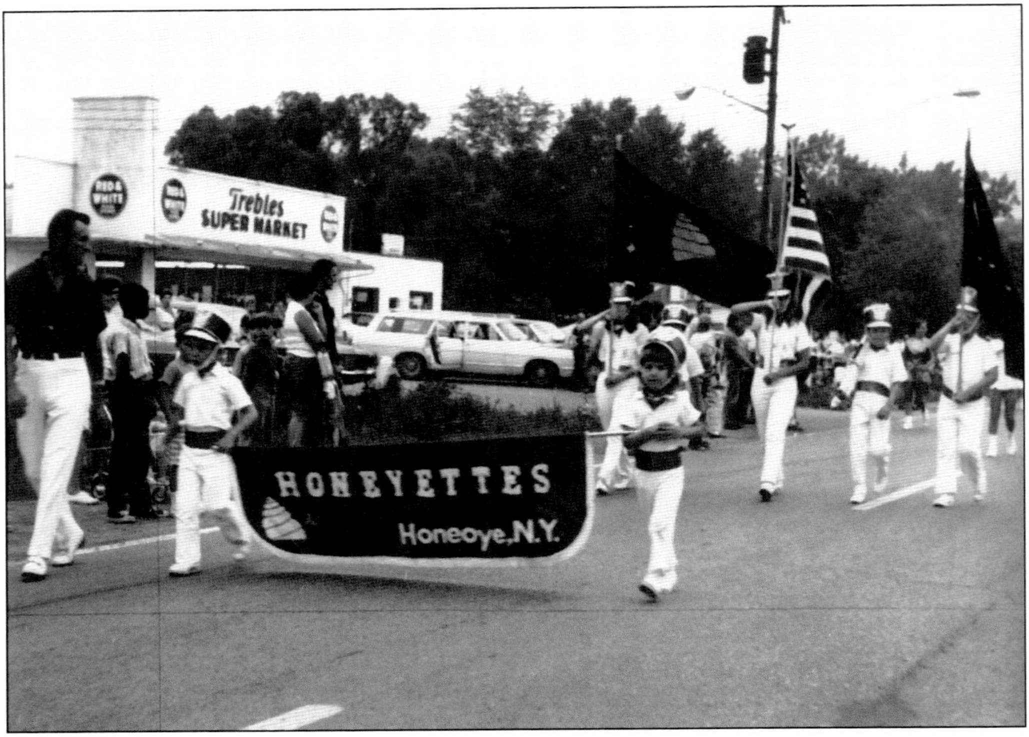

The Honeyettes marched in the fireman's parade down Main Street in Honeoye in 1971.

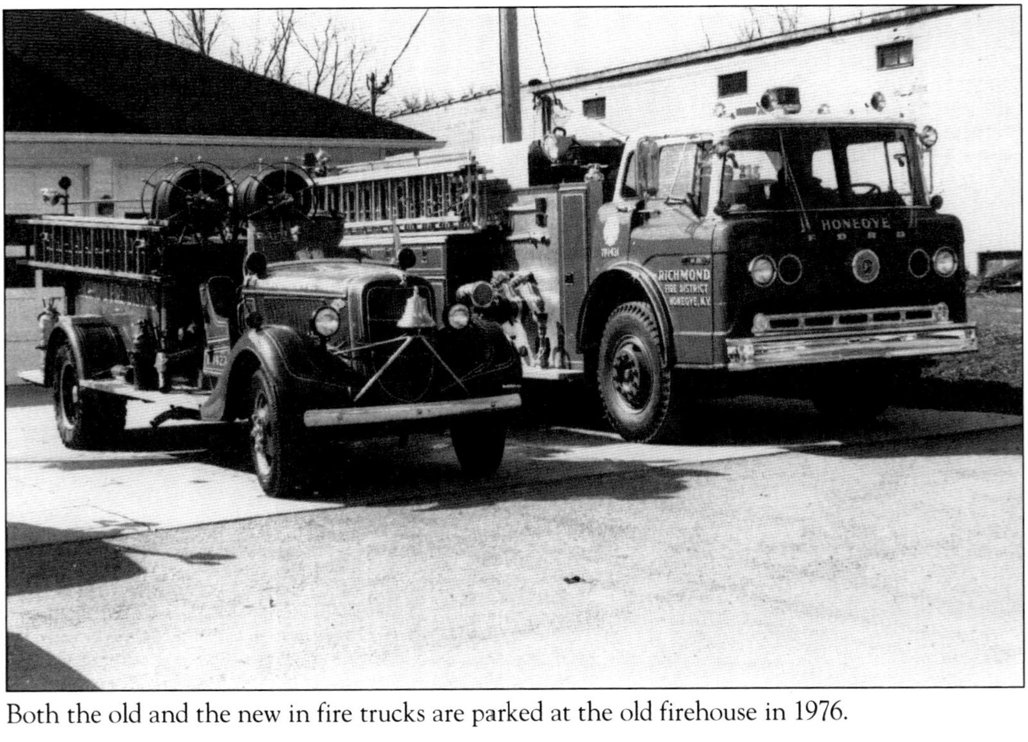

Both the old and the new in fire trucks are parked at the old firehouse in 1976.

Nine

SCHOOLS

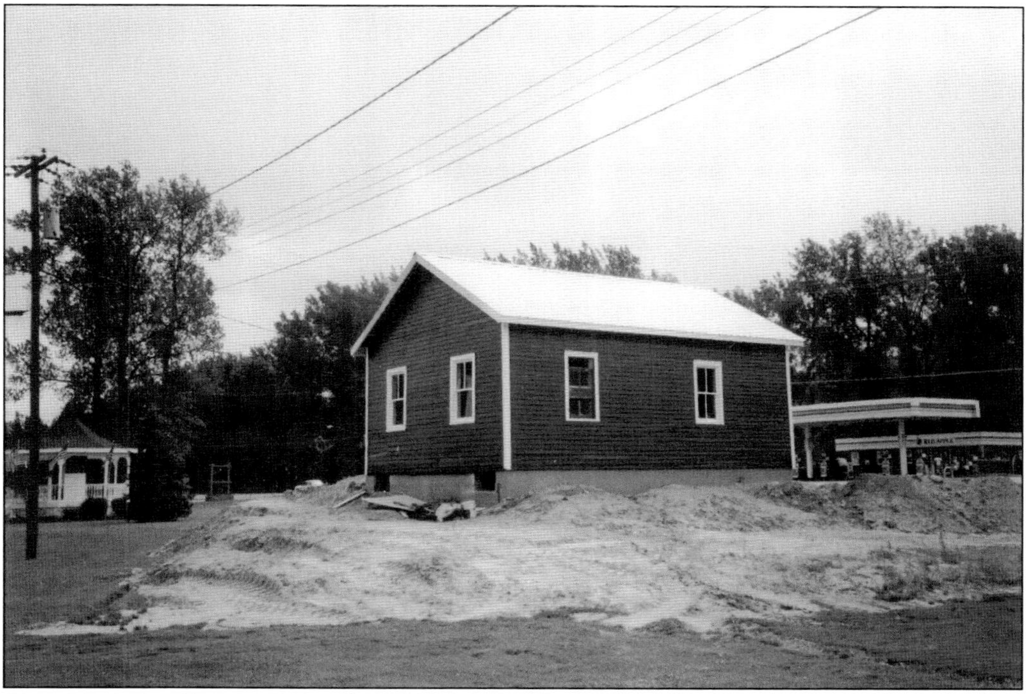

One-room schoolhouses sprouted up as hamlets formed in the towns of Richmond and Canadice. This photograph shows the District No. 1 school as it was being restored on Main Street in Honeoye. It was moved from its original location on East Lake Road and given to the Town of Richmond; the Honeoye Historical Society restored it so it could become an agricultural museum with donations from local residents.

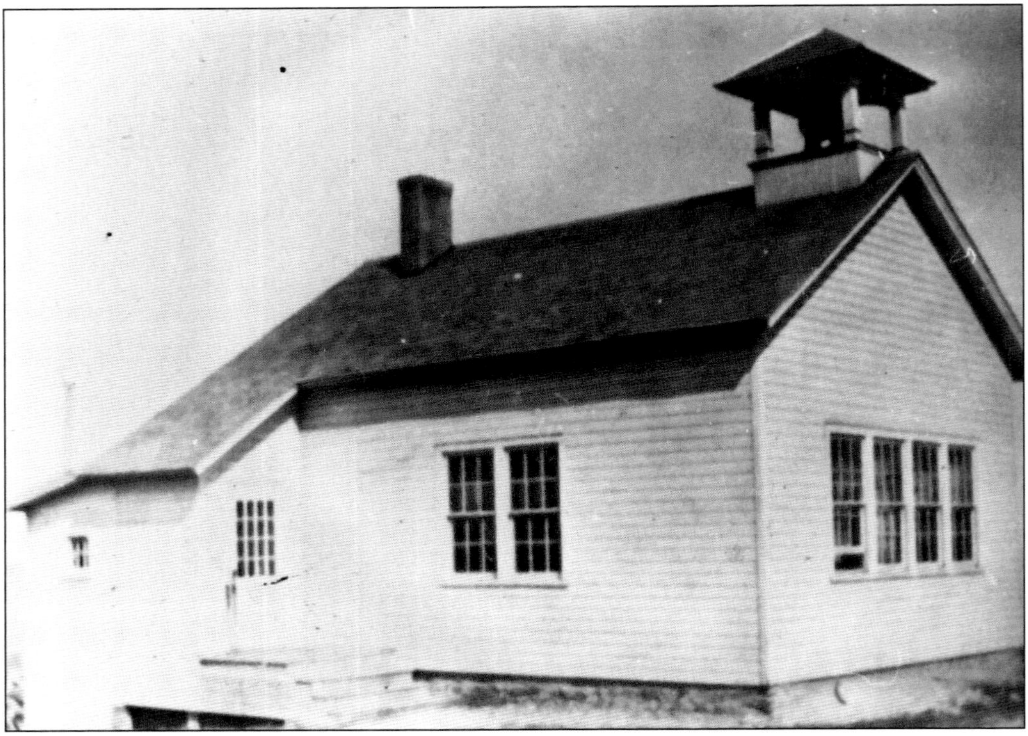

This photograph is of Canadice District No. 1, located on Bald Hill Road in 1933.

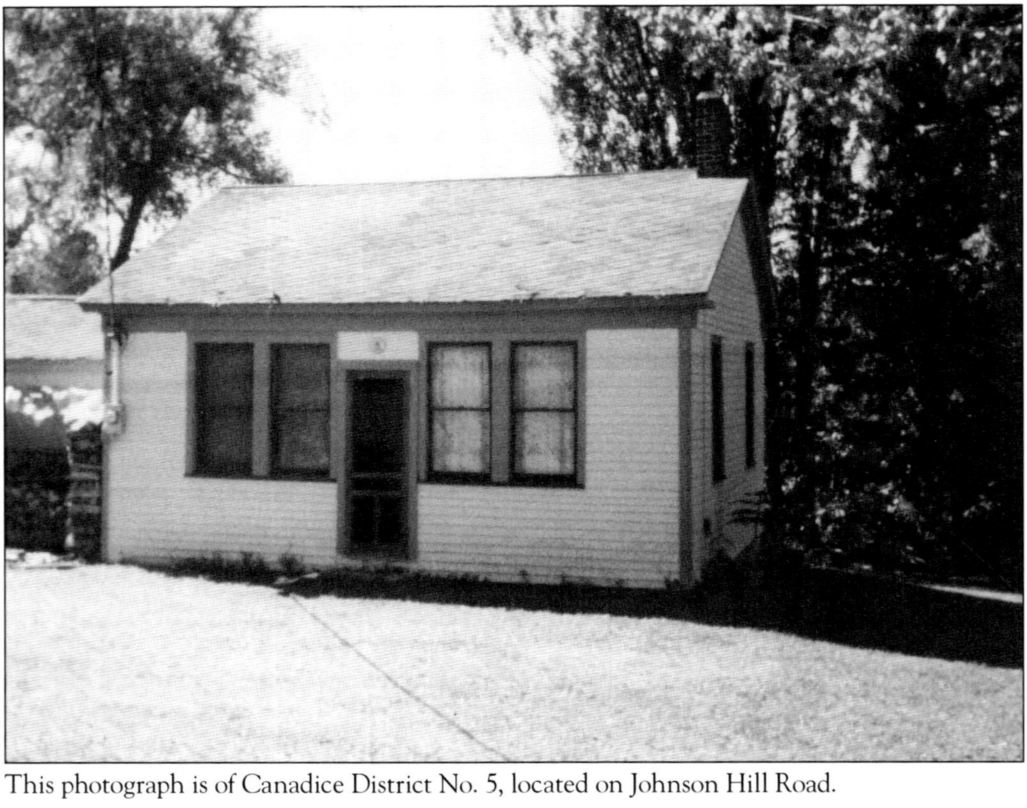

This photograph is of Canadice District No. 5, located on Johnson Hill Road.

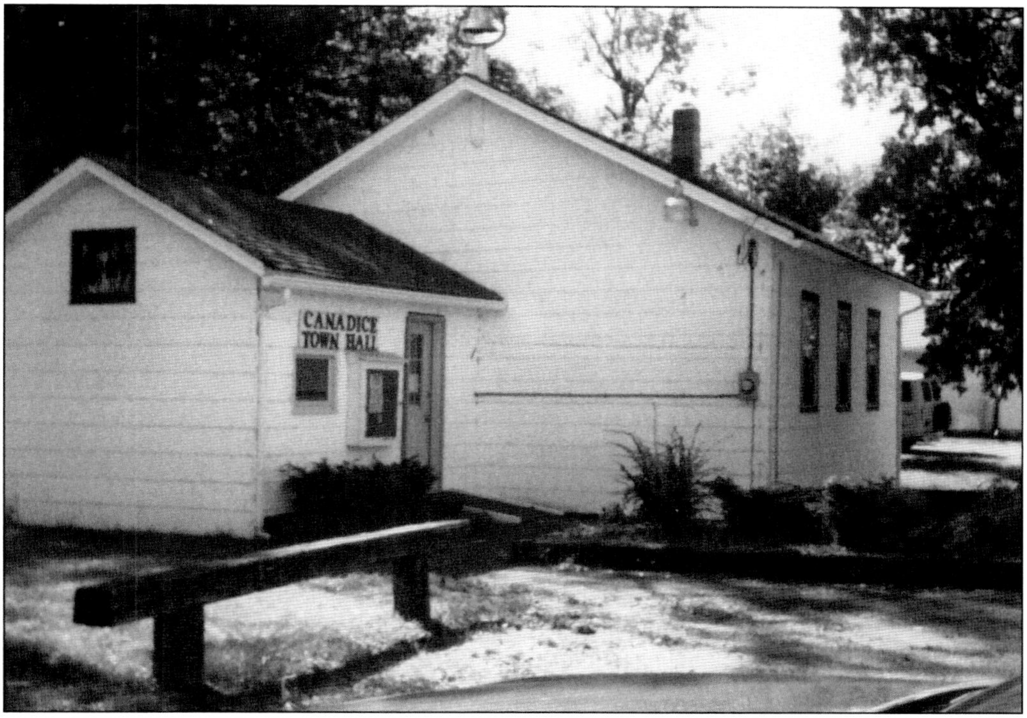

Canadice District No. 7 became the Canadice Town Hall when the school districts centralized in 1945. It was used for many years until a new town hall was built.

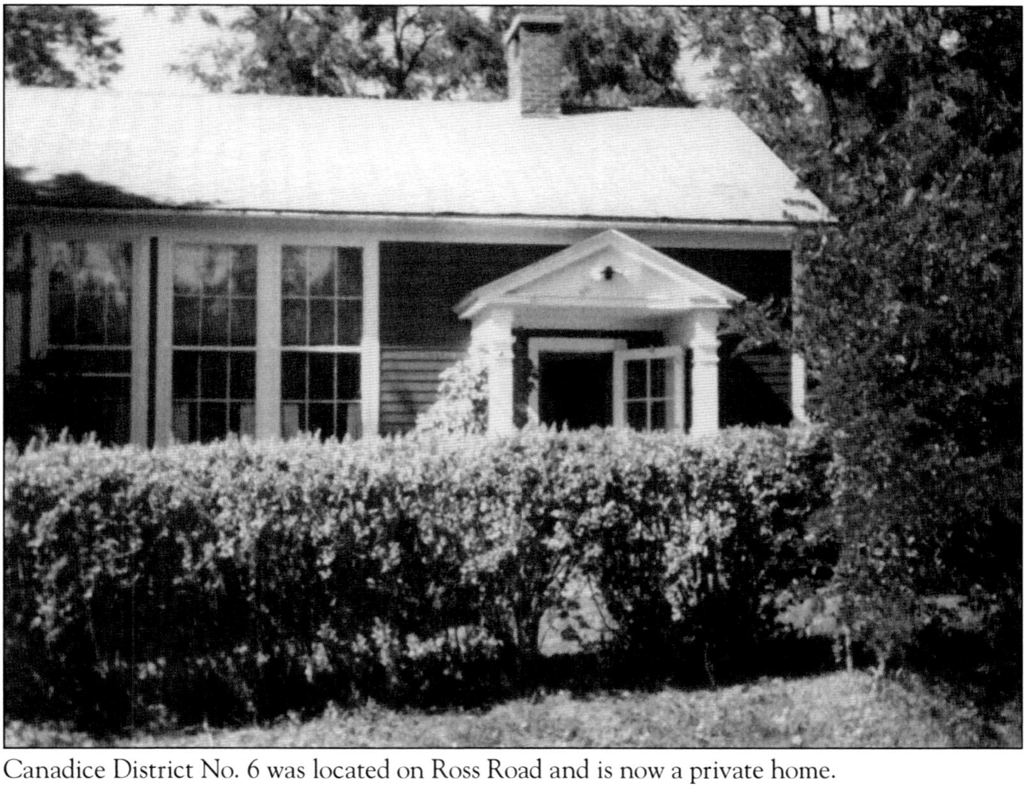

Canadice District No. 6 was located on Ross Road and is now a private home.

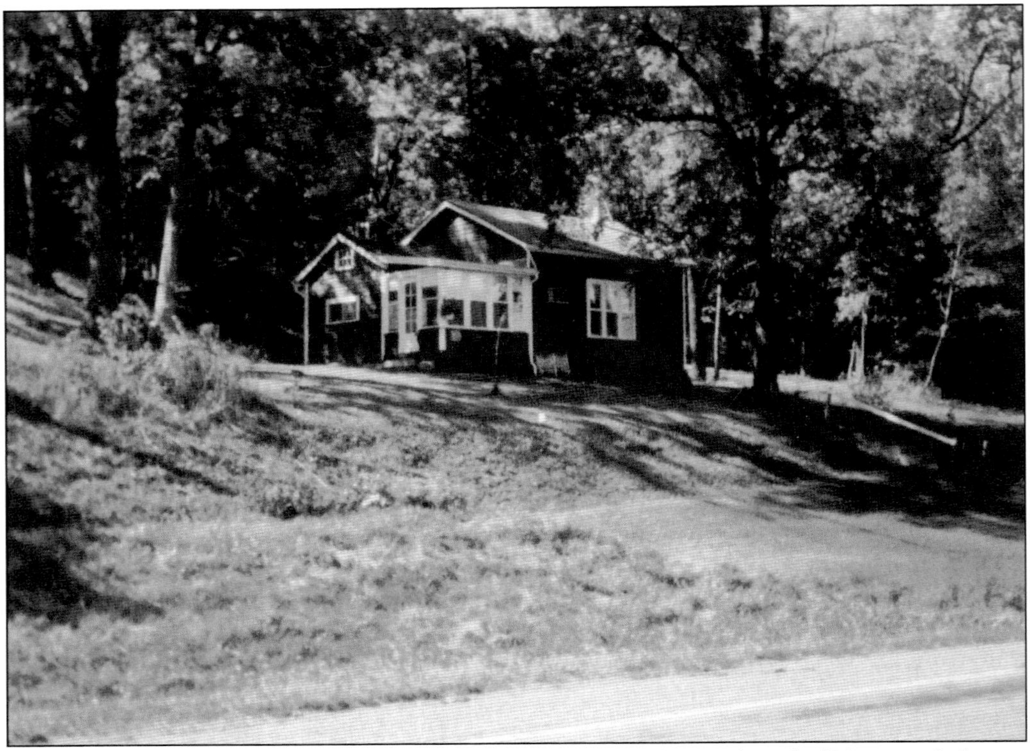

Canadice District No. 9 is now a private home located near the south end of Honeoye Lake.

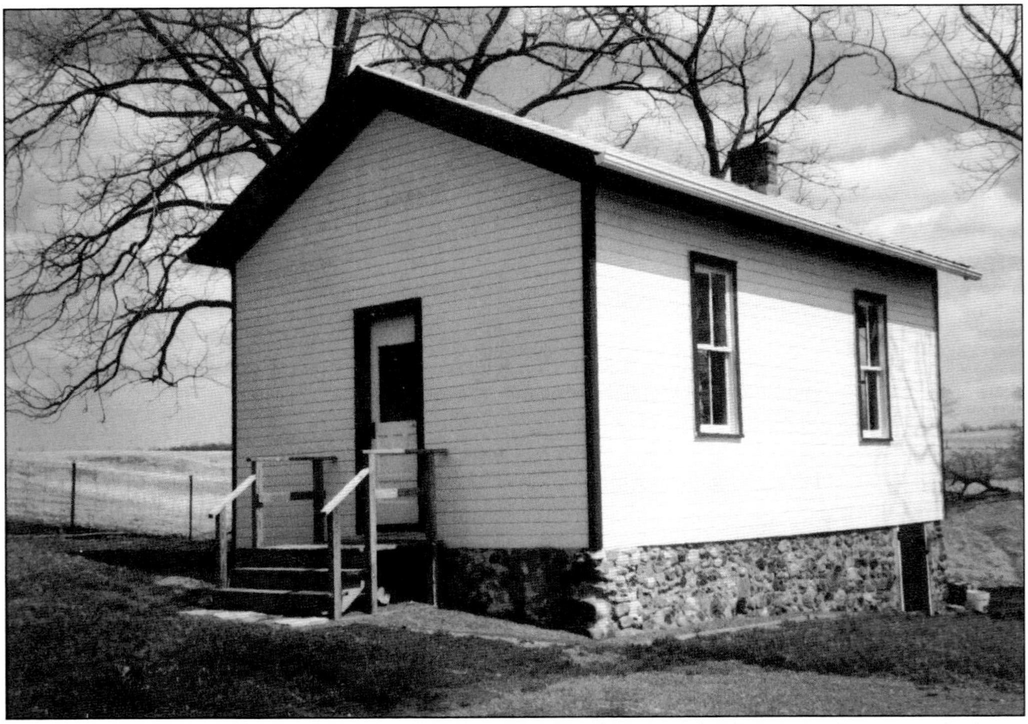

Richmond District No. 6 is located on Abbey Road and is completely restored as it might have been in the 1870s.

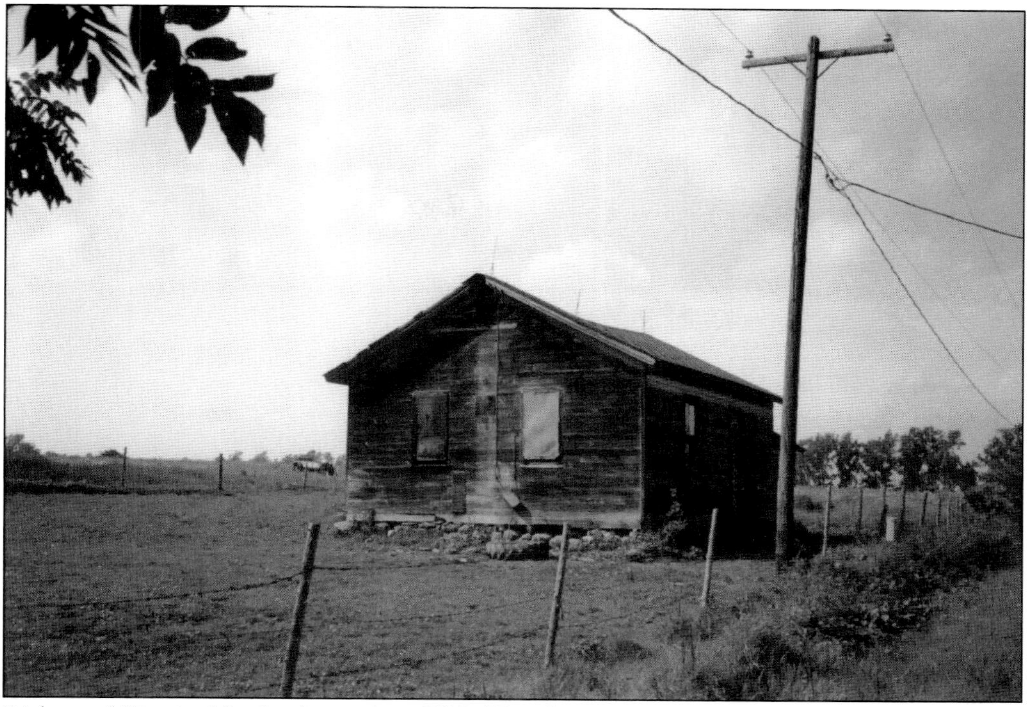
Richmond District No. 3 is located on O'Neil Road.

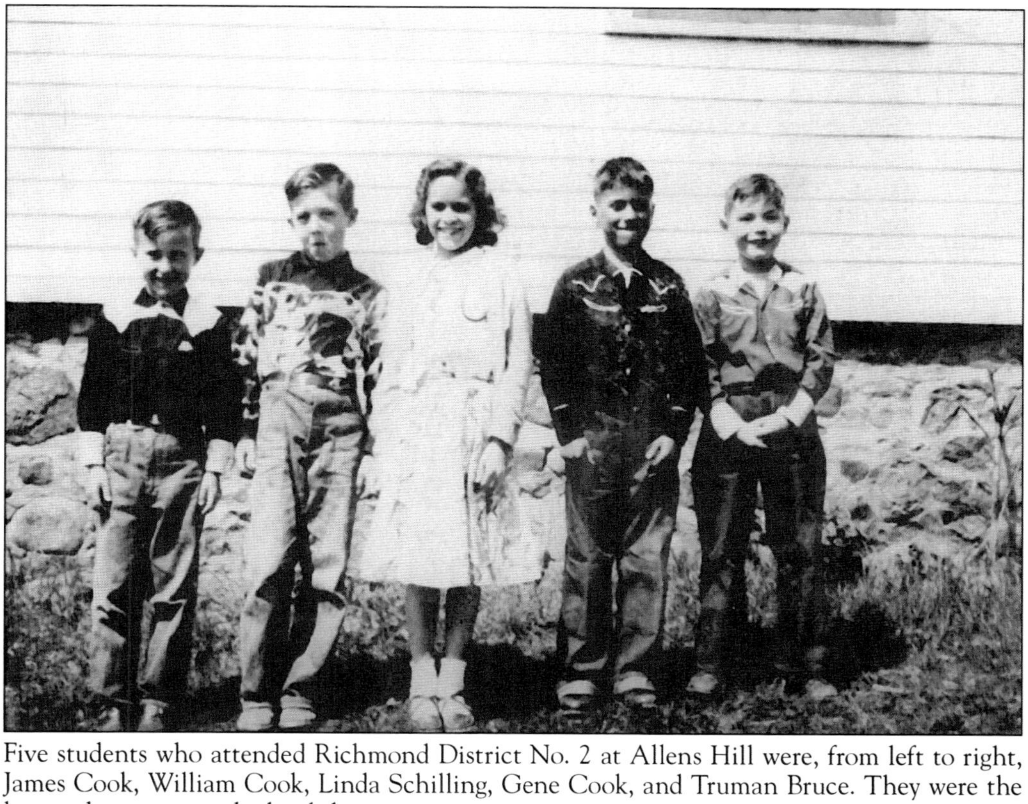
Five students who attended Richmond District No. 2 at Allens Hill were, from left to right, James Cook, William Cook, Linda Schilling, Gene Cook, and Truman Bruce. They were the last students to attend school there.

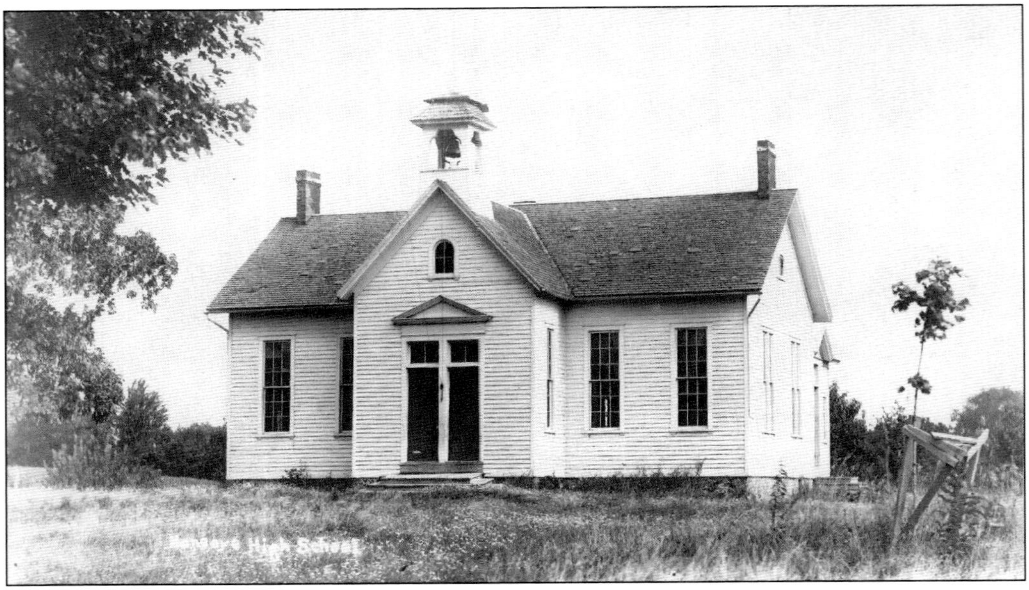

The Briggs Street School started with two classrooms. With an increase in attendance, more room was needed; an addition was put on the back, and later classrooms were built into the basement. When it was no longer used as a school, the Honeoye Amusement Co. turned it into a community center. When a dance was to be held in January 1940, the furnace was turned on to warm up the building and exploded, destroying the building.

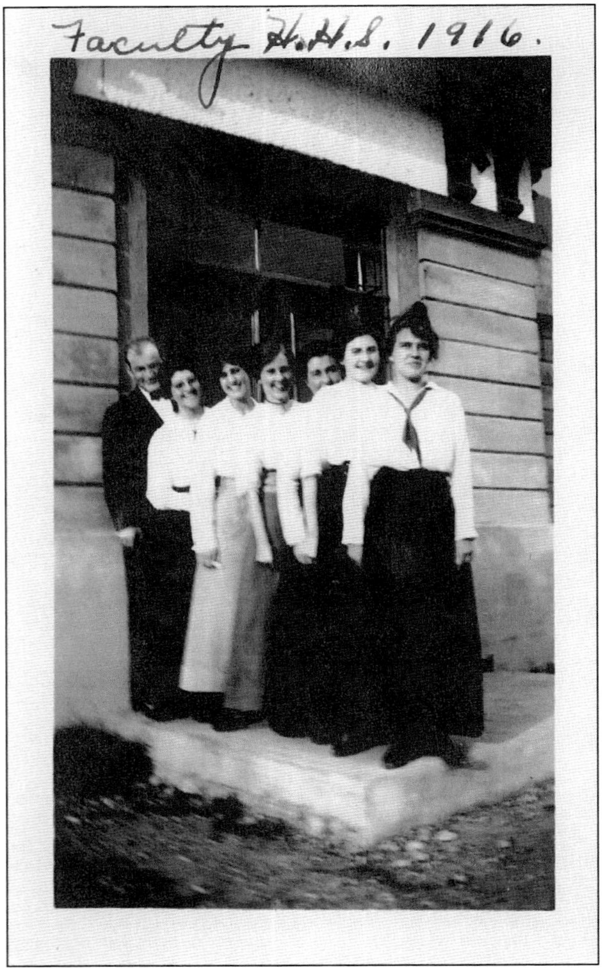

These teachers were on the faculty at the Honeoye High School in 1916. They are not identified.

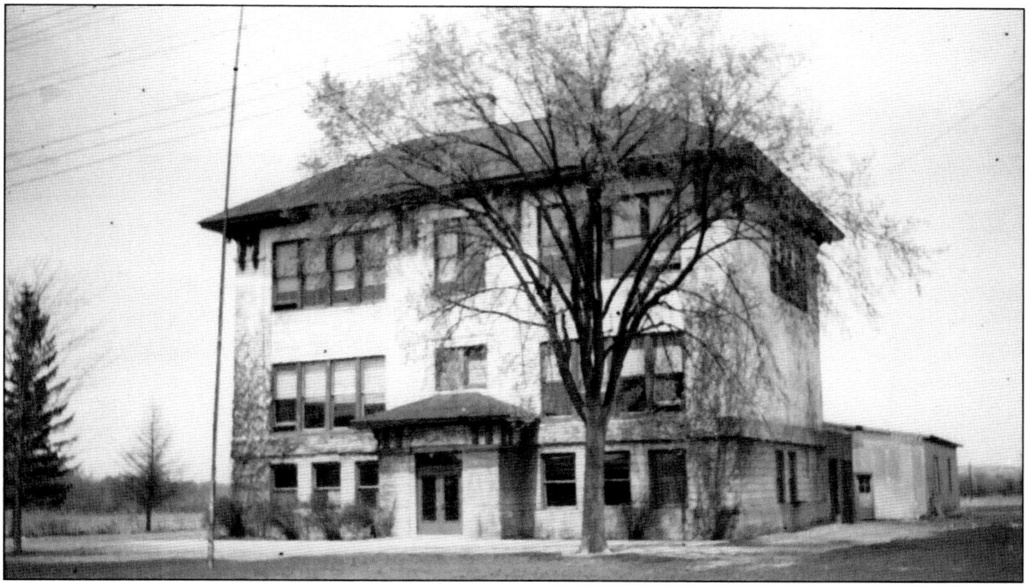

The Honeoye High School was often referred to as the "stucco building". It was used as the high school from 1913 to 1951. It is still standing on Main Street but is vacant. Eventually, it probably will be torn down to make way for a parking lot.

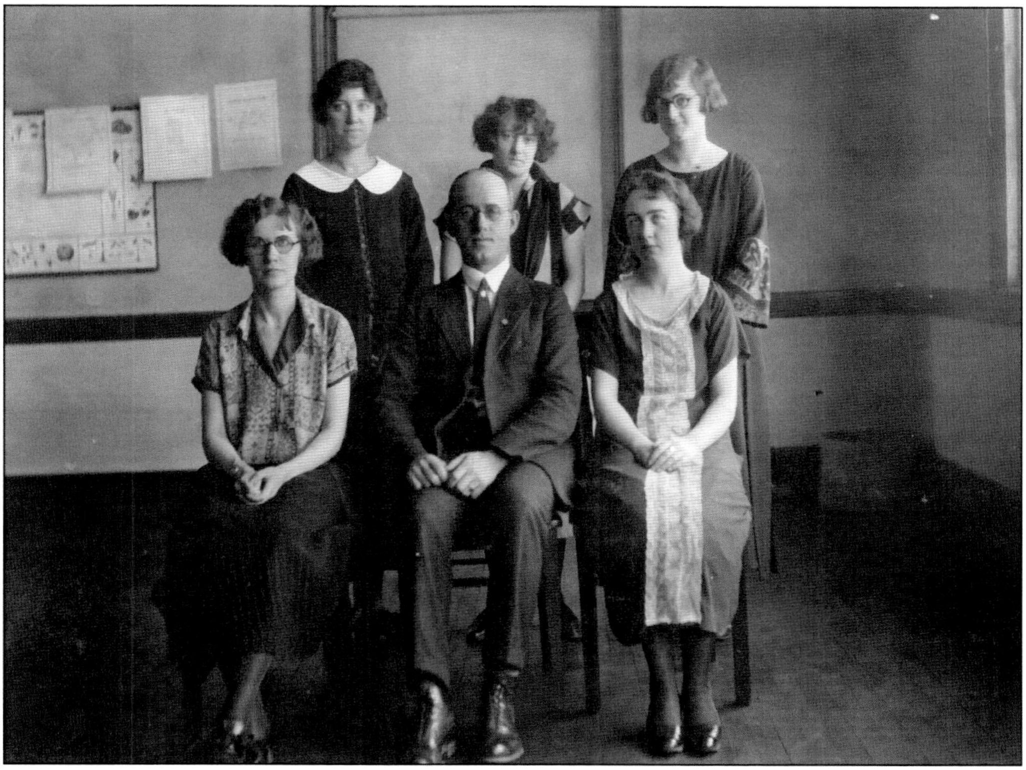

The 1914–1915 faculty at Honeoye High School was, from left to right, (first row) Miss Walter, Mr. Calkins, and Miss McCarthy; (second row) Miss Schmidt, Miss Perkins, and Miss Tague.

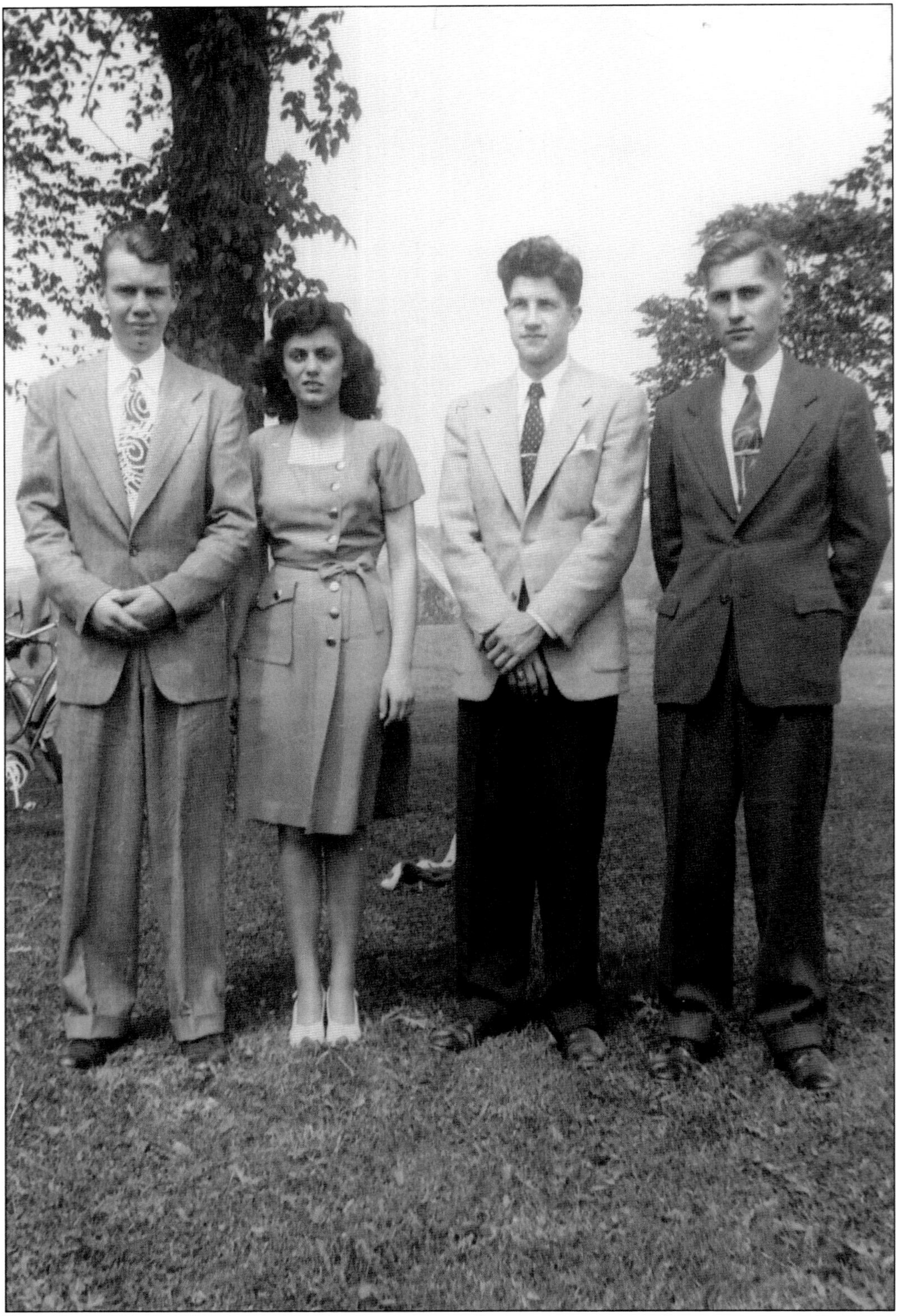

The class of 1947 from Honeoye High School was, from left to right, James Sullivan, Frances Angelo, David Green, and Arthur Treble.

Ten

Winter Carnival

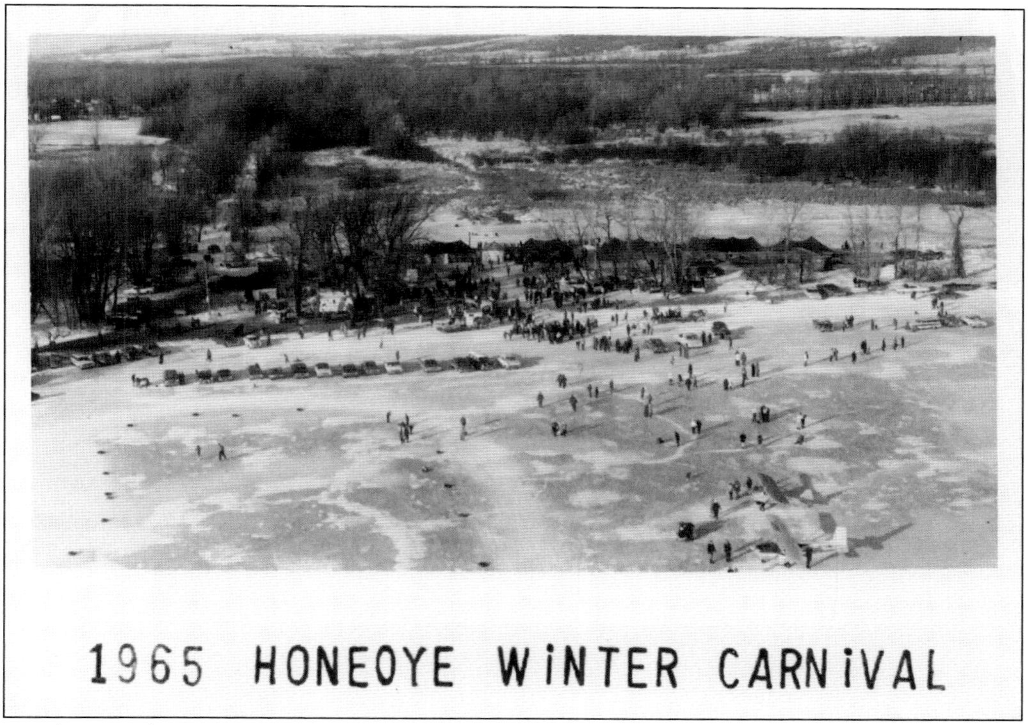

People came from near and far to attend the variety of events that were scheduled for two days every winter from 1962 to 1971. The idea for a carnival came from three local residents—George Baker, Henry Klemann, and Otto Uthe. They originally hoped for attendance of about 5,000 people. It was a big surprise over the years when the attendance hit estimates of 10,000 to 25,000 for the two-day affair.

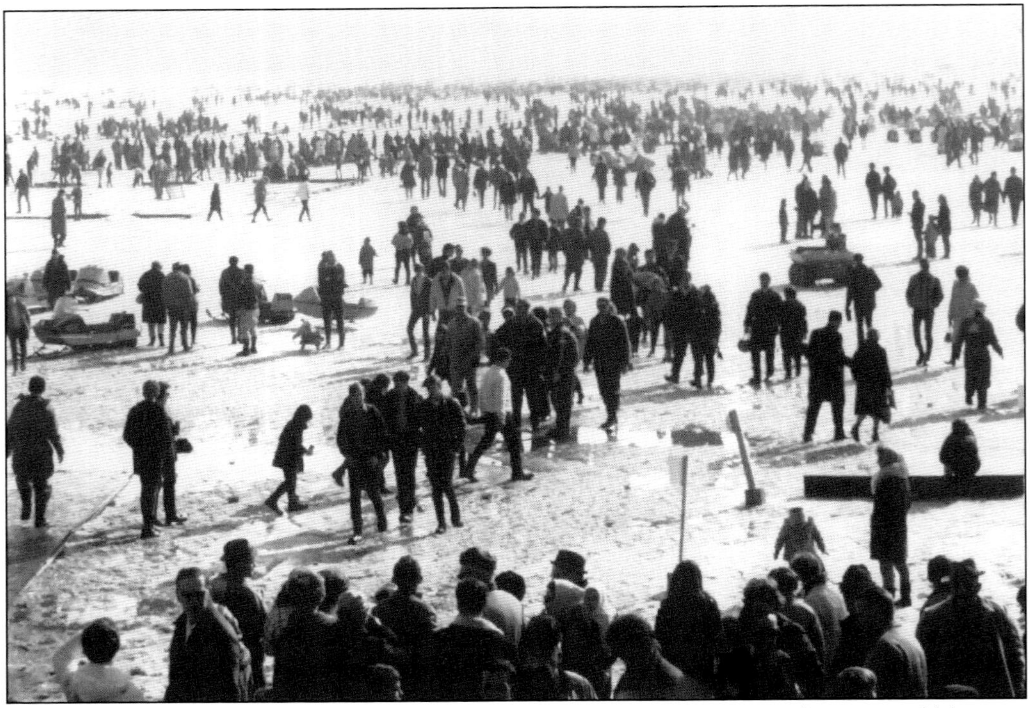

Huge crowds would gather on the frozen lake. The bus company in Rochester would bring a busload of spectators down from the city. The public address system was used to announce when the bus was ready to return to Rochester.

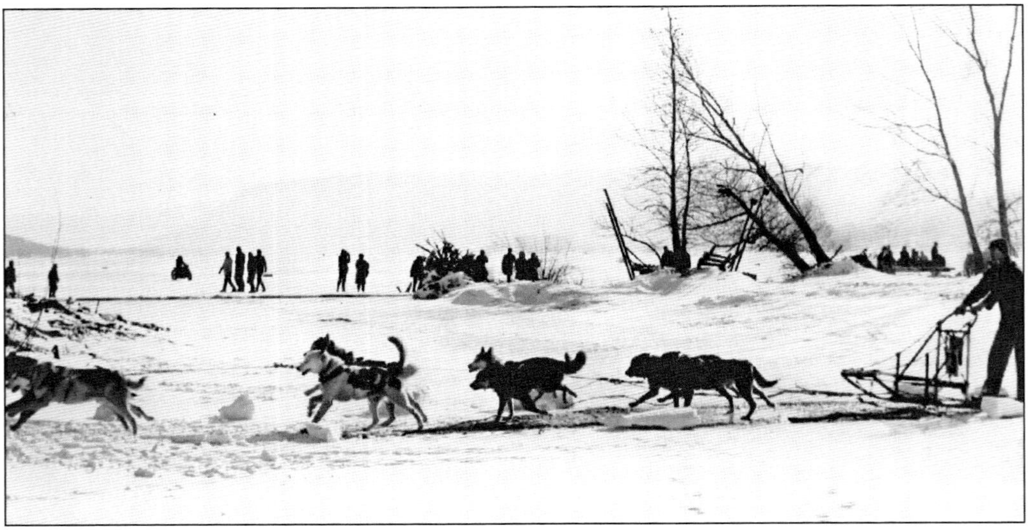

Dogsleds were a popular activity on the ice. Visitors were surprised that not all the dogs were huskies. Other breeds also were able to pull the sleds such as English Pointers, Siberian Malamutes, and Samoyeds. The Northern Sled Dog Club would attend the carnival and organized the races. Teams ranged from five to nine dogs, plus the driver. They would reach a speed of 30 miles per hour over the frozen lake surface. It was emphasized to visitors that they needed to leave their own dogs at home, as the racing dogs did not take kindly to interference by other dogs. With the dogs pulling at the sleds, their masters would shout, "mush," "gee," or "haw." Attendees said the carnival changed their opinion of winter and snow.

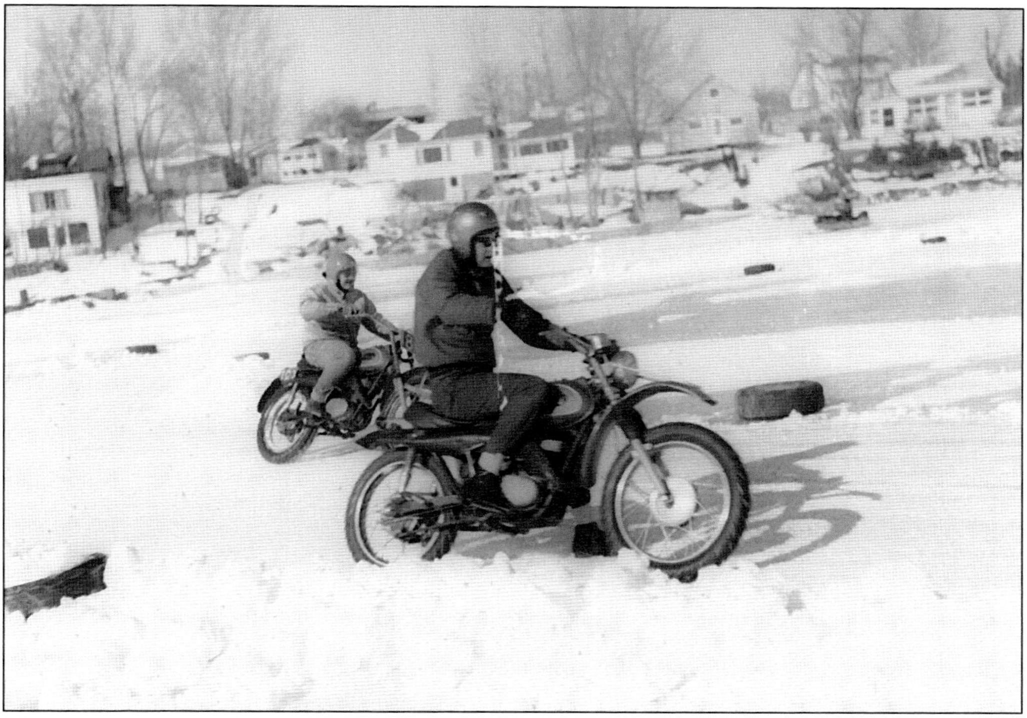

There were motorcycle races on the ice on laid-out courses. The tires had studs driven into the rubber to gain traction on the ice. The Wayne County Motorcycle Club attended for the first four years, and in the fifth year, the Goodyear Tire Company gave them national coverage. Male and female drivers raced on a half-mile oval course with top speeds of 60 miles per hour.

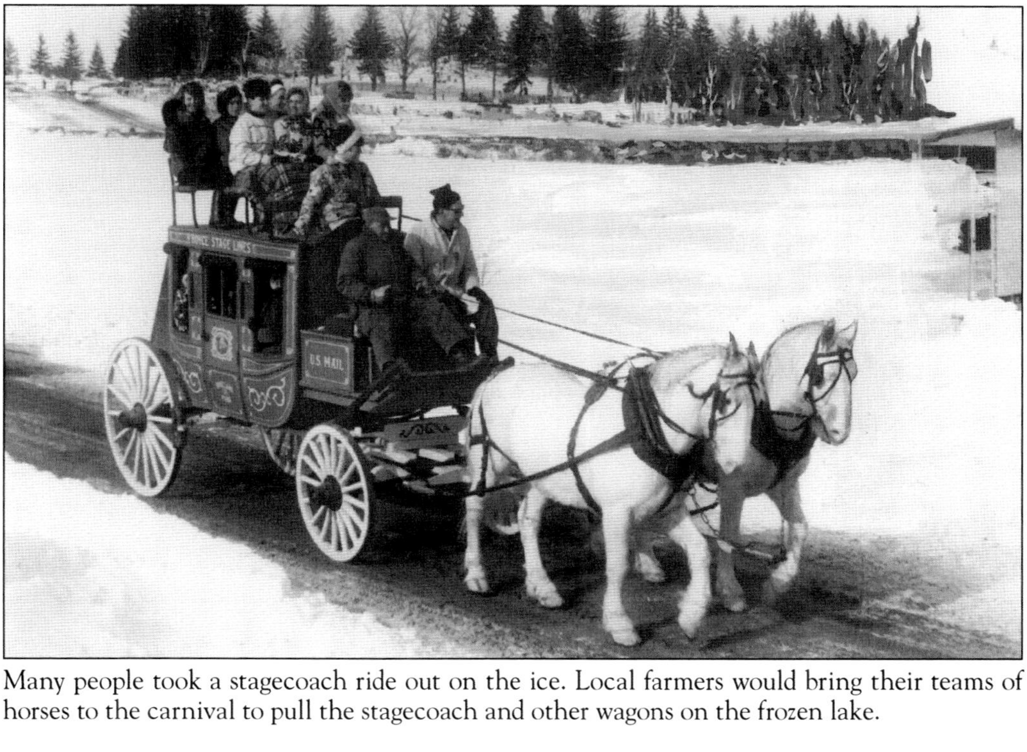

Many people took a stagecoach ride out on the ice. Local farmers would bring their teams of horses to the carnival to pull the stagecoach and other wagons on the frozen lake.

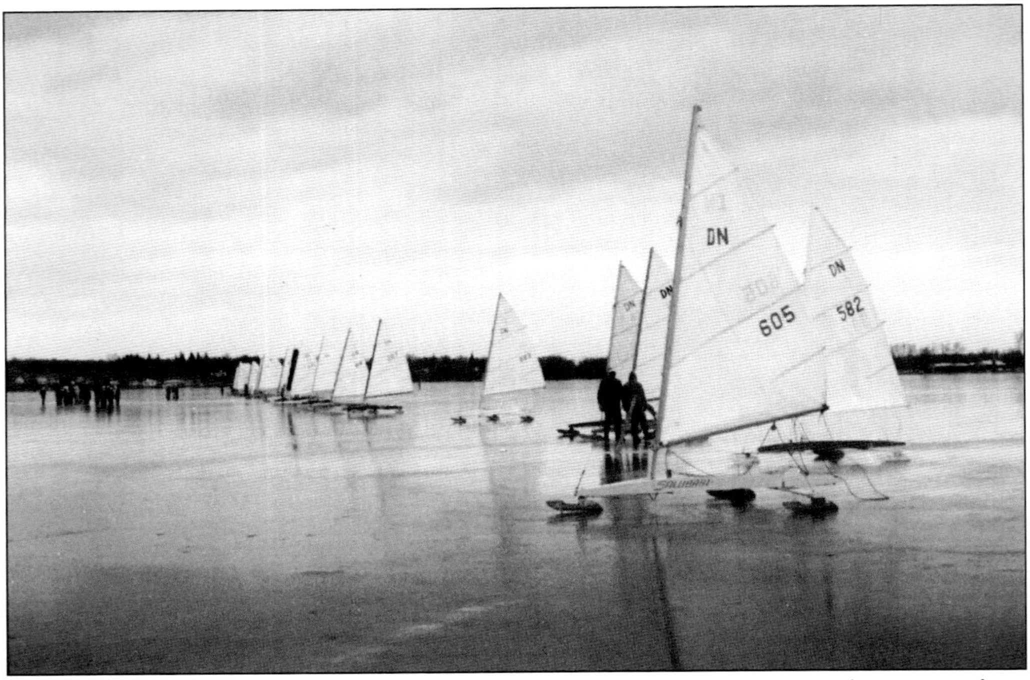

The frozen lake was a great place for an iceboat ride. The ice boat regatta drew racers from Canandaigua, Sodus, Irondequoit, and Bath Ice Yacht Clubs. This was one of the fastest and most inspiring winter sports on the lake. When asked how to stop an iceboat, one of the racers was said to have stated that he would just have to crash into the shoreline or hit another boat, as they don't have brakes.

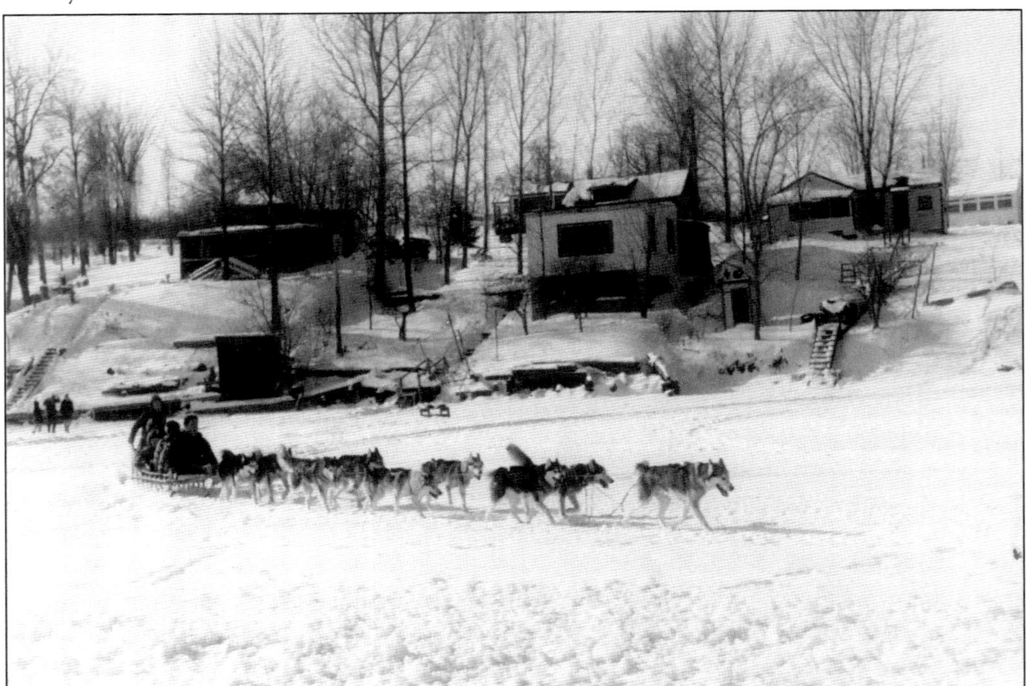

This dog team pulled a sled that held several visitors around the ice-covered lake.

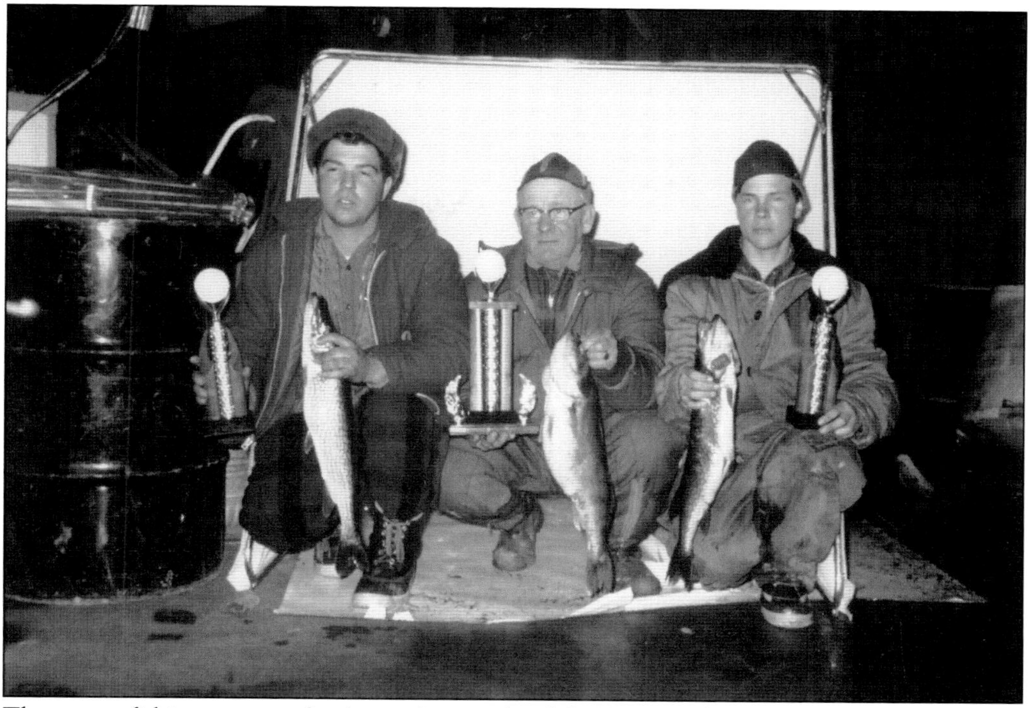

There were fishing contests for those who cared to fish. Here are three winners. Walt Cratsley, a veteran fisherman on the lake, stated that there were lots of walleyes and pickerels under the ice and bait was available at the Cratsley Bait Shop on West Lake Road in Canadice.

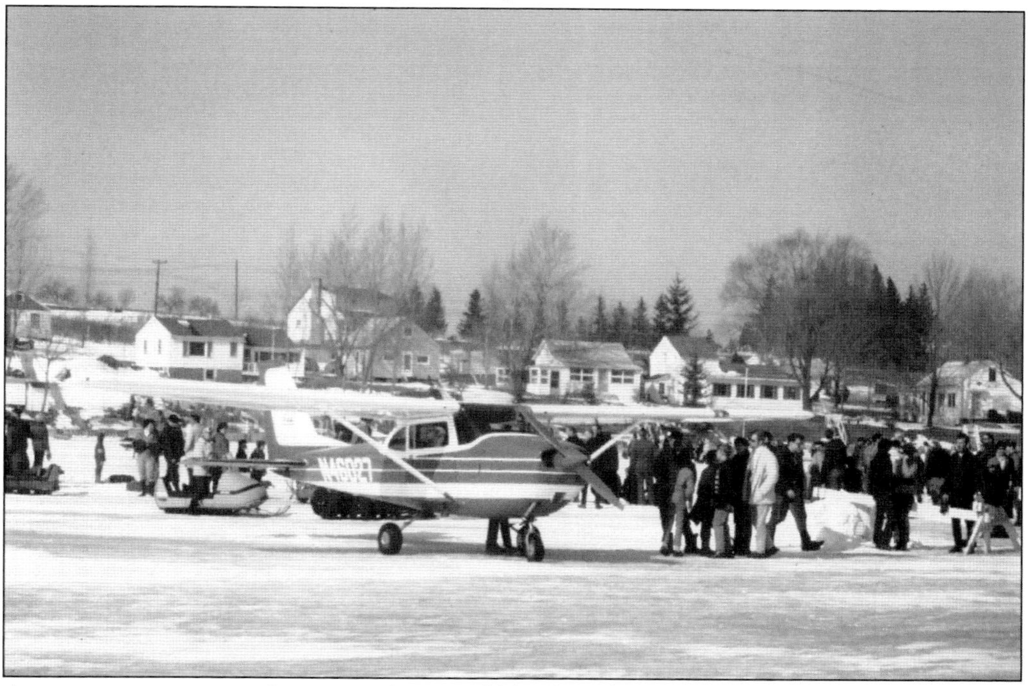

A major attraction was when an airplane would land on the ice. However, one year, a plane went through the ice and the pilot had to be rescued. The Flying Farmers were local small plane enthusiasts. Visitors could take plane rides to get an aerial view of the lake and surrounding area.

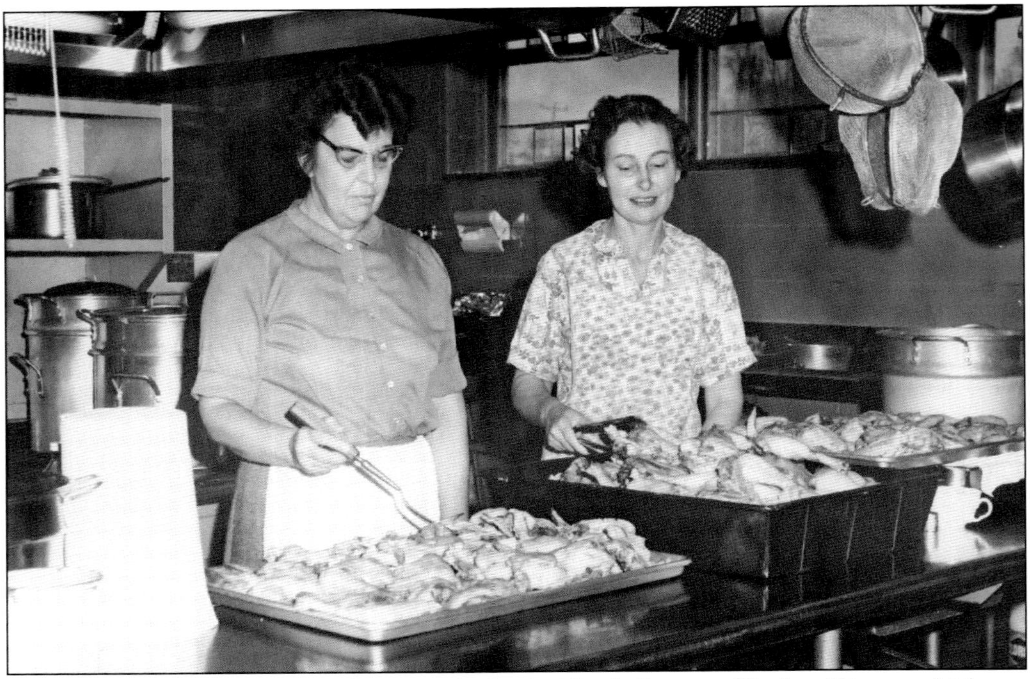

Elsie Van Fleet and Jane Barnard were cooks for the North Country Chicken Dinner, which was cooked at the Honeoye Central School cafeteria. Served along with the chicken were biscuits, squash, and pies. The profits were split between the Chamber of Commerce and the United Church of Christ. Local residents donated some of the food.

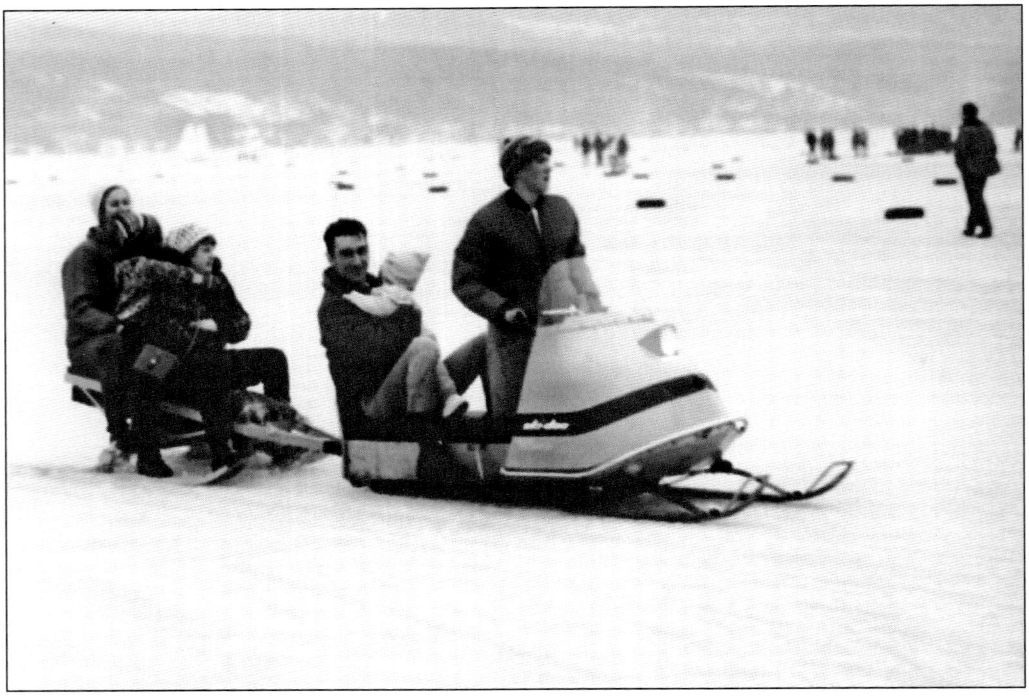

Snowmobiles were a big family attraction. Races were held on the ice in front of the California Ranch in Canadice. Plows would pile the snow up along the racecourse to protect the spectators.

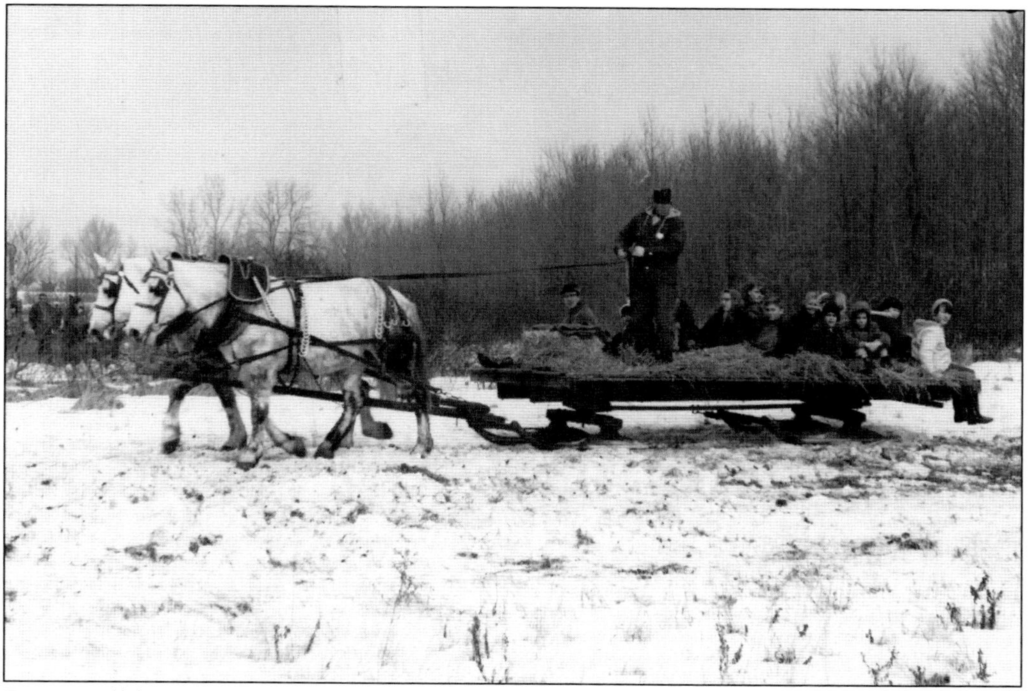

Everett Affolter's team of horses gave visitors a wintertime version of a hayride on a sleigh.

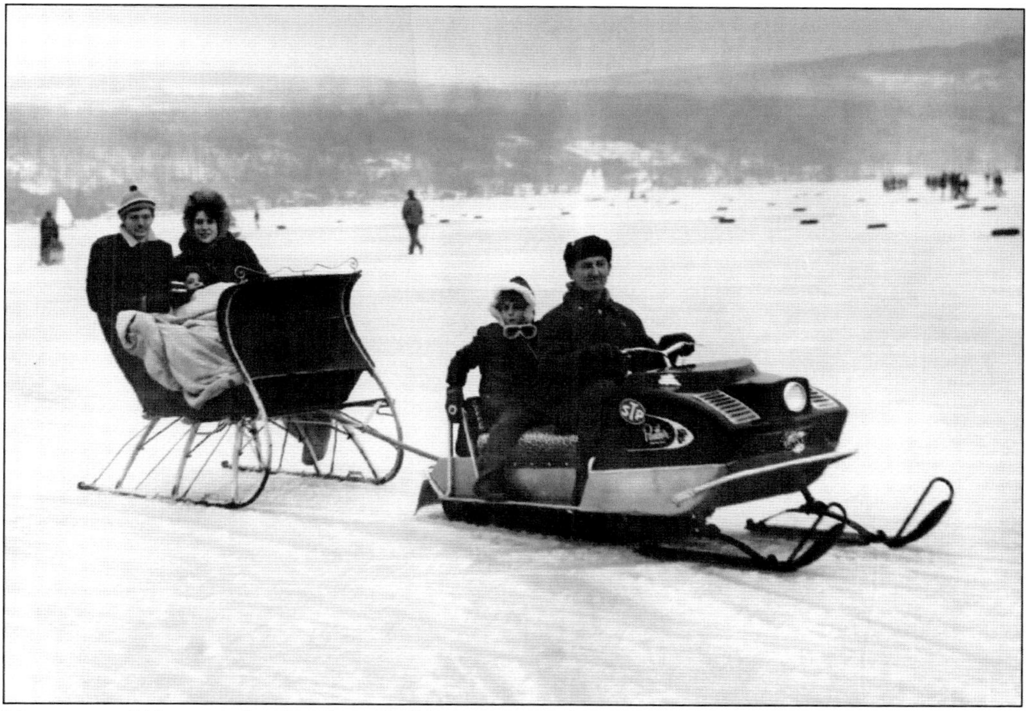

Visitors could have a sleigh ride pulled by a snowmobile. It was a good way to view the crowds and the lake while keeping as warm as possible.

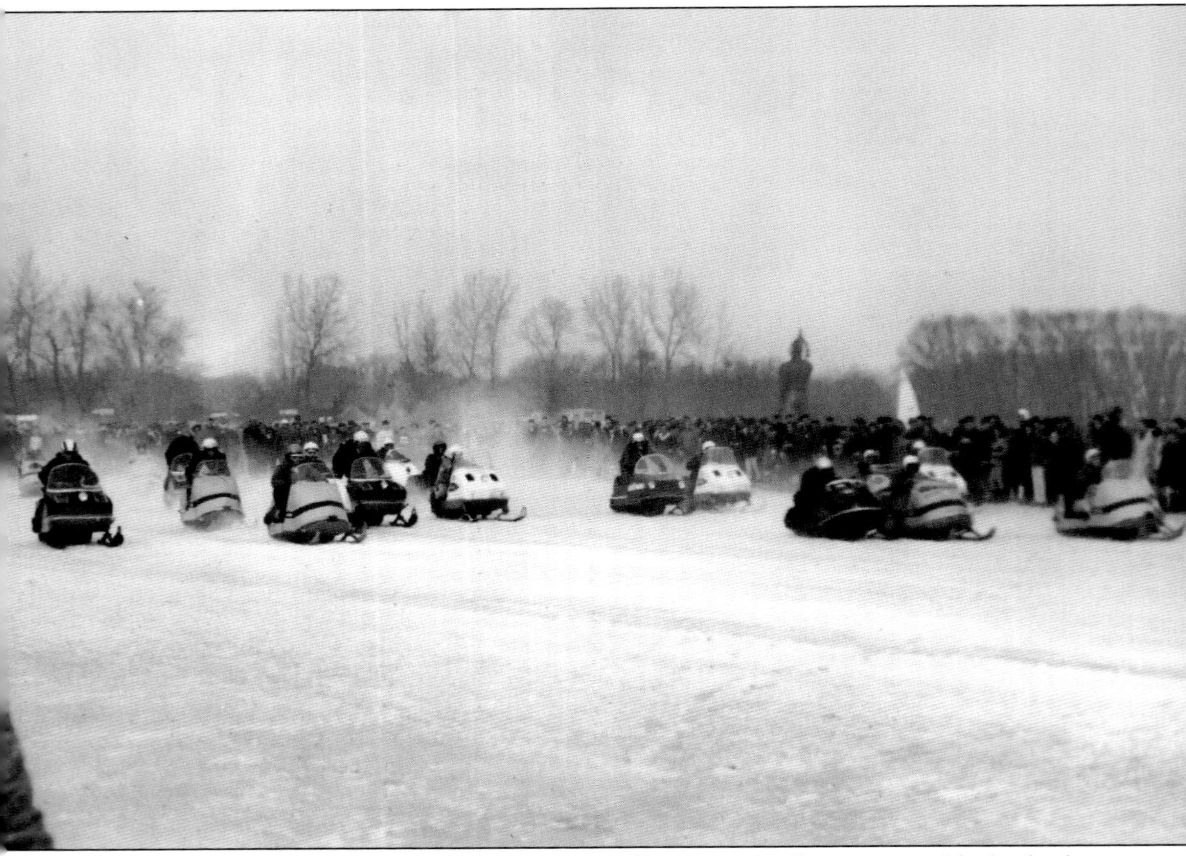

The snowmobile cross-country event generated much excitement. The course would take the drivers off the lake and onto land in Richmond and Bristol before returning to the carnival area.

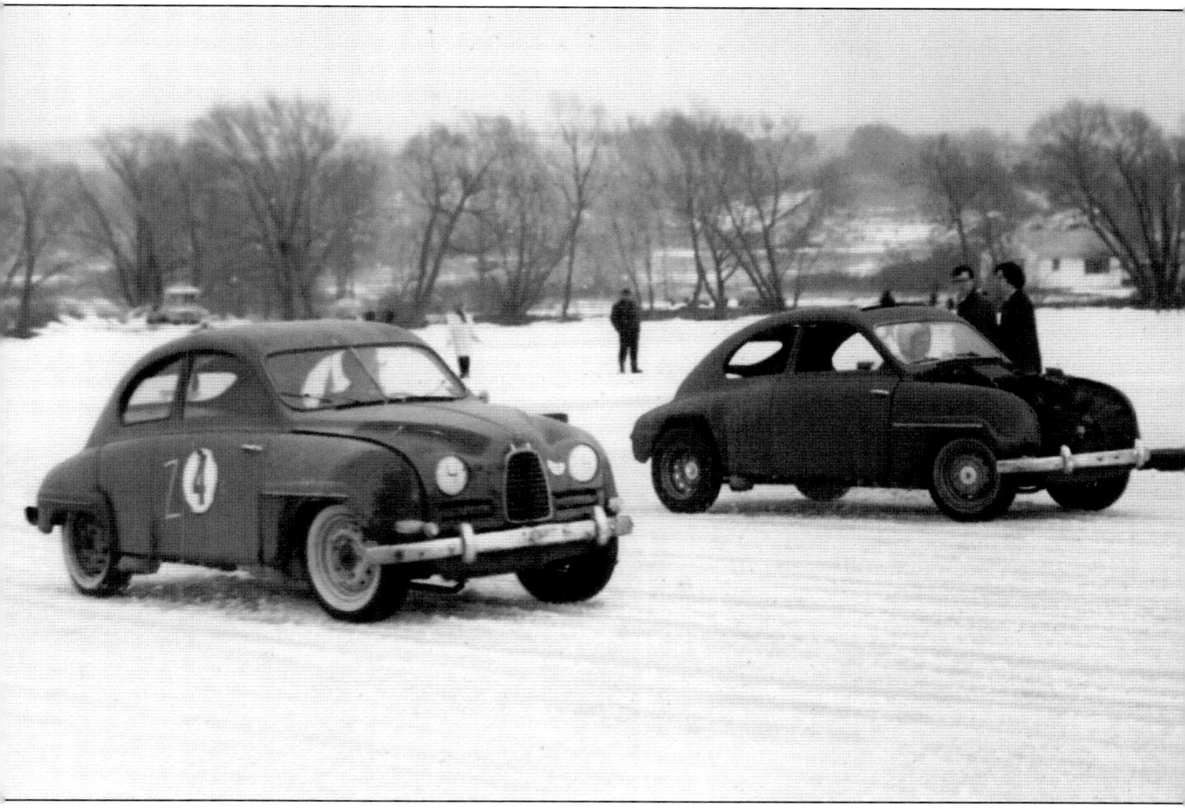

Cars would race on the ice on plowed courses. The racecourse was laid out by plows piling up the snow along the way. Tires would have studs to hold the vehicles on the ice. The snow piles also offered protection to the many spectators of the car races and other activities.

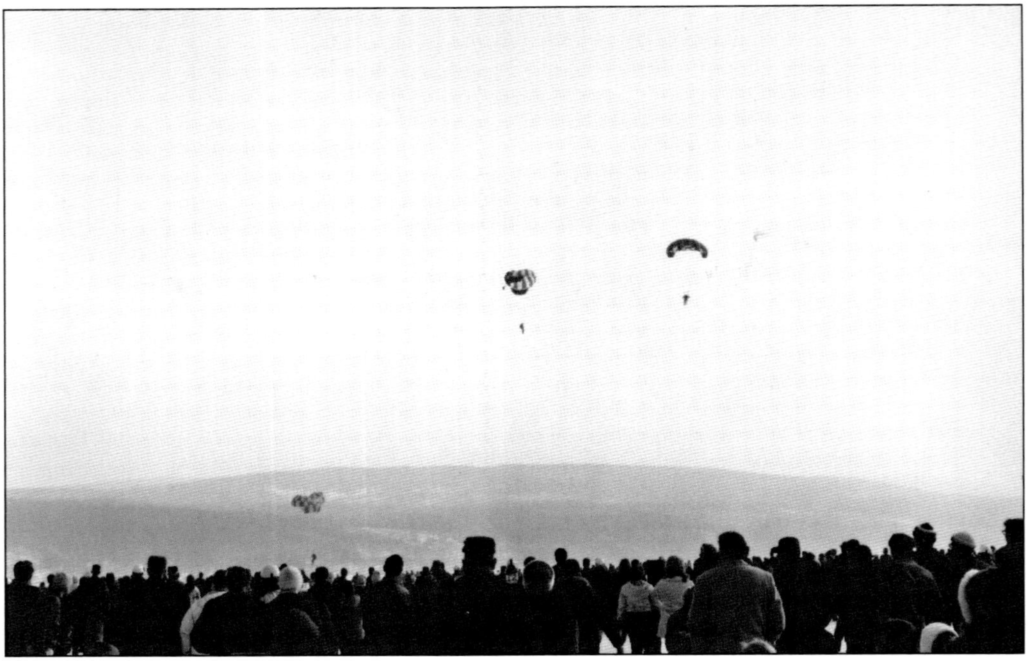

Parachuting was another way to arrive at the carnival. Some local people enjoyed jumping out of airplanes with parachutes strapped to their backs. They would head for a target on the ground, which consisted of two strips of 3-foot-by-25-foot black plastic shaped into an X. The jumpers required five eight-foot tables to repack their chutes to get ready for another jump.

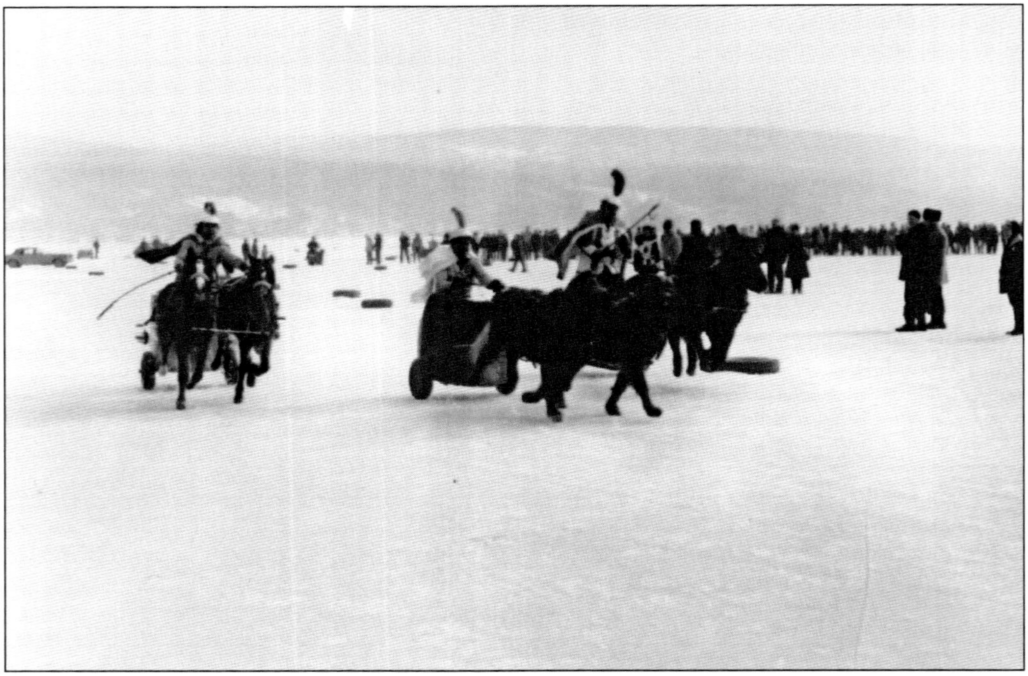

Honeoye had charioteers at carnival time. Local pony cart drivers would dress up as charioteers and in the appropriate carts, looked very much the part as they raced over the ice. They called themselves the Ben Hur Club.

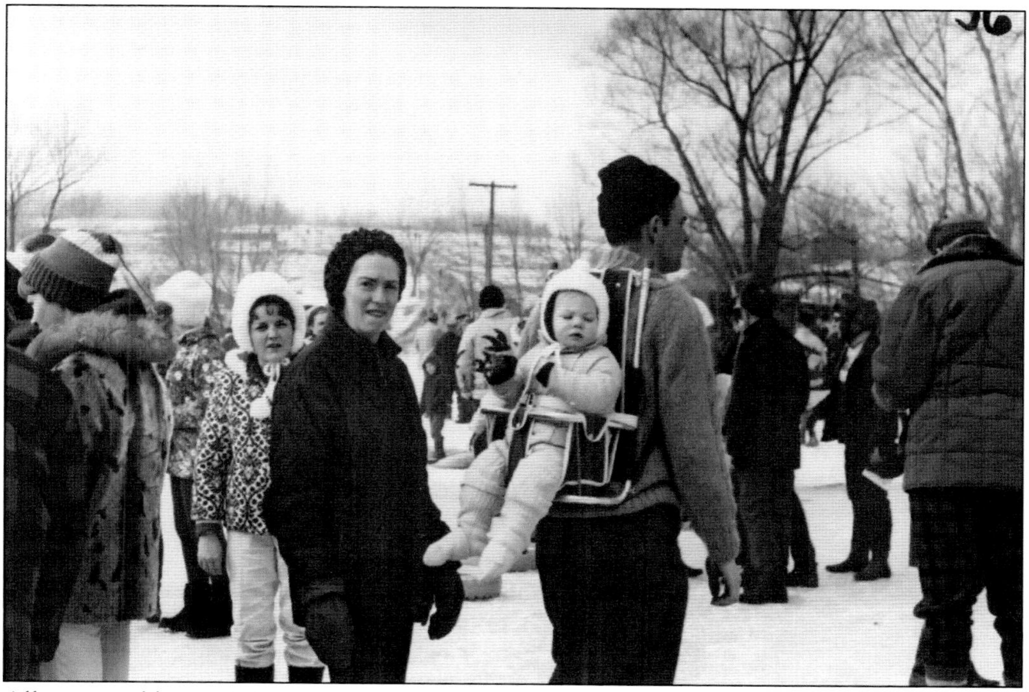

All ages would attend the carnival. From the burning of Christmas trees at the California Ranch property to start the carnival, to the Snow Ball dance at the end on Saturday night, the Honeoye Winter Carnival had something for everybody.

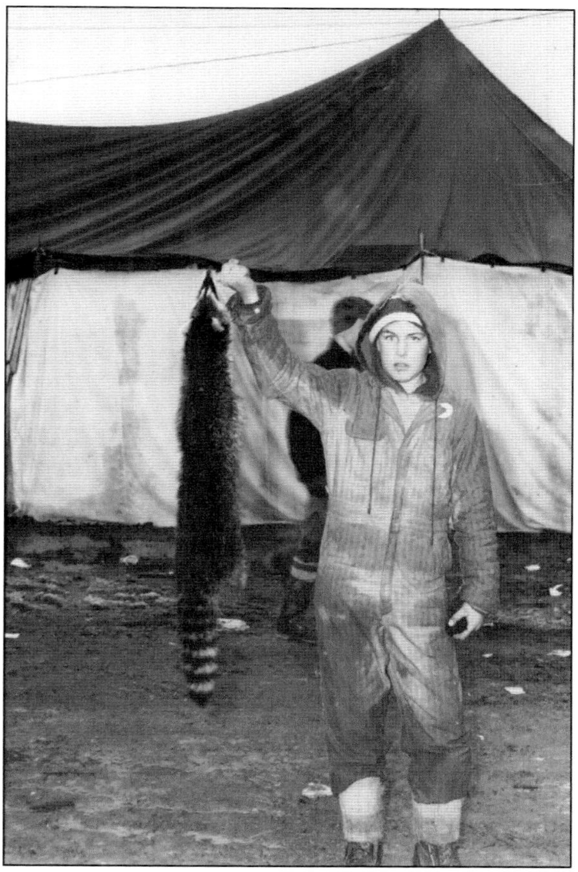

A pelt was a prize to this boy. The Genesee Valley Fur Trappers exhibited their pelts and also ran a muskrat-skinning contest at the carnival. They also felt they were educating the public on correct trapping and skinning. Working with furriers, the trappers provided fur coats for the Winter Carnival Queen candidates to wear over the weekend.

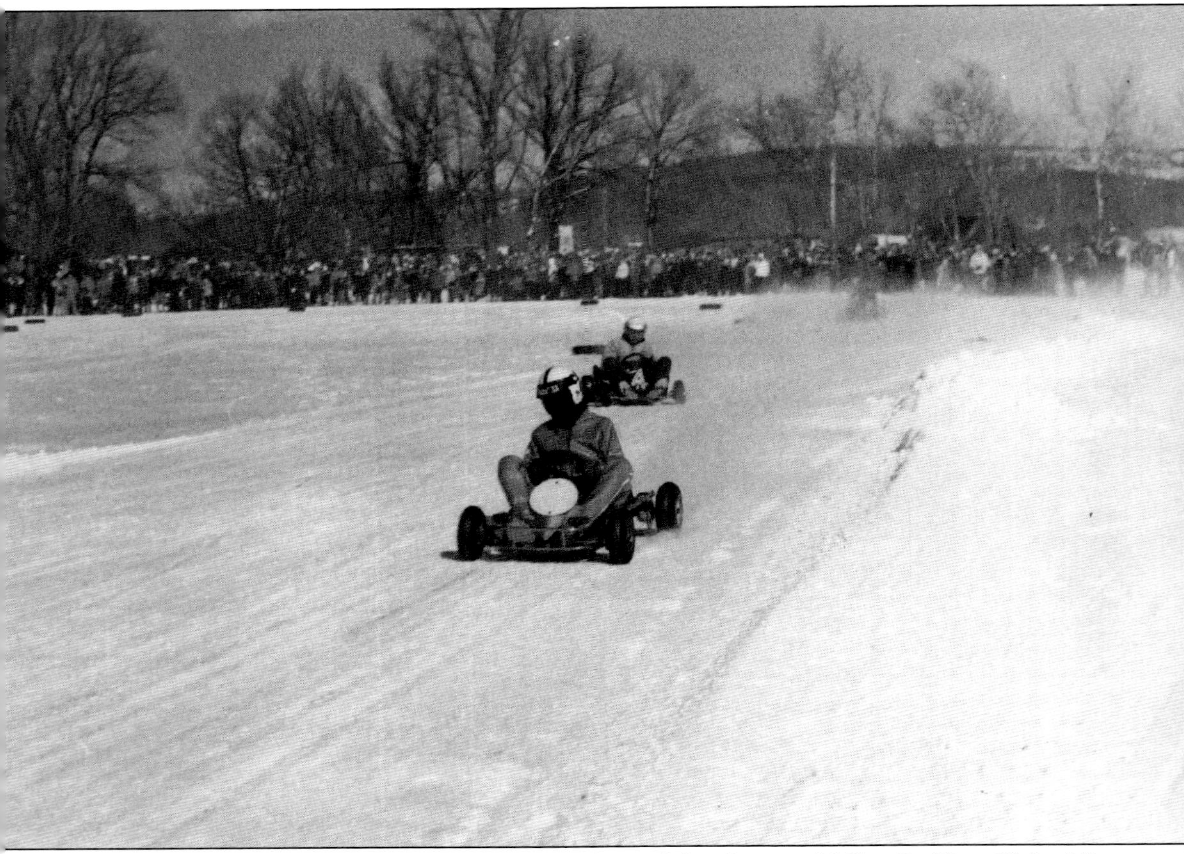

Go-carts had their turn out on the ice. Members of the Genesee Valley Go Kart Club of East Avon had specially equipped carts with runners instead of wheels in the front. The races were run on a 4/10-mile course on the ice. Different methods were used to obtain traction for the rear wheels, such as studded tires.

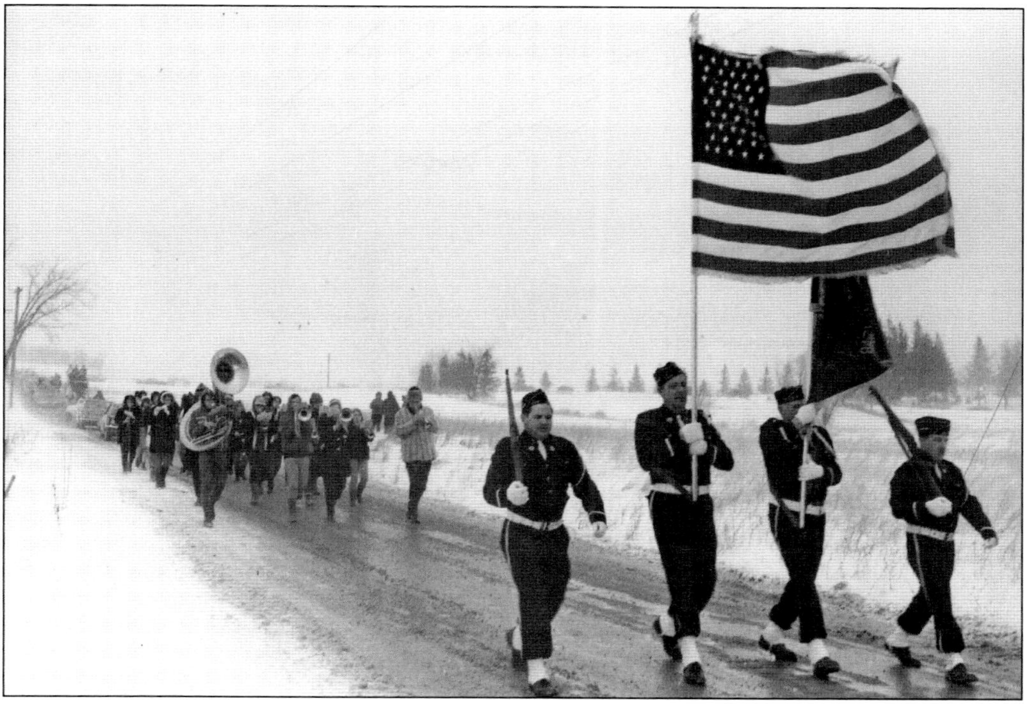

A parade was part of the festivities. The color guard was from the Hemlock-Honeoye American Legion. The legion also allowed parking on their property, which was nearby, as well as on the property of John Evans.

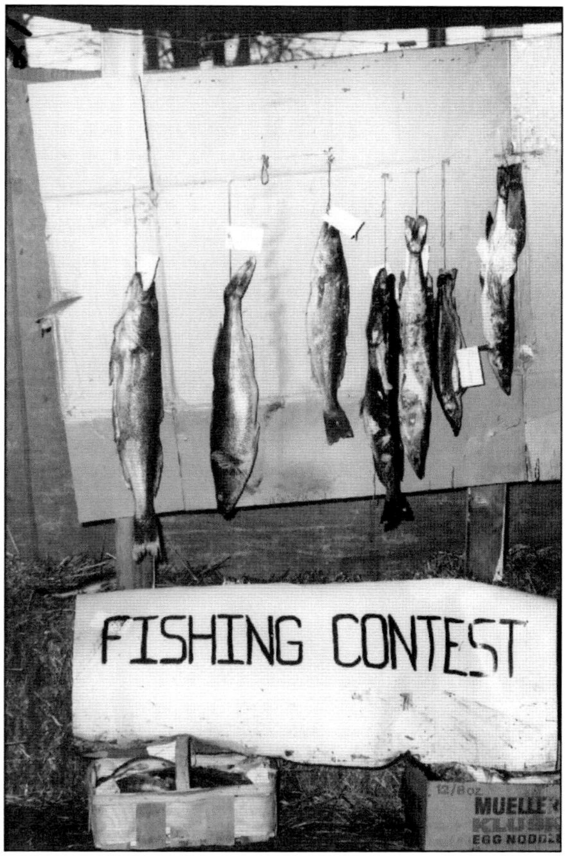

Fishing was encouraged down on the lake in front of the Cratsley Bait Shop on West Lake Road.

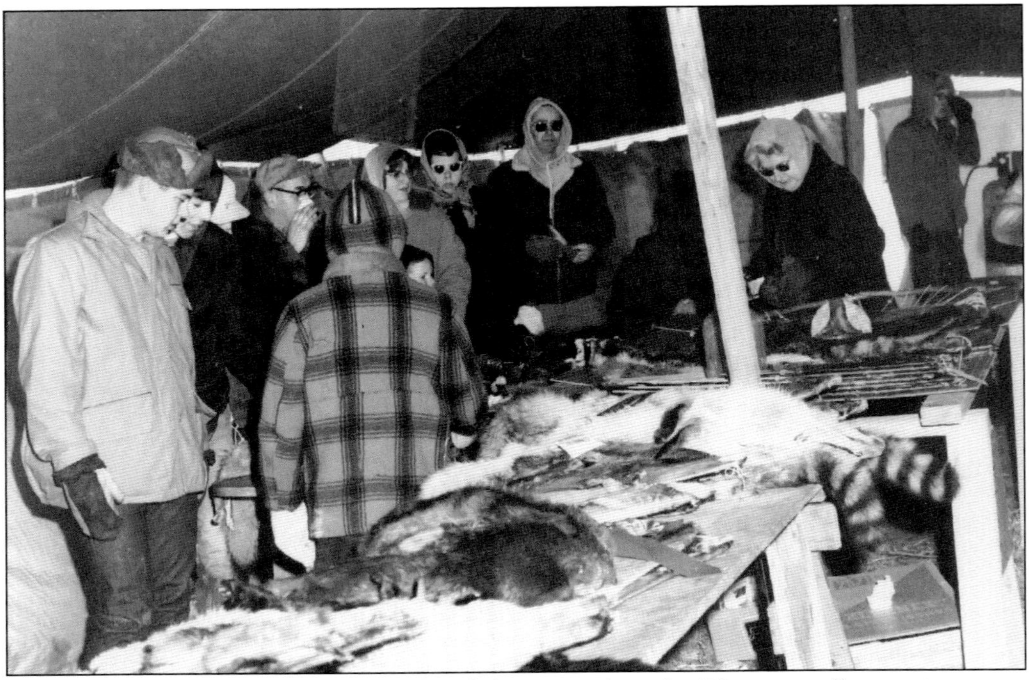

The Genesee Valley Fur Trappers exhibited their prize fur pelts. They are still an active group, promoting positive trapping procedures to be used in the area.

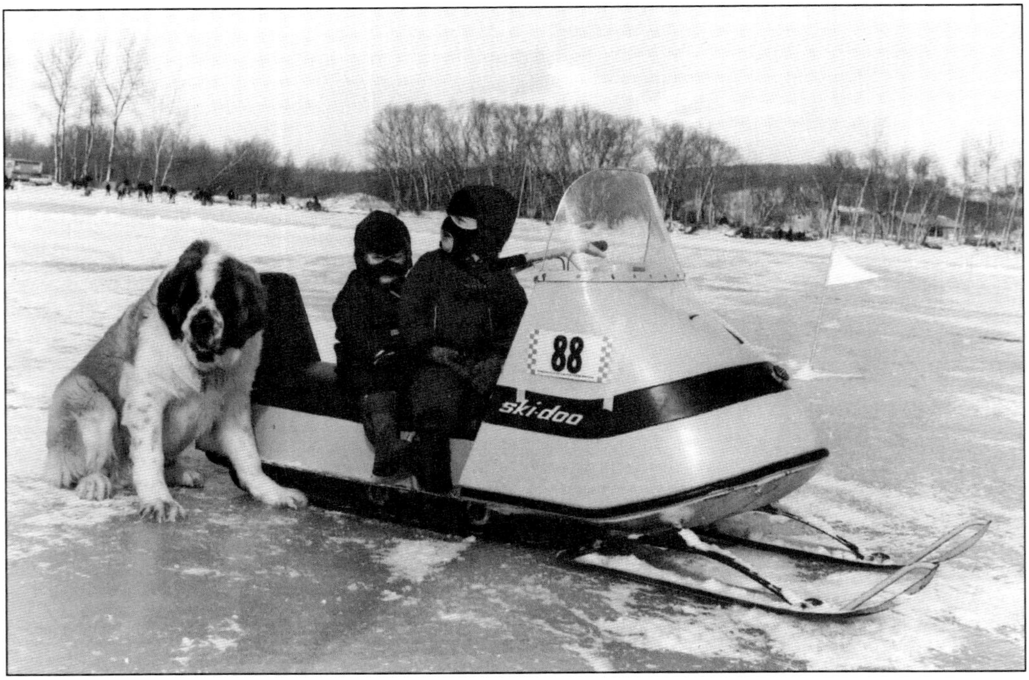

A few attempts to start up the Winter Carnival have been made, but without much success. It probably will stay a thing of the past for Honeoye Lake, Richmond, and Canadice. One year, an unexpected blizzard hit the area, which stranded some of the visitors. The central school was opened up to take in those who could not get home.

Bibliography

History of Ontario County, New York, 1876. Everts, Ensign & Everts, Philadelphia, PA.

Miliken, Charles F. *A History of Ontario County New York and Its People*. New York: Lewis Historical Publishing Co., 1911.

Nelson, Julie R. *Have We a Cause: The Life of Helen Pitts Douglass 1838–1903*. Shippensburg, PA: Shippensburg University, 1995.

The Honeoye Lake Book. Honeoye Lake Watershed Task Force, 1999.

Waite, D. Byron. *History of the Town of Canadice, Ontario County, NY*. Springwater, NY: Arthur N. Johnson, Printer & Publisher, 1908.